CH00821913

The Path of
Christ or Antichrist

CLIMB THE HIGHEST MOUNTAIN® SERIES

The Path of the Higher Self

The Path of Self-Transformation

The Masters and the Spiritual Path

The Path of Brotherhood

The Path of the Universal Christ

Paths of Light and Darkness

The Path to Immortality

The Path of Christ or Antichrist

———————

Predict Your Future:
Understand the Cycles of the Cosmic Clock

The Masters and Their Retreats

CLIMB THE HIGHEST MOUNTAIN SERIES

The Path of Christ or Antichrist

Mark L. Prophet · Elizabeth Clare Prophet

The Everlasting Gospel

SUMMIT UNIVERSITY PRESS
Gardiner, Montana

THE PATH OF CHRIST OR ANTICHRIST
by Mark L. Prophet and Elizabeth Clare Prophet
Copyright © 2007 by Summit Publications, Inc.
All rights reserved

No part of this book may be reproduced, translated, or electronically stored, posted or transmitted, or used in any format or medium whatsoever without prior written permission, except by a reviewer who may quote brief passages in a review. For information, please contact Summit University Press, 63 Summit Way, Gardiner, MT 59030-9314, USA. Tel: 1-800-245-5445 or 406-848-9500.
Web site: www.summituniversitypress.com
E-mail: info@summituniversitypress.com

Library of Congress Control Number: 2006940764
ISBN: 978-1-932890-10-5

SUMMIT UNIVERSITY � PRESS®

The Summit Lighthouse, *Pearls of Wisdom,* Science of the Spoken Word and Keepers of the Flame are trademarks registered in the U.S. Patent and Trademark Office and in other countries. All rights to their use are reserved.

Printed in the United States of America

Cover: *The Last Angel* (1942), a painting by Nicholas Roerich.

Note: Our understanding of life and the universe is that all things are in polarity: plus/minus, Alpha/Omega, yang/yin, masculine/feminine. The worlds of Spirit and Matter are in polarity as two manifestations of God's universal Presence. In this relationship, Spirit assumes the positive-yang-masculine polarity, and Matter assumes the negative-yin-feminine polarity. Thus, we have used masculine pronouns to refer to God and feminine pronouns to refer to the soul, the part of ourselves that is evolving in the planes of Matter. Also, in order to avoid the sometimes cumbersome or confusing expressions of gender-neutral language, we have occasionally used masculine pronouns to refer to the individual. These usages are not intended to exclude women.

11 10 09 08 07   5 4 3 2 1

And I saw another angel fly in the midst of heaven, having the everlasting gospel to preach unto them that dwell on the earth, and to every nation, and kindred, and tongue, and people,

Saying with a loud voice, Fear God, and give glory to him; for the hour of his judgment is come: and worship him that made heaven, and earth, and the sea, and the fountains of waters.

REVELATION

Contents

3 Antichrist   131

IMPORTANT NOTE

No guarantee whatsoever is made to anyone by Summit University Press or Elizabeth Clare Prophet that the spiritual system of the Science of the Spoken Word, including meditation, visualization, dynamic decrees and spiritual healing, embodied in this book will yield successful results for anyone at any time. The functioning of cosmic law is a direct experience between the individual and his own higher consciousness. In Jesus' time, some were healed and some were not—according to their faith or lack of it (see Matt. 8:13; 9:2, 22, 29; 15:28; 17:19–20; Mark 6:6; etc.). The same laws apply today. Karma and the Divine Providence must be the final arbiter of each one's application of the sacred fire. We can only witness to our personal healing—body, mind and soul—through the use of the suggested mantras and spiritual disciplines. Each man may prove or disprove the Law for himself. The practice and proof of the science of Being rests with the individual. No one can do it for another. These spiritual techniques do not replace medical treatment or diagnosis.

Preface

THE *PATH OF CHRIST OR Antichrist* is the eighth book in the Climb the Highest Mountain series. This volume explores some of the challenges of the spiritual path as well as providing techniques for dealing with these challenges.

Chapter 1, "Prayer, Decrees and Meditation," may be one of the most important in the whole series. It explains the various means of communion with God and with the Higher Self. It especially deals with the power of the spoken Word to bring change within man and in the world.

The Gospel of John tells us, "In the beginning was the Word," and that without that Word, "was not anything made that was made." In the teachings of the East, the Word itself contains the power to create and to uncreate. Thus in the Word—in the Science of the Spoken Word that the Masters teach—there is the means to meet the challenges of Light and Darkness in the world. It is the key to undoing the conspiracy of Antichrist.

Chapters 2, "Black Magic," and 3, "Antichrist," reveal the

origins of Evil and the battle of Light and Darkness in the world. Saint Paul wrote of his battle against principalities and powers of spiritual wickedness in high places.[1] And just as Jesus and all Avatars have had their confrontations with the dark ones, we must also learn to deal with these forces today in our own path of overcoming. The knowledge of the enemy and his strategy is an important step to maturity on the Path. It can open the door to a new liberation of the soul.

Chapter 4, "The Summit," tells the story of the Ascended Master El Morya and of The Summit Lighthouse, the organization he founded in 1958. In this cooperative endeavor of the Masters with their students, we see an example of the plans of the Brotherhood to bring Light to the world.

If this is your first exploration of the Climb the Highest Mountain series, we welcome you to your study of these Teachings from the Ascended Masters, which have been called the Everlasting Gospel,[2] the scripture for the age of Aquarius. For those who are taking up this book after reading previous volumes, we wish you God-speed in your continuing journey to climb the highest mountain.

THE EDITORS

Introduction

THE ASCENDED MASTERS ARE OUR Elder Brothers and Teachers. It has ever been so. They, the wayshowers of our spirits' fiery destiny, have from the Beginning held the vision of epochs of perfection we once knew.

For we, too, were embodied on ancient Lemuria, a civilization and a Motherland that brought forth the highest development of culture, science and technology ever known on this planet. Her golden ages exceeded in every field of endeavor the most advanced developments of modern man. Indelibly inscribed in the records of our own subconscious is the memory of an era when the life span of a people was measured in centuries rather than decades, when we, too, walked and talked with the Immortals, were never separated from our twin flame, and beheld our Teachers face-to-face.

When life on the continent of Mu was corrupted by aliens and fallen angels with their grotesque genetic miscreations, mocking the Godhead and violating the sacred science of the Mother by engaging men in wars of the gods, the Masters withdrew from the masses and gathered their initiates in

Mystery Schools to guard the Light of the Mother flame and her wisdom.

Just before the climactic end when the desecration of the holy shrines and the abominations of the flesh of man and beast had all but extinguished the divine spark in her people, the warning was sounded by the Hierarchs of the Cosmic Council that the Great Law would return full circle and in full force the vileness of mankind's deeds. And the children of Mu, the few who heeded their prophets and got out in time, beheld from afar as their beloved Motherland went down midst smoke and fire in sudden violent cataclysm such as the world has never seen—neither before nor since.

In more recent ages, prior to the Egyptian civilization, we recall the land of Poseid—also known as Poseidonis, Atla or Atlantis—portions of which were nigh the Azores. We recall the capital of Caiphul described by Phylos the Thibetan in his book *A Dweller on Two Planets:* "the Royal City, the greatest of that ancient day, within the limits of which resided a population of two million souls." The author says its broad avenues were "shaded by great trees; its artificial hills—the largest surmounted by governmental palaces, and pierced and terraced by the avenues which radiated from the city-center like spokes in a wheel. Fifty miles these ran in one direction, while at right angles from them, traversing the breadth of the peninsula, forty miles in length, were the shortest avenues. Thus lay, like a splendid dream, this, the proudest city of that ancient world."[1]

Some of us recall these early experiences as though it were yesterday. Twelve thousand years ago Atlantis was a part of our world. It is recorded in Genesis that before the Flood that sank the mighty continent of Atla, "the earth was corrupt before God, and the earth was filled with violence.... And God said unto Noah, The end of all flesh is come before me; for the earth is filled with violence through them; and, behold,

I will destroy them with the earth."[2]

The same cycles of vileness and wickedness that had destroyed Lemuria were now closing in on titanic Atla—the continent, they said, that "even God couldn't sink"—and would later crystallize the judgment of Sodom and Gomorrah, Pompeii, and other cultures corrupted by the love of pleasure before God.

As man's love for God and the devotional exercise of his heart to the living Word deteriorated, the flame within the temples went out and the heart flames of the people flickered and waned. Then came the day when all was buried by mud. So passed the glory of the gods that were made of clay and with them their mechanization man—dust to dust, mud to mud.

The people of that continent have continued to reembody throughout the ages, some descending to the same levels of darkness, others rising to win their ascension. And free will is the sole survivor of every (man's) cataclysm—the free will to make it right and build again in the next round. What else can you do when all of your past lies in rubble and ashes at your feet?

Thus, under the direction of the Brotherhood, Mystery Schools emerged here and there—in ancient China and India and more recently in the appearance of the Hebrews and their prophets, the Sangha of the Buddha, Pythagoras' Academy at Crotona, the Druids, the Essenes, Christ's community of the called-out ones and the School of the Sangreal at King Arthur's court.

And so we see that at Luxor and various Mystery Schools across the planet, the torch of the Mother and the Motherland has been passed. But it has not been seized by the majority, although many have benefited from the various flames that still burn in etheric octaves in the retreats of the Masters around the world.

It is in these flames that we discover we are not that far apart from each other—Christian and Jew, black and white man, Chinese and Indian. For these too were there on Atlantis —and some that had no Life in them. Nevertheless, all races and peoples upon the face of the Earth in whom there burns the divine spark are made by one God for one destiny.

The destiny must be grand. It must be noble. It must be worthy. And if we will it so, we can be a part of that destiny. Or we can deny ourselves that destiny by indulging ourselves in the enmeshing concepts of hatred (which is always "self"-hatred in one form or another) directed against ourselves and other selves and, beyond these, against the Great Creative Self, yes, the singular object of many men's contempt. For many are wed to the dweller-on-the-threshold, the seething, touchy synthetic self.

The retreats of the Brotherhood were kept on Atlantis midst the marbled geometric cities—schools of the mysteries. There was also the prevailing thought that finally caused the sinking of that continent. All of this has ripened to the present hour. The continent was destroyed, and approximately twelve thousand years later we are facing the same initiations. All of the traditions of Atlantis have returned and are full grown, standing before us, as choices we must make.

The vast majority of the people on the planet are not making choices—they are the victims of intellectual and philosophical systems that can be traced back to Atlantis. The very few, the intellectual elite, the power elite descending from the fallen ones of Atlantis, are making very definite choices. The few who remain in touch with the Mystery Schools, the chelas of the Ascended Masters, are also making choices. In the middle there are those people who are dedicated, religious, patriotic, who would like to make choices, who are for all the right things—but for all intents and purposes are noneffective. Their beliefs are right, but they have no dynamism of the

Spirit, no sword of Truth, no interaction with the Hosts of the LORD to change the course of history, to change civilization.

All that the fallen ones created without access to the living Word is maya, is illusion. It looks like a tremendous monolith of civilization and the buildup of nuclear weapons, and we fear and tremble before the councils of war of the Nephilim— the fallen angels. And we wonder what is coming upon us.

But in the face of all this, we have no reason to fear, because God is in us and "greater is he that is in you, than he that is in the world"[3]—the worldly consciousness. We must defeat the enemy of fear, of absence of self-worth and of an orthodox tradition that tells us that God is not in us and that he was only in one son of God, Jesus Christ.

Ever since the Nephilim were cast down, the Earth has been the scene of an epic battle that the scriptures record and that we are seeing played out to this very day. The power of the Word is greater than the might of armies. But if we fail to remember our ancient heritage as sons and daughters of the Most High and the all-power of heaven and earth that he gave to us in the Beginning, if we fail to remember the wickedness of the wicked clearly recorded on Sumerian tablets and in the records of akasha, if we fail to remember the countless Avatars who have come to expose the fallen ones and been murdered over and over again by them, if we fail to perceive their present massacre of our holy bands, then we will be condemned as the generation of Lightbearers who lost an age, an entire evolution, and perhaps our very own souls.

Those who have the will to choose to do something about the persecution of the people and their intended destruction of an entire planet must turn swiftly to call upon the name of the LORD, to invoke a higher science and a higher law. This is the only means whereby this Earth and her evolutions and their very souls can be saved.

The Spirit of the LORD came upon the prophet Joel, and he

wrote:

> And it shall come to pass afterward, that I will pour out my spirit upon all flesh; and your sons and your daughters shall prophesy, your old men shall dream dreams, your young men shall see visions....
>
> And I will shew wonders in the heavens and in the earth, blood, and fire, and pillars of smoke. The sun shall be turned into darkness, and the moon into blood, before the great and the terrible day of the LORD come.
>
> And it shall come to pass, that whosoever shall call upon the name of the LORD shall be delivered: for in mount Zion and in Jerusalem shall be deliverance, as the LORD hath said, and in the remnant whom the LORD shall call.[4]

The LORD is calling you and me today to be the remnant who will use his name—the sacred name of AUM, the sacred name of the I AM THAT I AM, the sacred name of Jesus Christ, of Gautama Buddha and every saint—to intone the Word, and release the Light for the healing of the nations.

Brothers and sisters, God has given to us the answer. It is this liberating power of the Word. We welcome you to join with us in experiencing and experimenting with this, the very sacred fire of creation itself.

Mark L. Prophet

Elizabeth Clare Prophet

MARK AND ELIZABETH PROPHET
Messengers of the Masters

Chapter 1

Prayer, Decrees and Meditation

*So shall my word be that
goeth forth out of my mouth:
it shall not return unto me void,
but it shall accomplish that
which I please, and it shall
prosper in the thing whereto
I sent it.*

Thus saith the LORD, *the
Holy One of Israel, and his
Maker, Ask me of things to
come concerning my sons, and
concerning the work of my
hands command ye me.*

ISAIAH

Prayer, Decrees and Meditation

MANY STATEMENTS FROM HOLY Writ affirm the power of the spoken Word. That which comes to mind most readily is "In the beginning was the Word, and the Word was with God, and the Word was God. The same was in the beginning with God. All things were made by him; and without him was not anything made that was made."[1]

The Power of the Spoken Word

With these immortal words, John, the beloved disciple of Jesus, reminds us that it was the fiat of the LORD that brought forth the world of form out of the void. Creation came forth from the Mind of God when he gave the command, "Let there be Light."[2] And it will come forth from the Mind of Christ as individual man utters the same command in His name: "Let there be Light!" By the Word, the Elohim were summoned, and lo, creation was born.

The Word, the Logos, is the principle of all energy flow. Decrees, fiats, prayers, meditations, songs and mantras connect you to that Principle, that Source. They are words in combination, words in rhythm, words in cadence. Some are sung, some are chanted. Some are spoken softly like a summer rain, some are released like lightning and thunder that clears the air and quickens the mind. All invoke the Word without which "was not anything made that was made." To be—I AM—is to create—I AM *that* I AM. To create, we invoke the Word.

We all sense the power within the atom of transcendent Being. Many have sought to unleash it. Many have propounded methods. But only the Word can create. By it all things were made.

The Science of Energy Flow

The Ascended Masters teach the science of energy flow as the release of the Word through all of the chakras. But for the thrust of creativity in the here and now, for the challenging of Darkness and the intoning of Light, for attainment and the balancing of karma and the mastery of a self and a cosmos, they train their chelas in the Science of the Spoken Word.

Spoken prayer is at the heart of all true religion. Christians, Jews, Moslems, Hindus, Buddhists and others offer devotions in the form of daily prayers, recitations of scripture and mantras to the Deity. These include the Our Father, the Hail Mary, the Shema and Amidah, the Shahadah, the Gayatri and the Heart Sutra.

For thousands of years, formulas of the Word—as sacred ritual, as science, as mathematics—have been the key to the elevation of consciousness and to the materialization of the God flame. Formulas of the Word have been the bridge between the finite and the Infinite. Man has approached his

God through prayer and songs of praise. He has meditated on the Image, the name, the essence of Being—and thereby he has discovered the mantra, the "thoughtform," of the object of his worship.

Mantra

The mantra is the translation of the original Word, a gift of the Lawgiver whereby souls evolving in time and space might trace the flow of Life from the nonpermanent to the permanent—from the outer manifestation to the inner pattern.

The mantra is a worded matrix that conveys the frequencies of the Master's consciousness to chelas moving toward self-mastery. The mantra is inseparable from the Master's vibration. Those who pronounce it with devotion to the fiery blueprint of creation merge with the Electronic Presence of the Master.

The mantra is the nexus of worlds. It is the bridge over which we pass from the natural to the spiritual order of things. The mantra is the mediator: it is the Christ. The mantra is the means whereby we transcend ourselves and find ourselves alive in God.

A mantra is a sacred formula the Master imparts to his disciple. Through the mantra, the Guru gives the gift of Selfhood to his chela. Sanskrit mantras have come down from the Manus of the early root races, who intoned the sacred Word on Lemuria. And from the Motherland and the Mother flame, the Word released the origin of all culture, all science, all religion.

Jesus gave a mantra of Mu to his disciples when he pronounced the fiat: "I AM the resurrection and the life."[3] This was a formula of the Word given to him by his Guru, Lord Maitreya, who holds the focus of the Cosmic Christ. By repeating it, you realize the resurrection and the Life of the God flame. By this mantra and other sacred formulas of the Law, Jesus proved the victory of Life over death. He taught that we could do the same—that we must do the same.

In this chapter, we will explore mantra, prayers, decrees and meditation, and the differences between them. Each method has its place in attuning the soul with God and invoking his blessings, to which all are entitled.

The Authority of the Divine Similitude

Paul's admonishment to the Philippians, "Let this mind be in you, which was also in Christ Jesus,"[4] was given because he knew that the Mind of Christ embraces the power, the pure forms, the all-knowing love and the fires of perfection that are required not only to bring forth creation, but also to restore, to resurrect and to recharge the being and consciousness of those in whom the wholeness of the Son of God has been temporarily eclipsed.

Paul goes on to explain why Jesus was able to manifest the fullness of the Mind of Christ and thereby to do his healing work: "Who, being in the form of God, thought it not robbery to be equal with God."[5] Jesus recognized himself as a Son of God, and he knew that it is the preordained destiny of every son of God to "be in the form of" his Maker, i.e., to live after the perfect pattern of the Divine Image in which he was made.[6]

Jesus knew that if he were to maintain his oneness with that Image and would depart not from the consciousness of God, it would not be "robbery to be equal with God,"[7] for he would be expressing only that which God intended him to have and to be. The beloved Son becomes a co-creator, a joint heir, for he is found in the similitude of his Maker.

Jesus realized that when man was given free will, he was

also given the full responsibility for his words, his thoughts and his deeds; for these are the consequences of man's use or misuse of his free will. Therefore, he said, "By thy words thou shalt be justified, and by thy words thou shalt be condemned."[8]

He knew that man could be neither justified nor condemned in matters in which he bore no responsibility. He also knew that the responsibility that he was given cannot be transferred to another, albeit the Christ Self bears the burden of Light that will lighten not only his load but also his way. It is the Christ who lives within that enables him to complete his course and to balance his karma without being overburdened by a false sense of responsibility.

It is this false sense that sees man as the doer and does homage to the lower self instead of to the Christ. Let us pursue a deeper understanding of this mystery in order that we may establish man's authority for giving prayers, decrees and meditations.

Your Divine Inheritance

Those who truly understand the mystery of the Christ have seen that even as there is one God, one Father, so there is one Christ, one Son. It is the nature of the "Infinite One" to multiply Selfhood infinitely and still remain one. (One times one times one ... ad infinitum, always equals one.) Thus, God the Father and God the Son may be actualized in man over and over again and still remain inviolate as the Divine One.

All men share in this oneness and have within themselves the essence of the Divine Nature—God individualized as the I AM Presence of every man, and the Christ, individualized as the Christ Self of every man. Without God and the Word, the Christ, which was with God in the Beginning, no manifestation was made. In other words, no man was created without being infused with a portion of God and a portion of the Christ.[9]

The Chart of Your Divine Self (facing page 12) reveals how these manifestations of God are individualized within you as the Father-Mother God, in the I AM Presence (upper figure); as the Son, in the Holy Christ Self (middle figure); and as the Holy Spirit, who, when you have prepared yourself, may take up his abode in the body temple God provided for your soul's sojourn on planet Earth (lower figure). The Chart shows the fulfillment of the Psalmist's trust:

> He that dwelleth [in consciousness] in the secret place of the most High shall abide under the shadow of the Almighty [the mighty I AM Presence].
> I will say of the LORD, He is my refuge and my fortress: my God; in him will I trust.[10]

God told Moses to tell the children of Israel that his name was I AM THAT I AM and that "I AM hath sent me unto you." Moreover, he said, "Thus shalt thou say unto the children of Israel: The LORD God of your fathers, the God of Abraham, the God of Isaac, and the God of Jacob, hath sent me unto you: this is my name for ever, and this is my memorial unto all generations."[11]

The Jerusalem Bible translates the last sentence: "This is my name for all time; by this name I shall be invoked for all generations to come."

When we call upon the name of the LORD, as the prophets tell us to do,[12] we use the name I AM THAT I AM or simply I AM. Addressing "our God with us" in prayer we say, "Beloved mighty I AM Presence…"

The Almighty, the Maker of heaven and earth, has manifested himself to each one of us as the I AM THAT I AM, who goes before us as the LORD went before the children of Israel, "by day in a pillar of a cloud and by night in a pillar of fire."[13]

The I AM Presence and the seven spheres of Light that surround it (the color bands) make up the body of First Cause, or the Causal Body. These spheres are the "many mansions" of our Father's house where we lay up for ourselves "treasures in heaven."[14] Our treasures are our words and works worthy of our Creator, positive thoughts and feelings, our victories for the right, and the virtues we have embodied to the glory of God. And as Jesus said, where our treasure is, there will our heart be also[15]—in this our heaven-world.

When we judiciously exercise our free will, the energies of God that we harmoniously qualify automatically ascend to our Causal Body. These energies are deposited in the spheres of Light that correspond to the seven chakras and the seven color rays we use in our creative activities. They accrue to our lifestream as "talents," which we may increase as we put them to good use lifetime after lifetime.

John the Beloved saw and described the I AM Presence, calling it a mighty angel: "And I saw another mighty angel come down from heaven, clothed with a cloud: and a rainbow was upon his head, and his face was as it were the sun, and his feet as pillars of fire."[16]

The Holy Christ Self is the Mediator between God and man. This Universal Christ is the only begotten Son of the Father—the Light-emanation of First Cause. It is the Christ of Jesus and the Christ of you and me. Yet there is but one LORD and one Saviour.

Your Holy Christ Self overshadows you wherever you are and wherever you go. He endows you with the capacity to be "Christ conscious" at all times or, to put it another way, to have the "Christ consciousness" all ways. This beloved Friend and Teacher and Comforter is actually your Real Self, whom you will one day become if you follow in the footsteps of your Saviour.

The lower figure is shown enveloped in the violet flame within the tube of light, which descends from the I AM Presence in answer to your call. This cylinder of steely white Light sustains a forcefield of protection twenty-four hours a day—so long as you guard your harmony.

Your lower self consists of your soul and your spirit dressed in the garments of the four lower bodies. Your soul is the nonpermanent aspect of being that is evolving through the four planes of Matter. The soul is made permanent through the ritual of the ascension.

Your spirit is the distilled essence of your self. It is the pervading and predominating presence by which you are known. It is the animating, or vital, principle of your Life that you take with you throughout your soul's incarnations, molding it after the likeness of the Spirit of the living God.

Through the ascension, the soul is become the Incorruptible One. Henceforth to be known as an Ascended Master, the soul receives the crown of everlasting Life. This is the consummate goal of Life, greatly to be desired. The ascension is freedom from the cycles of karma and the rounds of rebirth; it is the entering in to the joy of the LORD.

The Chart of Your Divine Self is thus a diagram—past, present and future—of your soul's pilgrimage to the Great Central Sun as year upon year up the spiral staircase of initiation you go, drawing nigh to God as he draws nigh to you.[17]

The Gift of Life
from Your Divine Parents

The threefold flame is your divine spark, the gift of Life, liberty and consciousness from your Divine Parents. Also called the Holy Christ Flame, it is the essence of your Reality, your potential for Christhood. It is sealed in the secret chamber of your heart.

The three plumes of the threefold flame are the blue (on your left), the yellow (in the center) and the pink (on your right), corresponding to the primary attributes of power, wisdom and love, respectively. Through the power (of the Father), the wisdom (of the Son) and the love (of the Holy Spirit) anchored in the threefold flame, your soul exercises her* God-given free will to fulfill her reason for being in the physical plane and throughout all time and eternity.

The crystal (or silver) cord[18] is the stream of Life that flows from the heart of the I AM Presence to the Holy Christ Self to nourish and sustain the soul and her vehicles of expression in time and space. John saw the crystal cord and described it as "a pure river of water of life, clear as crystal, proceeding out of the throne of God and of the Lamb."[19]

You can think of the crystal cord as an "umbilical" cord through which the Light/energy/consciousness of God flows all the way from the Great Central Sun to child-man embodied on the far-flung planets. It enters the being of man at the crown, giving impetus for the pulsation of the threefold flame as well as the physical heartbeat and all bodily functions.

Shown just above the head of the Holy Christ Self on the Chart of Your Divine Self is the dove of the Holy Spirit descending from the Father. This signifies that the Comforter attends each lifestream until the soul is spiritually ready to receive the cloven tongues of fire and the baptism of the Holy Spirit. To that end, the son of man, embracing the will of God, matures in Christ Self–awareness as a Christ-filled being day by day. As he gains greater love and greater wisdom as the foundation of his self-mastery, he enters into true communion with his Holy Christ Self.

---

* Whether housed in a male or female body, the soul is the feminine complement of the masculine Spirit and is addressed by the pronouns *she* and *her*.

The Divine Mother, the Sacred Fire and the Chakras

The Divine Mother is focused and adored in the temple of man through the sacred fire that rises as a veritable fountain of Light from the base-of-the-spine chakra to the crown chakra. The seven chakras are the spiritual centers in the body that distribute the Light of the Mother ascending from the base of the spine, and the Light of the Father descending from the I AM Presence.

The coming together of these two radiant streams of Life-energy, pulsating from above and below, establishes the union and the balance of the plus-minus (yang-yin) forces in the chakras. Thus each chakra becomes a center for the release of the Light of the Father-Mother God. Each focuses one of the seven color rays and one of the seven planes of Being.

In the spiritually developed, the Mother's sacred fire (known in the East as the Kundalini) rises up the spinal stalk for the quickening of the soul and the awakening of the Inner Christ and the Inner Buddha. Our Divine Mother, ever present with us, guards and guides our footsteps, teaching us how to attain our self-mastery by taking command of our soul and our spirit, our four lower bodies, and the sacred fire that we release through our chakras.

The Chart of Your Divine Self

The Four Lower Bodies

The four lower bodies are four energy fields. They are interpenetrating sheaths of consciousness, each vibrating in its own dimension. And so you have a flesh-and-blood body that is your physical body. You have a mind that cogitates, which is your mental body. You have emotions and feelings, which express through your astral, or desire, body (also called the emotional body). And you have a memory that is housed in your etheric, or memory, body, the highest vibrating of the four, which also serves as "the envelope of the soul."

These four lower bodies surround the soul and are her vehicles of expression in the material world of form. The planets also have four lower "bodies" demarcating the etheric, mental, astral and physical planes in which their evolutions live and evolve. These four quadrants of being correspond to the fire, air, water and earth of the ancient alchemists.

Our four lower bodies are intended to function as an integrated unit like "wheels within wheels." Or you might think of them as interpenetrating colanders. When the "holes" are lined up, your four lower bodies are in sync. This means they are aligned with the blueprint of your lifestream that is sustained by your Holy Christ Self, enabling you to direct the Light through your chakras without obstruction to bless and heal all Life.

But most of us don't have our "holes" lined up. We are out of alignment with our Real Self, and so we don't experience the full benefit of our just portion of the Light that descends over the crystal cord from our mighty I AM Presence.

The problem we have to deal with if we are to emerge from earth's schoolroom as an integrated personality in God is this: During our stay on this planet we have gotten our spiritual pores clogged up with a lot of human karma and astral effluvia (i.e., the dust and debris of the misqualified energy of the centuries). In addition, each of us is carrying a percentage of the total planetary karma in our four lower bodies.

As we have misqualified God's pure Life-stream perpetually flowing from our I AM Presence for our use here below, it has accumulated in the subconscious as rings on our tree of Life and in the collective unconscious of the race. Like it or not, we are bearing one another's karmic burden, simply because we are a part of this evolution.

What Is a Decree?

To assist Jesus and the Masters of the East, the Hierarchy of Ascended Masters who constitute the Great White Brotherhood* have set forth for Western chelas on the path of Christhood sacred formulas called decrees.

Like the mantras of the East, these thoughtforms are specific formulas for a specific purpose. Each one connects you with the source of all Life and energy, your own I AM Presence. Each one is based on the law of love and the principle of the Christ. All are formulated on the will of God for every soul: freedom, enlightenment, self-mastery, purity, harmony, love.

Decrees written by Ascended Masters—those who like Jesus and Gautama have mastered time and space and entered into the center of the AUM, the I AM THAT I AM—are matrices of cosmic consciousness. The Masters call them cups of Light. They convey the waters of eternal Life—the energy

---

* The Ascended Masters of the Great White Brotherhood, united for the highest purposes of the brotherhood of man under the Fatherhood of God, have risen in every age from every culture and religion to inspire creative achievement in education, the arts and sciences, God-government and the abundant Life through the economies of the nations. The word "white" refers not to race but to the aura (halo) of white light surrounding their forms. The Brotherhood also includes in its ranks certain unascended chelas of the Ascended Masters. Jesus Christ revealed this heavenly order of saints "robed in white" to his servant John in Revelation.

flow of vital, ascendant Being.

This is the water of which Jesus spoke when he said: "Whosoever drinketh of the water that I shall give him shall never thirst; but the water that I shall give him shall be in him a well of water springing up into everlasting life."[20]

First of all, let us define our term *decree*. The *Oxford English Dictionary* defines *decree* as follows:

> *Decree, noun:* An ordinance or edict set forth by the civil or other authority; an authoritative decision having the force of law. *In theology*, one of the eternal purposes of God whereby events are foreordained.
>
> *Decree, verb:* To command (something) by decree; to order, appoint, or assign authoritatively, ordain; to ordain as by Divine appointment, or by fate. To decide or determine authoritatively; to pronounce by decree. To determine, resolve, decide *to do* something, *obsolete* or *archaic*. To decide, determine, ordain.

The decree, as we use it, is the most powerful of all applications to the Godhead. It is the command of the son or daughter of God, spoken in the name of the mighty I AM Presence and Holy Christ Self, for the Light to descend from the Unformed to the formed—from the world of Spirit to the world of Matter. The decree is the means whereby the kingdom of God becomes a Reality here and now through the power of the spoken Word.

Meditations and visualizations are an important part of daily devotions, but dynamic decrees are the most powerful method of directing God's Light into manifestation for individual and world action. Decrees are often accompanied by prayers, invocations, mantras, chants, fiats, affirmations and calls to the one God and the saints, whom we refer to as the Ascended Masters, and the Heavenly Hosts.

The decrees that we teach have been dictated out of the geometrization of the Ascended Masters' own Causal Bodies. In their affirmation of Truth and their denial of error, they are the highest expression of Divine Science and all branches of metaphysics that issue therefrom.

The Divine Mother's decrees crystallize her sacred fire for the transmutation and perfectionment of our worlds. They are the tools by which the children of God might once again "pull up" the Mother flame (the sacred fire from the base-of-the-spine chakra) and "pull down" the Father Light (from the I AM Presence). When their practice is accompanied by a loving service to all Life, a study of the scriptures and an obedience to the Laws of God, the practitioner can achieve soul purification, the balancing of karma and union with God through the living Word.

Who Shall Decree?

To decree means literally to decide. Who in this world has the authority to decide, to make decisions? Only he who holds within his hands the power to implement the Universal Will and those to whom he has extended the authority of his will through the gift of free will.

That man who can say, "All power is given unto me in heaven and in earth,"[21] has the authority to make decisions because he has the power to implement them. One who decrees is ordained by God to command, to order, to fore-ordain and to appoint the bounds of His creation. There is only one such man, and he is the Christ.

Having the gift of free will, yet having been confined in time and space and having been given a limited creative potential, man (the lower self), also, may make decisions, but these can be effective only within the limited framework of his personal karma.

"Thou shalt also decree a thing and it shall be established unto thee!"[22] The promise holds true no matter what the level of man's individual consciousness. For as El Morya said, "Every moment, each man or woman creates his own future. Life, which is a God-given gift, continually acts to fulfill man's spoken or unspoken desires. Human thoughts and feelings are decrees in themselves and do produce with certainty and justice after their kind, whether joy or sorrow."[23]

The decrees or decisions that are made from the level of the human consciousness are limited in their effect because they proceed from the finite mind, but those made from the level of the Christ—the Holy Christ Self of every man—are unlimited (1) because they proceed from the infinite Mind of God, which is expressed through the Christ, and (2) because the Christ who lives in every man was ordained by God to be a co-creator with Him.

To decree or to command the energies of Life is the prerogative of the Christ-identity, or Higher Self, of every man. The human self, being imperfect and incomplete, has not yet been given the authority to utter fiats of creative direction; and thus, he must always preface his decrees by saying: "In the name of the beloved mighty victorious Presence of God I AM in me and my own beloved Holy Christ Self..."

The decree or divine fiat, the decreer and the answer to the decree comprise a threefold manifestation of God himself. The decreer must recognize that "God in me is giving this decree; it is God's energy that flows forth to obey his command, and he is the fulfilling of the Law by the power of the spoken Word that is manifesting in me."

Man (the lesser self) is thus an instrument for the Light that comes forth from the heart of God to coalesce as manifest perfection. He is not the source of the Light, neither is he the

dictator of creation; and he does not have any power of his
own to cause that Light to obey his command.

Therefore, if the disciple will determine to raise his
consciousness to the level of his Christ Self and know that he
is, in reality, that beloved Son, he, being one with God, may
present himself a living sacrifice—consecrated to purity in
order that God's Light, God's Word and God's decree may
flow through him to manifest the perfect work of the Creator.

Thus, having established in mind the realization of who is
"the doer" (the "door"*), the disciple may begin the sacred
ritual of offering decrees in the name of the Father (the
Presence of God, or the I AM Presence), the Son (the Universal
Christ, which manifests in every man as his own beloved
Christ-identity or Holy Christ Self) and the Holy Spirit (the
energies of the sacred fire that endow form and consciousness
with the essence of God that is Life).

The word "decree" is defined in the dictionary as an order
having the force or the authority of the law. According to our
usage, "the Law" is the will of God, and the authority or
"force" of the Law is in the power of the spoken Word.

A decree implies a foreordaining will. In our use of
decrees, we understand that it is the supreme will of God that
is the foreordaining power of the spoken Word. Above all,
decrees are the affirmation of the covenant between God and
man that has been in effect since "the Beginning."

Prayer and Meditation

Let us now examine prayer and meditation, realizing that
these are also forms of decrees, because they are the consequences of man's decision to seek the aid of his Creator and to
realign his energies with their Source. Prayer and meditation

---

* "I AM (God in me is) the open door which no man can shut" (John 10:9; Rev. 3:8).

may or may not make use of the power of the spoken Word, whereas decrees are scientifically based upon this principle.

The Ascended Masters Jesus and Kuthumi have written a series of teachings on the subject of prayer and meditation.[24] These, together with *The Science of the Spoken Word*,[25] should be studied by all who would gain a better understanding of the relationship between prayer, decrees and meditation.

Beloved El Morya has explained that these three forms of worship, when correctly used, comprise a balanced activity of the threefold flame. Prayer that is not based on a fear of punishment or a desire to gain personal favors from the Deity is intended to focus in the supplicant's heart the purity of God's love for him, even as he, through adoration, builds a ladder of love to God.

Meditation, when properly engaged in, opens the doors of the mind to the wisdom of God that enables man to understand and implement God's love. And decrees are invocative of the power and the faith that activate the flame of God's wisdom and his love and make these practical in our daily living.

Thus, prayer magnetizes the love ray, meditation establishes the wisdom ray, and decrees focus the power ray. The regular, rhythmic use of these three avenues of communion with the Holy Spirit blends the individual's energies with the white Light of the Christ, in whom he may contact every aspect of the consciousness of God. The following definitions of prayer and meditation were given by beloved Kuthumi in the above-mentioned series:

"Prayer and meditation are as twins, framing the pathway to holiness and delight. Just as prayer or entreaty makes contact with God, drawing down into the world of the seeker the rays of divine intercession, so meditation lifts up the Son of man that he may be bathed in the radiance of the Eternal.

"Meditation is an aerating of the mind, a flushing-out of silt and misconception. Meditation is for purification. It is the thought of man about his Creator. The dust of the world must be blown away, the threshing floor of the heart of man swept clean. In prayer, man makes intercession to God for assistance. In meditation, he gives assistance to God by creating the nature of God within his own thoughts and feelings....

"The admonishment of your beloved Hilarion, known unto many as Saint Paul, was 'Think on these things.'[26] To meditate, then, is to let the thoughts of God that flow into the heart rise into the head, that the Knower may also become the known. Meditation is an exchange of man's imperfect thoughts about himself and his Creator for the perfect thoughts held for him by the Creator.

"Identifying now with the eternal God, who is his Creator, the highest in his nature becomes the joint creator of himself. Thus, in a very real sense, as man draws the perfection of God into his world, he becomes the arbiter of his own destiny—a co-worker in the sublime—and he becomes as God is, self-created and creating."[27]

"Prayer is invocative; meditation is convocative. The Word goes forth; and the Word is the burning power of the Spirit that abides in the flesh but consumes it not, that transforms it, that raises the whole man, with his passion for Reality, vibrationally, emotionally, mentally, etherically and spiritually. For the entire being of man must be touched by the power of Truth, and Truth is the nature of God."[28]

Impediments to a Higher Communion Removed through Decrees

God knows our every need, but his outreach to us is hampered by the debris of our own human creation and by the misalignment of the internal patterns of our own thoughts and feelings. It is therefore imperative, even before prayer, that the great magnet of the God Presence and of the Ascended Masters' momentum of perfection be invoked by the power of the spoken Word.

This is done in order to bring about (1) the transmutation of all that impedes the penetration of God's Light into our consciousness, and (2) an inner realignment of our energy patterns, in order that the four lower bodies might be made fitting chalices for the Holy Spirit.

It should be understood that from time to time it becomes necessary for the following reasons for the individual to recharge his energies according to the divine pattern:

(1) the long period of man's disobedience to the Laws of Life has left many untransmuted records in his world,

(2) he has created chaos within his own forcefield through his disobedience, and

(3) he has contaminated his aura by contact with discordant energies from without, which are magnetized to his forcefield by the above two conditions.

Due to the fact that it is not visible to most people, the human aura is often permitted, through neglect or a lack of awareness, to become a repository of misqualified thoughts and feelings instead of being guarded as a chalice for the consciousness of God. Often the energies within the subconscious mind (the electronic belt) seethe with discord that never makes so much as a ripple on the surface of the conscious mind until they are triggered by sudden confrontation with discord from without.

The giving of decrees, then, desensitizes these virulent energies that lurk beneath the surface of man's conscious mind (before they can act or encroach upon his manifestation of Life's perfection), and thus he becomes less susceptible to the forces without that seek to catch him unawares. The recharging of the individual's entire forcefield, his energies and his consciousness according to the will of God can be done with complete safety through the giving of decrees.

Beloved Kuthumi has said: "Prayers or decrees can be used prior to the period of meditation. The Ascended Masters know that for mankind, caught as they are in the snares of human feelings and thoughts, a decree session given in full voice before the meditation period will serve to insulate, to protect and to harmonize the four lower bodies so that each life-stream can be best prepared to receive the fruits of his own meditation."[29]

For those who have the goal of the ascension before them, decreeing is a daily necessity. The giving of decrees that have been written by the Ascended Masters, and which therefore contain the pattern and the momentum of their Ascended consciousness, will heighten the spiritual sensitivities of the devotee.

As he contacts his own Christ Self and the Mind of Christ as it expresses through the Ascended Masters, he finds that that Mind which was in Christ Jesus[30] is also expressing through his own mental body. He notes a quickening of his perceptions as the Holy Spirit infuses his entire being with its enlivening power.

Through the giving of decrees, he is thus drawing into the chalice of his four lower bodies those God-qualities that are already in manifestation in his three Higher Bodies. Through the affirmation of the name of God, he is fulfilling the ritual "as Above, so below," and the kingdom of God is coming into realization in the world of form through the nexus of his own consciousness.

Decrees are magnets of divine love that draw to the decreer needed gifts and graces. These may come in the form of renewed health and the fulfillment of every requirement of body, mind and soul. The power of the Christ that is invoked through decrees will reverse riptides of negatively qualified energy that the disciple may encounter; it will cast out demons and entities; it will transmute wrong thoughts and feelings; and it will attune the soul and the four lower bodies with the consciousness of the Christ.

Through the giving of decrees, the inner sight and hearing can be restored and the music of the spheres can once again be heard. The sound of the flames of God will actually be heard "as the noise of many waters."[31] And the rushing of the wind of the Holy Spirit will become audible. These enveloping tones will resound within one's very bones and produce by cosmic harmonics the correction of those imperfect patterns that cause disease, accidents and old age; the tone produced by the "singing" of the elemental beings within the flames will automatically reverse negative currents of imperfect human thinking and feeling.

The drawing of the Light of God's love through the giving of decrees has such a harmonizing influence on the world of the individual that it is truly a great misfortune that some choose to maintain a closed mind concerning the Laws that govern the scientific release of divine power through decrees.

As the Word of the LORD came to Ezekiel, "Son of man, thou dwellest in the midst of a rebellious house, which have eyes to see, and see not; they have ears to hear, and hear not: for they are a rebellious house,"[32] the disciple should understand that his four lower bodies have become "a rebellious house" and their rebellion against the will of God has taken the form of a misqualification of His energy.

The energy that the individual allows his lower bodies to misqualify through wrong thought and feeling settles in these bodies as the dust of the centuries. Layer upon layer it accumulates through his many unenlightened incarnations until finally the spiritual centers (the chakras) are completely buried.

Thus, it comes to pass that the Word of the LORD given to Ezekiel is fulfilled in everyone who has turned from the path of righteousness (the "right use" of God's Laws and his energy). Having eyes to see, they see not, and having ears to hear, they hear not, for the wheels of their spiritual centers have become clogged with their own misqualified substance.

As archaeologists of the Spirit, we must dig up the artifacts of True Being that, in discovering our ancient heritage, we might become all that we were intended to be. As alchemists of the sacred fire, we must use the sword of the living Word to transmute the base metals of our human creation into the refined gold of spiritual perception. These are practical goals that can be accomplished through the power of the spoken Word as it is implemented in the giving of decrees.

Jesus Christ Taught Us to Decree

It was none other than Jesus Christ himself who taught us to decree. When Jesus gave us the Lord's Prayer, he said, "After this manner therefore pray ye."[33] Jesus taught us not only what to pray but also how to pray. And the manner in which he taught us to pray has been entirely overlooked, although it is as important as the prayer itself.

First Jesus taught us to address the Father, "Our Father which art in heaven," thereby establishing the contact of loving adoration from our heart to the heart of God. He then taught us to recite seven commands. Each one is spoken to our Father not as a request but as a decree in the imperative mode:

1. Hallowed be thy name!
2. Thy kingdom come!

3. Thy will be done on earth as it is in heaven!
4. Give us this day our daily bread!
5. And forgive us our debts as we forgive our debtors!
6. And lead us not into temptation!
7. But deliver us from evil![34]

When we give commands such as those Jesus taught us in the Lord's Prayer, we are actually commanding the moving stream of the River of Life that flows to us over the crystal cord from our mighty I AM Presence to crystallize into form in fulfillment of our spoken Word.

These are not the pleas of miserable, guilt-ridden sinners groveling before a wrathful god. They are the commands of children of the Light and loving sons and daughters whom God has entrusted with the wise and judicious use of his Word, who know they are joint-heirs with Jesus of the Christ Light.

What we learn from our Lord's prayer is that as sons and daughters of God, we need not beg our Father for our daily needs. We need only ask—in the form of the command—and he will release his Light, energy and consciousness to us in the form we specify.

The Lord's Prayer— Formula for Commanding the Father

When we command the Father, we use the scientific principle of bringing forth, or precipitating, from Spirit to Matter that which is the intent of our free will harnessed to God's will. We are confirming the commission spoken to the issue of God: "Be fruitful and multiply, and replenish the earth, and subdue it: and have dominion..."[35]

God would not have given us this commission without the means to fulfill it. Therefore he gave us the Word in a twofold way, as: (1) the personal Christ—*the Word Incarnate* in Jesus Christ and in our Holy Christ Self, who serves as Mediator of our soul's communion with God and by whose authority we command God's Light, energy and consciousness; and (2) the impersonal Christ—the spoken Word whereby we ratify in the Matter cosmos what God has already ordained in the Spirit cosmos.

But our power to command by the Word is not without circumscription. Jesus included in the Lord's Prayer certain qualifying commands that he intended us to insert in all our prayers or decrees. Again, this is why he said, "After this manner pray ye."

In telling us to follow our address to the Father with the command "Hallowed be thy name!" Jesus is teaching us that the name of God I AM THAT I AM or any other name ascribed to the Godhead must be hallowed, that is, "made holy" and adored with all our heart and soul and mind. Supreme respect for and veneration of our Father-Mother God and the Great Law that girds the cosmos is the foundation of our faith and our dynamic decrees.

In this first command of the Lord's Prayer, Jesus is affirming the first of the Ten Commandments: "Thou shalt have no other gods before me."[36] Those who pray, "Hallowed be thy name!" affirm their allegiance to the one God and are thereby signifying that God is Lord of their temple and ruler of their household—"Hear, O Israel, The LORD our God is one Lord."[37]

Therefore, in effect, they do petition that any prayer or command that is inordinate or unlawful in his sight be answered not according to the human will but the Divine. This is the safety valve that protects every devotee of God from the misuse of the Science of the Spoken Word and the consequent misqualification of God's Light.

The second command is "Thy kingdom come!" and the third is "Thy will be done on earth as it is in heaven!" In affirming these, the supplicant agrees that God's kingdom and only his kingdom shall come into manifestation as a result of his decrees and that God's will and only his will shall be done in his life. In other words, he agrees that he shall exercise his free will and the authority God has given him to command spiritual and material resources in His name in order that the earthly patterns may be established after the heavenly patterns according to God's will.[38]

When a son of God gives a command, the "plus spirals" of the Spirit creation are transferred through the nexus of the Christ to the "minus spirals" of the Matter creation. And that which is Above is manifest here below: God's kingdom is come "on earth as it is in heaven." God's will is done and that which is below is become the mirror image of that which is Above.

The fourth, fifth, sixth and seventh commands are predicated on the prior affirmation of and consent by the supplicant to the first three. These four commands are examples of our most basic physical, psychological and soul needs. They are: (4) to "Give us this day our daily bread," (5) to "Forgive us our debts as we forgive our debtors" and (6) to "Lead us not into temptation," (7) "But deliver us from evil."

God is ready to hear other commands that pour forth from

our hearts and to fulfill them—as long as we subordinate them to the first three. For unless we submit our commands to God's will, even when we think we know what is best for ourselves, our loved ones, our country and our planet, we run the risk of misusing or "misdirecting," "misapplying" or "misqualifying," as we say, the crystal-clear stream of the River of Life that flows to us unceasingly from the Source.

If we use God's power to create other than as God would have us create, we defile this sacred science of the Word and therefore God himself. The consequence is injury to Life and negative karma that we must one day painfully and painstakingly undo, thread by thread, as we serve to set Life free.

When we create negative karma, we get out of alignment with the will of God and drift farther and farther into the delusions of thinking man, who thinks he alone is true. But unless he is one with Christ, his mind one with the Christ Mind, how can he be sure? For the plumb line of Christ Truth is the measure of our "trueness." And Paul said, "Let God be true, but every [mortal] man a liar."[39]

Now, when we understand the Word as the incarnate Christ, who is our true inheritance when we walk in the footsteps of the Master, and when we understand the power of the Word when spoken in the manner Jesus taught us to pray, we can follow Jesus' example in any situation we find ourselves in.

For instance, when Jesus came upon the barren fig tree, he cursed it with the command: "Let no fruit grow on thee henceforward for ever!" And when the disciples marvelled, "How soon is the fig tree withered away!" Jesus said:

> Verily I say unto you, If ye have faith, and doubt not, ye shall not only do this which is done to the fig tree, but also if ye shall say unto this mountain, Be thou removed, and be thou cast into the sea; it shall be done.

And all things, whatsoever ye shall ask in prayer, believing, ye shall receive.[40]

Whether it be the fig tree or the mountain or any other offense or obstacle, we understand from this vignette that when Jesus says "whatsoever ye shall ask in prayer,..." he often means "whatsoever ye shall command, believing, ye shall receive."

The final statement of the Lord's Prayer—it is actually the eighth command—is for the sealing of our prayer: "For thine is the kingdom, and the power, and the glory, for ever. Amen."[41]

The sealing is our affirmation that everything we have called forth from the heart of the I AM Presence belongs to God. It is his omniscience, his kingdom (i.e., his consciousness); his omnipotence, his power; and his omnipresence, his glory, that forever sustain his decrees and ours, when they are in consonance with his.

The "Amen" serves a function similar to that of the Sanskrit "Aum." It is the sealing of the prayer in the heart of God for his disposition. Man has proposed, God will now dispose. Man has propounded, God will now compound.

In our sealing, we are acknowledging God as the original Decreer, as the Decree and as the Answer to our Decree. We must acknowledge that the entire creation that came forth from him, ourselves included, belongs to him—that we are his, that the kingdom is his, that the power is his and that the glory is his, forever. This final command is for our protection —lest we take God's kingdom, power and glory for the adornment of the lesser self.

Within this Allness that is God, he has made his sons and daughters to be co-creators with him. So long as we create to his kingdom, to his power, to his glory and for the very love of him, our commands for the qualification of the Waters of the River of Life that flow through us will be accomplished.

Decrees: The Fulfillment of Prophecy

Early in the 1930s, the Ascended Master Saint Germain released the knowledge of the science of decrees as the most effective means whereby unascended man might redeem the energies of God that he had vested with his imperfect qualifications. And thus another prophecy was fulfilled—that the days should be shortened for the elect.[42] For by invoking the transmutative power of the violet flame, the individual not only lightens his aura by requalifying and recharging his energy patterns with their original perfection, but he also lightens the burden of his karma, thereby shortening the days of his travail.

How is this possible? The explanation is simple: personal karma is recorded in the dense misqualified substance lodged within the four lower bodies of man. As his misqualified substance is transmuted, so is his karma transmuted.*

It is karma that determines the length of man's days in earth's schoolroom. Therefore, by transmuting his karma in the flames of the Holy Spirit and by consecrating his energies in dedicated service to Life when he is not decreeing, his days may be shortened, and he may win his immortal freedom from the round of rebirth.

Whenever personal karma is balanced through the use of the flames, both the individual and those whom he may have wronged in the past are blessed and freed from the burdens of their mutual karma. These blessings are given from the hand of the God Presence whether or not there is contact on the

---

* It should be noted that the transmutation of personal karma is accomplished not only through the giving of decrees but also through service rendered to God and man.

personal level.

It does not matter who was to blame; as long as the individual desires to forgive, to forget and to be free, the flames of freedom will liberate the energies, the soul and the consciousness of all concerned. How great is our God and how great is his mercy![43]

Thus it came to pass that in the 1930s, groups of students gathered in many cities in the United States and elsewhere in the world for the purpose of expanding the Light within themselves and on behalf of all mankind. Among the organizations that first sponsored decree work, some have continued to use decrees; whereas others, following the edicts that from time to time are issued from "the rebellious house,"[44] changed the patterns that the Masters had given until their decrees became nothing more than innocuous statements, devitalized of the radiant, vibrant energies of the Christ, which are so necessary in producing in the consciousness of the race the manifestation of the living Word.

Affirmations of Truth: Mind over Matter?

Now, there is an apparent similarity between decrees and the affirmations or "statements of Truth" that have been advocated by various metaphysical movements. In these groups, often without their realization, greater emphasis is placed on the power of the mind—"mind over matter," as some say—than upon the Christ. In this case, the "mind" they refer to is the lower mental body, although they aver that only the power of the Christ Mind (the Higher Mental Body) is used. We would point out that merely to affirm that this is what is happening does not necessarily make it so.

Some practitioners of mental science who are adamant

against hypnotism, thought transference and thought control actually use elements of all three to bring about the healing of mind and body and the "desired" changes in the consciousness of those who come to them for help. Others have truly entered into the consciousness of the Christ, and we would be the first to acknowledge that this Higher Mind works through them to bring about the healing of the patient.

A word of caution is in order here: when the lower mental body is used to bring about an apparent healing by means of the human will, the cause, effect, record and memory of the disease is not cured. This is because only the fires of the Mind of Christ have the power to transmute misqualified energy—to purify and cleanse the waters of Life—to change Darkness into Light.

What happens, then, to the cause, effect, record and memory of the disease when the lower mental body and the human will are employed as the instruments of healing?

These karmic factors and their symptoms (which may have begun to manifest as disease on the physical, mental or emotional level) are forced back into the etheric body (the memory body) from whence they must one day come forth again to be expiated through one or more of the lower bodies.

Therefore, we see that the individual may elect, by his free will, not to balance his karma (to "atone for his sins," in Christian parlance). Using "mental physics," hypnotism and other systems of karma-dodging, he will neither (1) let the cause, effect, record and memory of the disease run their course through the four lower bodies, nor will he (2) invoke the flames of God through his four lower bodies, thereby transmuting the karmic factors and also much, if not all but a token, of the suffering these may entail.

In most cases the postponement of his own "day of salvation" (day of Self-elevation—the elevation of the Real Self in his consciousness) comes about as the result of his recycling of his karma. The individual has used his free will to change the programming of his returning karma, which was arranged by the Lords of Karma and his own Christ Self for the evolution of his soul. But the result will be that he may have to wait one or more embodiments before the opportunity will again be given him to stand, face and conquer this particular element of his own human creation.

Through such unfortunate and misguided use of the Law, the days are actually lengthened for these individuals, even though to all outer appearances it would seem that they are leading a charmed existence. Based on the evidence that their problems and their ills disappear, they conclude that they are practicing the true and lost science of healing as it was demonstrated by Jesus Christ.

Engaging the Total Being of Man in the Spiritual Quest

Various methods of the reunion of the soul with God have been advocated. Many schools do not realize that their methods take into account only one of man's lower bodies. For instance, metaphysics places its emphasis on the mental body; evangelism works mostly through the emotional body; Eastern forms of religion in which meditation leading to Samadhi and Nirvana is stressed work primarily through the etheric or memory body; and those religions that are based on form and ritual appeal to those whose orientation is in the physical body.

This fact should not detract from the good that is to be found in all religions, nor should it compel the teachers and followers of these religions to leave their churches. Nevertheless, those seeking total reunion must come to the place where they begin to reexamine the path they are following with a view to making their religious experience well-rounded according to the highest and most complete teachings that are available.

This can be done without unnecessary upheaval simply by adding a deeper understanding of Life's mysteries to the Truths they have already been given and by eliminating those concepts that, in the light of the higher criticism, are found to be in error.

In the work of The Summit Lighthouse, as it comes under the direction of the Spiritual Hierarchy of Light, the total being of man is engaged in serving the Light and in developing its outreach toward perfection. The three Higher Bodies,

(1) the I AM God Presence,

(2) the Causal Body and

(3) the Christ Self, or Higher Mental Body,

and the four lower bodies,

(1) the etheric body,

(2) the mental body,

(3) the emotional body and

(4) the physical body,

are all intended to be the instruments of Truth, chalices to consecrate man's higher nature, to raise him to the summit of his being.

The etheric body, or memory body, was designed to record the purity of God and the original pattern of man's perfection, the acceptance of the perfection of God. The mental body was built to focus the Christ, the golden Light of the sun of illumination. The emotional body was uniquely patterned to radiate God's love universally, without dissimulation. The physical body, so noble in its artistic structure, was intended to hold the ray of power in the world of form.

As these four bodies are cleansed by the action of the sacred fire—baptized by the Spirit Most Holy—they magnetize the Presence of the three Higher Bodies through the fulcrum that is the threefold flame within the heart. The four lower bodies are the vehicles into which perfection descends from the dimensions of the Spirit into the dimensions of Spirit's materialization in form. Only by a total religious experience, which must include the seven bodies of man, can the whole man be made whole, and only by this means can the four lower bodies be raised into the ascension in the Light.

Certain Dangers to Be Avoided in Meditation, Prayer and Decrees

One of the dangers involved in entering into meditation without having first given at least the Violet Fire and Tube of Light Decree (see page 43) is that the protection of the consciousness has not been established in order to insure contact with the Mind of God during the period of meditation.

Without first building a forcefield of Light around oneself, steadfast concentration on the God Presence may become difficult; the mind may wander and subtle vibrational patterns of negation may flow into the subconscious mind and later surface as emotional or psychic disturbances. Such unhappy states may be avoided by first giving decrees and then by directing one's meditation toward specific levels of the divine character, such as the love, peace, joy, wisdom and harmony of the Holy Spirit.

On the other hand, Kuthumi points out that "meditation ought not to be prescribed by the meditator. He may choose a subject of the higher order upon which to reflect; but he should always permit the hand of God to lead him in thought, that the meditations of his heart and mind may be directed exclusively by his Holy Christ Self and mighty God Presence, I AM.

"Among the dangers in meditation that many have faced is the altogether human penchant for the psychic (because it is so readily available) and the wish to find a unique teacher in the higher realms or perhaps a 'spirit guide' who will convey some exclusive concept that one can then parade before his fellow men.

"If the aspirant for higher meditation will only understand that the childlike simplicity and trust of the seeker enables him to contact the Reality of the living God, he will cease to be led by the curious elements of his own lower nature into the byways of ego-centered ventures that can never reward him with the spiritual bliss that his soul craves. For even as God's love flows to all in equal measure, he does convey a specific motif of exquisite and unique beauty to each monad according to his infinite purposes."[45]

One of the dangers of decrees is that the decreer may forget who is giving the decrees, that it is his own Christ Self and not his outer consciousness who speaks the lost Word that compels the freedom of his soul. He should be careful not to strain his voice or to force the flow of God's energy, nor should he give in to the temptation to use decrees to implement his human will instead of the divine will. The danger of this is especially great when he thinks he knows what the will of God is.

Therefore, regardless of his conviction, he should always conclude his prayers and his decrees with a statement such as, "In the name of my I AM Presence, I ask my Christ Self to adjust this petition according to the will of God and his plan for all concerned."

Prayers and decrees should always be given in the same spirit that prompted Jesus to say, "Nevertheless, not my will, but thine, be done,"[46] and also in the spirit of the Psalmist, who said, "Let the words of my mouth, and the meditation of my heart, be acceptable in thy sight, O LORD, my strength, and my redeemer."[47]

Above all, the decreer should remember the words of Jesus concerning the Christ, "My Father worketh hitherto, and I work.... Verily, verily I say unto you, The Son can do nothing of himself, but what he seeth the Father do: for what things soever he doeth, these also doeth the Son likewise.... For as the Father raiseth up the dead, and quickeneth them; even so the Son quickeneth whom he will."[48]

One of the dangers of prayer is that the supplicant may dwell in a sense of incompleteness and separation from the God he seeks in prayer. The need to ask God's help may cause the individual to accept the subtle suggestion that he does not already have that help or that his prayers are not already answered before he gives them. Neither should he fall into the trap of asking God to do for him what he, through the power vested in his own Christ Self, may do for himself by the simple practice of God's Laws.

The Science of Decrees

The Ascended Master Saint Germain has given his thoughts on decrees: "When we contemplate methods of God-realization, we dare not exclude the power of the spoken Word.

"For many years, the so-called orthodox religions have used ritual and form, together with spoken mantras. In the West these have been called responsive readings, for they require the response of the congregation, or audience participation. In some instances, the prayers of mankind have become vainly repetitious and devoid of meaning, but I for one would rather see individuals involved in rote than enmeshed in the wrong kinds of vocalized expression....

"Decrees are not careless words; they are careful words. And the patterns we recommend are invocative of the highest good for man.

"Decrees are generally composed of three parts, and they should be thought of as letters to God:

"(1) The salutation of the decree is invocative. It is addressed to the individualized God Presence of every son and daughter of God and to those servants of God who comprise the Spiritual Hierarchy. This salutation (the preamble to the decree), when reverently given, is a call that compels the answer from God and the Ascended Ones. We could no more refuse to answer this summons in our octave than could your firemen refuse to answer a call for help in yours. The purpose of the salutation, then, is to engage immediately the energies of the Ascended Masters in answering the body of your letter to God, which you so lovingly vocalize individually or in unison.

"(2) The body of your letter is composed of statements phrasing your desires, the qualifications you would invoke for self or others, and the supplications that would be involved even in ordinary prayer. Having released the power of the spoken Word through your outer consciousness, your subconscious mind and your superconscious, or Higher Self, you can rest assured that the supreme consciousness of the Ascended Masters whom you have invoked is also concerned with the manifestation of that which you have called forth.

"(3) Now you come to the close of your decree, the acceptance, the sealing of the letter in the heart of God, released with a sense of commitment into the realm of the Spirit whence manifestation must return to the world of material form according to the unerring laws of alchemy (the all-chemistry of God) and precipitation.[49]

"Those who understand the power of the square in mathematics will realize that when groups of individuals are engaged in invoking the energies of God, they are not merely adding power by the number of people in the group on a one-plus-one basis, but they are entering into a very old covenant of the square, which squares (multiplies) the release of power to accomplish the spoken Word by the number of individuals who are decreeing and by the number of times that each decree is given.

"We heartily recommend individual decrees to accomplish untold blessings in the lives of those who will discipline themselves in this ritual of invoking Light to a darkened world. But group decreeing, when accompanied by an intense visualization of the good desired, is more efficacious on a world scale than individual decreeing and will result in a speedy response to those engaged in it, not only to themselves but also on behalf of all mankind.

"It should be borne in mind that whenever Good (God) is invoked in the world of form, surrounded as the world is today by a great accumulation of mortal effluvia, the Good (the Light) that is released from on high in answer to the call (because of the high frequency of the vibrations of the Light) is automatically opposed by the negative vibrations already existing in the atmosphere of the earth (because of the low frequency of these vibrations).

"Rhythm is also important in decrees. Proper rhythm creates a most penetrating projection of spiritual vibrations that will magnetize all over the planet the qualities of God that are being invoked through the decrees. The momentum of these waves that form undulating circles over the planetary body creates an intensification of Light wherever devotees come together to participate in a like endeavor.

"The laws governing the manifestation and distribution of physical light also apply to the flow of the currents of spiritual Light. Spiritual qualities are distributed around the planetary body from every radiating focus of Ascended Master love.

"Let no one feel, then, a sense of separation in his service to Hierarchy; for by the power of decrees, issued forth at any point upon the Earth's surface, the currents of Light, Life and Love from the heart of God can be unleashed as electrical, radiating waves to make their impact in the world and bring back to the invoker the God-ordained response....

"We know full well that individuals who come into our meetings and encounter these decrees for the first time without understanding the Laws governing them or the beautiful results that can be obtained through their use can well come under the influence of certain negative forces and entities in the world that quite naturally are diametrically opposed to the use of dynamic decrees.

"Too frequently, individuals who stress their desire for quiet meditation fail to take into account that there is a time and a place for quiet meditation, a time and a place for prayer and a time and a place for decrees. All three can be used in religious service. All three can be used in the home, individually, or in groups, as one desires. But one form of worship is not a substitute for the other....

"After all, consciousness is one. The individual who dwells in God can pour out his heart to God in prayer, in song, in decrees, or sit silently meditating upon an aspect of Deity. Thought precedes worded expression, or at least it should. Therefore, to meditate or to think upon God is one way of expressing him. Decreeing is another.

"When the children of Israel brought down the walls of Jericho, it was by a great shout, a great use of the consummate power of divine energy.[50] The sinister force has perverted this knowledge, which has been a part of the forte of the teachings of the Great White Brotherhood for thousands of years.

"Some groups have taken to training young people in the

wrong use of this law involving the power of the spoken Word. Their followers chant in unison and in rhythm, thereby summoning or magnetizing power and projecting it forth upon a vibratory wavelength that is charged with personal and group hatred. The effect of these momentums of mass misqualification can be disastrous upon those who encounter them, for when correctly used, this power did bring down the walls of Jericho....

"Decrees are synthesized manifestations of the heart flame of each one who decrees. Decrees draw together and focalize the power of the spoken Word, the visualization of the Christ Mind and the rhythm of the divine pulse. When you decree, you are releasing divinely qualified energy charged by your invocation and multiplied by the power of the Ascended Masters. It goes forth to do its perfect work for the amplification of the power of Light upon the entire planet.

"I can say little more than that which was spoken of old: 'Prove me now herewith, saith the LORD of hosts, if I will not open you the windows of heaven, and pour you out a blessing, that there shall not be room enough to receive it.'[51]

"The proper use of decrees takes practice. Individuals should not expect that the first time they make a call, the very perfection of the universe will sweep away all of the accumulated debris of their lives.

"Proper decreeing is an art, and as one gains greater proficiency, he will find it possible to speed up his decrees— that is, he will be able to speed up the rate at which they are given. He will also be able to understand what is taking place as he speeds them up. For this acceleration, by raising the rate of his own electronic pattern, throws off and transmutes negative thoughts and feelings in his world.

"Oh, what delight and peace you can bring to your family, to your friends and to yourself through the proper use of decrees! What a boon to freedom! How gloriously the world can be changed for the better!

"After all, blessed ones, Nature herself is not always silent. God speaks in thunder, in lightning and in the wind;[52] and the chattering of the many birds through the world, like the crickets in the swamp, certainly raises the decibels.

"By the power of the Word the Earth was framed,[53] and by the power of the Word the freedom of man shall be dominantly asserted in God's name. Use your decrees! Fear not the opinions of men, for the Hierarchy has spoken and those who heed will profit."[54]

The Tube of Light

Because men send out torrents of discordant thoughts and feelings each day through the misqualification of God's energy, the individual must find a means of protecting himself. Unless this be achieved through a conscious rejection of these ill-fitting thoughts, he will find that, either consciously or subconsciously, this effluvia will penetrate the domain of self.

The banal effects of such penetration invariably come to the surface later. But from the moment they gain entrance into the individual's subconscious world, they can produce a vibratory response to negativity that burdens the soul and produces feelings of unhappiness, depression and sickness, thus thwarting her total creative output.

There is a way in which every person on Earth can call to his Divine Presence and ask that Presence to enfold him in the seamless garment of the living Christ. This garment is a high-frequency manifestation of vibrating Light that can actually be drawn down daily and hourly to enfold the self with tremendous protection. Through regular devotion and invocation on the part of the supplicant, the power of this garment of Light can become more and more real.

It has been reported that some of the great adepts of India have developed such a momentum in drawing down this garment of Light into tangible manifestation that it has actually deflected a bullet from an elephant gun, the lead being flattened upon contact with the Light and falling to the ground a few feet from the body.

Of course, sensible students will neither claim nor test such development of the armour of God ("Thou shalt not tempt the Lord thy God"[55]). But they will maintain implicit faith and trust that when the need arises, the Light of God will defend them against all attacks on their person.

The seamless garment is a powerful thoughtform for the protection and sealing of the aura against negative thoughts and feelings emanating from the mass consciousness. You may put on this seamless garment as a surrounding tube of light by pouring out your love to your God Presence, saying:

O my constant, loving I AM Presence, thou Light of God above me whose radiance forms a circle of fire before me to light my way:

I AM faithfully calling to thee to place a great pillar of Light from my own mighty I AM God Presence all around me right now today! Keep it intact through every passing moment, manifesting as a shimmering shower of God's beautiful Light through which nothing human can ever pass. Into this beautiful electric circle of divinely charged energy direct a swift upsurge of the violet fire of freedom's forgiving, transmuting flame!

Cause the ever expanding energy of this flame projected downward into the forcefield of my human energies to completely change every negative condition into the positive polarity of my own great God Self! Let

the magic of its mercy so purify my world with Light
that all whom I contact shall always be blessed with the
fragrance of violets from God's own heart in memory of
the blessed dawning day when all discord—cause, effect,
record and memory—is forever changed into the victory
of Light and the peace of the Ascended Jesus Christ.

I AM now constantly accepting the full power and
manifestation of this fiat of Light and calling it into
instantaneous action by my own God-given free will and
the power to accelerate without limit this sacred release
of assistance from God's own heart until all men are
ascended and God-free in the Light that never, never,
never fails!

Or you can use this shorter prayer, which is also highly
effective:

> Beloved I AM Presence bright,
> Round me seal your tube of light
> From Ascended Master flame
> Called forth now in God's own name.
> Let it keep my temple free
> From all discord sent to me.
>
> I AM calling forth violet fire
> To blaze and transmute all desire,
> Keeping on in freedom's name
> Till I AM one with the violet flame.

There are certain activities in the flame involving elemental
life—the dancing electrons, the fiery salamanders and the very
energy components of the flame itself. These are magnetized in
the service of man through intense visualization. This visualization must include not only a mental image but also the
feeling of the heart—a great love for the Light and an empathy

with the flame that enables you to experience a unity with God bordering on spiritual ecstasy.

Focusing this powerful tube of spiritual light around your physical form insulates your mind and consciousness. As long as you sustain the action of the tube of light, you have an impervious armour that shields you against the play and ploy of the psychic effluvia of the planet.

But if you then become involved in any kind of discordant activity whatsoever (be it gossip, argument, anger or despair), you must quickly call upon the law of forgiveness and the violet transmuting flame and then invoke the tube of light once more. Any rent in the spiritual garment caused by the introduction of inharmony into your forcefield should be mended as soon as you have recovered your balance through the mercy of the Christ.

The Wall of Fire and the Glory in the Midst

The tube of light and violet flame are a source of daily protection to every lifestream who will use them. These are man's natural defenses against invisible agencies. The prophet Zechariah glimpsed the reality of this manifestation of Light's protection when he recorded the word of the LORD concerning the Holy City, "For I, saith the LORD, will be unto her a wall of fire round about, and will be the glory in the midst of her."[56]

The tube of light is every man's "wall of fire," and the violet flame is the "glory in the midst" of the tube of light. The tube of light, when invoked daily, is man's sure defense against all intruding negativity, and the violet fire pulsates in the center of the tube—in, through and around the very being of man—to consume the impurities of the self that are apt to hamper one's spiritual advancement from within. What a marvelous way to insulate oneself from without and from within! So simple and beautiful, and yet how scientific are God's Laws!

As you offer the prayer for the tube of light, look at the Chart of Your Divine Self (facing page 12). Visualize the tube of light as a concentrated stream of vital, intelligent energy that weaves an armour of invincible protection, a cylinder of spiritual Light substance around your whole being. You may think of yourself as standing in a giant milk bottle. Your tube of light is approximately nine feet in diameter and extends three feet beneath the soles of your feet into the earth.

As you balance and expand your threefold flame, the tube of light increases in stature. The tube of light of an Ascended Being such as Jesus the Christ or the Lord Buddha is as large as the planet.

The Violet Flame

When the ritual of invoking the tube of light is concluded, draw forth the violet fire of freedom's love in, through and around yourself within the tube of light. Through the conscientious use of the violet singing flame, the cause, effect, record and memory of all errors and harmful momentums of the past are loosened from your entire consciousness, being and world. By the power of the Light of God that never fails, these are actually changed "in the twinkling of an eye" into spiritual energy that may then be used to implement your forward movement and regeneration into the domain of freedom.

Originating in the heart of the I AM Presence, the Light ray descends into the forcefield of the individual. When it reaches the "ground," or the point of invocation, it springs up as a violet flame. It should be seen leaping and pulsating through the folds of one's consciousness as the purple lining of the seamless robe.

The power of the violet flame and of all of the flames of God is known as "the power of the three-times-three" because it contains within it the action of the threefold flame. Through this power to make one whole, the violet flame readies the aspirant for initiations to come.

As you know, the "zero" that is added to one to make ten introduces the next place in the column of figures. Spiritually speaking, the step from Grade 9, which is the power of the 3 x 3, to Grade 10 is the step of initiation. It is one's graduation into the next order of magnitude of the God flame within. Here the cycle of transformation moves into the ascending spiral of the transfiguration; here the disciple is expected to have readied himself through the ritual of transmutation for the divine testing.

Saint Paul referred to this test as a daily challenge when he said, "I die daily."[57] He also said, "The fire shall try every man's work of what sort it is."[58] For when the violet transmuting flame is called forth on the altar of being, it does ready man's consciousness for the cycles of initiation to follow.

The violet flame is like the pen of the Architect of man's noblest aspirations. It focuses the power, wisdom and love of the Holy Spirit that assists each one to transmute his negatives and to make way for the great positive onrush of divine perfection into his world.

The violet flame is not always felt, and it is usually not visible to one who is just beginning to practice this ritual. However, it can become visible and tangible in a very short time; therefore, when calling forth the flame, one should always hold in consciousness the vivid memory of a roaring, crackling violet fire.

The action of the flame should be envisioned intensely until you can literally feel and hear its pulsations. For the violet flame penetrates the pores of your physical body, your brain, your bones, your nerves as it vivifies every cell and atom of your being.

If you will call upon the violet flame at least once but preferably twice or three times a day, you will find that the causes and cores of unhappiness, fear, distress and a host of knotty human problems will gradually be eliminated from your world. This takes place as the lower self is stripped of its records and momentums of past errors and mistakes. As the energies you have invested in imperfection are transmuted by the violet flame, they rise into your Causal Body, where they are stored until such time as you have need of them.

As the penetrations of the psychic effluvia of the world and the wrong thoughts and feelings of others are dissolved by a generous application of the violet flame, there occurs what we may call a "washing of the water by the Word."[59]

This is a spiritual cleansing; it is the baptism by fire that was referred to by John the Baptist when he said, "One mightier than I cometh, the latchet of whose shoes I am not worthy to unloose: he shall baptize you with the Holy Ghost and with fire."[60]

Concentration, Visualization, Adoration— Essentials for Decreeing Effectively

Concentration is of the utmost importance while decreeing, for it is over the flow of man's attention that the energies of the Presence travel to fulfill the spoken Word. Contrary to the concept of most students who take up the science of giving decrees, concentration is a quality of heart rather than of the mind. Your center of attention should be in the heart flame at all times while you decree, for here is your own individual focus of God's power, wisdom and love. This practice will avoid mental strain and undue pressure on those chakras that are less developed in Western man.

Decreeing is a function of the heart and of man's devotion. The intellect, which has for far too long ruled the heart in most people, must be reeducated to obey the heart's call and to be obedient to the intuitive powers of the heart, which most often do reflect the inner voice of the Christ Self.

If the attention is riveted on the desired manifestation and the mind's eye is visualizing the decree made manifest, the results will be infinitely more effective than if the mind wanders, the feelings are absorbed in various distractions, and the eyes gaze at random about the room.

As you become more familiar with the words of the decrees, you may close your eyes and see taking place before you the action you are invoking. This process, known as *visualization*, is based on man's ability to "image forth" or to imagine. Use this creative faculty to "see" each word or descriptive phrase as a thought-pattern or "matrix," a "cup" or a "chalice" held steady in heart and mind in order that God's energy may flow into your cup of consciousness to energize and manifest perfection in the world of form.

Kuthumi explains some of the principles of the science of visualization: "When you are calling for a specific quality to manifest, do not fail to use the spiritual power of your vision. If you are calling for illumination's golden flame, then visualize yourselves and your contemporaries as surrounded by illumination's golden flame. If your power of vision and artistry is somewhat lacking, call to your Holy Christ Self and to your God Self to give you greater understanding as to how to construct, by mental patterns, these pictures of Light that attract to you the radiant atoms of eternity and form the matrix and mold into which the energies of your words may be poured.

"As you pour these words into this matrix, there is formed

in the atmosphere of the room in which you are decreeing a strong magnet, a thoughtform, charged with intense feeling, and this is used by the Ascended Masters in much the same manner that a radio receiver is used to receive a radio program from a distance. For as you create this tremendous, intense thoughtform, it magnetizes from the higher octaves the Light-energy that will help to manifest on mighty Light rays the very qualities for which you call.

"And this is the most scientific prayer known upon the planet. By it the walls of Jericho fell down. For as the people marched around the city, they gave a great shout, and they blew the trumpets and the walls of Jericho fell down.[61] You are modern Joshuas living today and using the power of your decrees to assist and implement the powers of Light, and I bless you for it."[62]

Use this creative faculty to see and to feel each word or descriptive phrase as a thought-pattern or matrix that is held steady in heart and mind in order that God's energy may flow into your cup of consciousness to energize and to manifest perfection in the world of form.

Some teachers of metaphysics have called this process "treasure mapping," others refer to it as "knowing the Truth." Whatever the term, you must recognize the importance of entering wholeheartedly into your meditations, prayers and decrees, and of employing the faculties of your four lower bodies as well as those of the Christ Mind. You must learn to energize your mental visualizations with the pure feelings of the heart, recording the memory and the momentum of the decrees in your etheric and your physical bodies in order that you may efficiently draw to yourself the qualities of God that you are invoking.

When you give the preamble to the decree, you should pour forth your love and adoration to God and to his Servant-

Sons, the Ascended Masters. The love that you release to the Heavenly Hosts forms a ladder from your world to theirs; and as the flame of adoration from your heart rises to meet the Christ, he will send his angels descending with bowers of blessings, messages of hope and the strength of the Almighty to assist you on your way. Truly, adoration to God opens the portals of heaven.

When you come to the body of the decree where the specific action of the flame is invoked, you should visualize its pulsing action enveloping your form, penetrating your mind and rekindling the fires of Life in the heart of each cell. Close your eyes and feel the currents of the Holy Spirit flowing through your body and know that this is the fire that will consume all unwanted habits, fears and frustrations—all that has hindered the expansion of God's Light within your soul.

The stronger the visualization, the stronger will be the action of the flame. And the action of the flame must be experienced with all of your spiritual faculties. In like manner, these faculties will come alive as you use the violet flame.

A simple method of visualizing the flames is to fix in mind the memory of a blazing campfire. Retaining the concept of the action of the physical flames, see them take on the color of the God flame you desire to invoke.

Now enlarge your image of the flames to fill your entire consciousness. Then visualize yourself in the center of God's flaming Presence. Feel his love enfold you as a thousand-petaled lotus—each flame a petal of God's all-embracing consciousness.

The assimilation of the flames of God by your four lower bodies will take place gradually and naturally without any uncomfortability to the body or to the psyche if you will visualize these flame colors as tangible, living fire, saturating your world with the God-qualities desired, while cleansing your being of all that is less than his perfection.

Before actually speaking the words of the decree, sit in a comfortable straight chair in a well-lighted room where you will be undisturbed, taking care that the room has been tidied, cleaned and well-aired. Dust, untidiness, stale air and poor lighting reduce the effectiveness of the decrees because these impede the flow of Light and repel the angelic hosts, who always assist the supplicant to amplify the release of God's holy energies.

Visualize the Presence of God above you (see the Chart of Your Divine Self, facing page 12), your lower self enveloped in the violet flame administered by your Christ Self, and visualize the threefold flame pulsing and expanding from your heart— the blue plume to your left, the pink plume to your right and the golden plume in the center.

Hold your spine and head erect, your legs and hands uncrossed and your feet flat on the floor. (Poor posture opens the consciousness to negative forces because the solar plexus, which is the doorway of the emotions, is not under control. Crossing the legs and hands causes a "short circuiting" of the energies that are intended to flow through the individual to bless all mankind.)

Therefore, remember Paul's words, "Know ye not that ye are the temple of God, and that the Spirit of God dwelleth in you?"[63] and let the energies of God flow through your body. Hold your book or the individual decrees at eye level so that you do not lean down while decreeing. You may prefer to sit at a desk or table where you can prop up your book in front of you, thus leaving your hands free and resting, palms up, to receive the blessings of God through the Masters.

Speak the decree slowly and clearly without strain until you can fully comprehend the meaning of its content. Then concentrate upon the rhythm and begin to give it more quickly. You will see how your mind can learn to follow with lightning speed the concepts and the release of power that come as you recite with greater facility.

It is important to breathe deeply and regularly, using the power of the Fire Breath of God to project the Light through your entire body and then out into the world to bless all of Life with the magnetization of God's energy focused through your own heart flame.

When decreeing for loved ones, first call to your own I AM Presence and Holy Christ Self—as worded in the preamble of the decree you are giving. Then insert in the preamble your call to the "mighty I AM Presence and Holy Christ Self of _____" (give the name of the person or persons for whom you wish to decree).

By calling to the God Presence of those in need of spiritual assistance, you open up the fount of heaven into their worlds so that all of the divine blessings of the Light may flow forth to heal whatever condition of imperfection may be manifesting therein. This service may be rendered without becoming personally involved in a given situation; for by your calls, the Ascended Masters are given the authority to move in and take command of any person, place, condition or thing to which you, in the name of God, may direct their attention.

You will note that the decrees published here have the following ending:

> And in full faith I consciously accept this manifest, manifest, manifest! (3x) right here and now with full power, eternally sustained, all-powerfully active, ever-expanding and world-enfolding, until all are wholly ascended in the Light and free!
>
> Beloved I AM, beloved I AM, beloved I AM!

The full acceptance of a decree made manifest in your

world is most important, for it is right here in the physical octave that the Light of God is needed. Through the giving of decrees, the supplicant draws down the Light from higher octaves of perfection to lower octaves of human imperfection.

We do not need to perfect God or his Christ; but we do require change in this world of chaos, disease, unhappiness and death. These changes can be brought about only by the drawing-forth of the Light of God and the conscious acceptance of that Light that never fails to give man his freedom whenever and wherever he determines to give of his energy in decrees until God can manifest His perfect work in him.

Without consciously accepting the answer to your decrees made manifest, the pure energies of God may very well remain in the higher octaves of Being—a matrix unfulfilled in Matter and untethered to the world of material form. The spoken Word is the key to drawing the Light from heaven to earth. You will remember that Jesus, when he healed, always spoke the command that released the Light in order to manifest on the physical plane that perfection that he acknowledged was already complete in the kingdom of heaven.

In the account of the raising of Lazarus, we note that Jesus employed the power of the spoken Word to release the energy from the plane of Spirit to the plane of Matter for the restoration of the Life-force. It is recorded that "they took away the stone from the place where the dead was laid. And Jesus lifted up his eyes and said, Father, I thank thee that thou hast heard me. And I knew that thou hearest me always: but because of the people which stand by I said it, that they may believe that thou hast sent me. And when he thus had spoken, *he cried with a loud voice,* Lazarus, come forth!"[64] It is also known that he *spoke* "as one that had *authority,* and not as the scribes."[65]

Decrees are thus *spoken* by man because it is the power of

the Word—and no other power in the universe—that is able to create, to resurrect, to transmute and to perfect the Divine Image in the sons and daughters of God. Therefore, decrees should always be given aloud; and only if it is impossible to do so should they be offered silently.

Light: The Alchemical Key

Those who decree understand that God already knows our need, as Jesus taught, and that he desires to help us. They understand that the way to receive that help is to identify their consciousness with God's.

This process of identifying with one's Source, with one's "very present help,"[66] of realigning one's being with all of the good in the universe, is accomplished most effectively through the exercise of all of one's faculties—mind, heart, soul and voice—in the offering of decrees, mantras and affirmations—call them what you will.

In the repetition of God's thoughts about man, in the affirmation of the Truth of Being—which God has declared from the Beginning and which Jesus expressed in his statement, "I AM the Way, I AM the Truth and I AM the Life"[67]— the soul, together with the four lower bodies, takes on the divine patterns that are to be found everywhere in the universe and that are held inviolate in each one's Causal Body.

We have included at the end of the chapter the Transfiguring Affirmations taught by beloved Jesus Christ to his disciples, because these affirmations may be offered to God as prayer, as meditation or as decrees. They fulfill the function of all three.

These scientific statements of Being were and are taught by one whose balanced threefold flame is able to impart the grace and the Truth of Law as a trinity of love, wisdom and power.

This is true of many of the decrees in The Summit Lighthouse decree book, "Prayers, Meditations, Dynamic Decrees for the Coming Revolution in Higher Consciousness."[68]

These invocations are actually decrees, meditations and prayers all in one, for they were written by the Ascended Masters, whose consciousness is poised in the heart of the cosmic threefold flame.

The sound of a large number of people decreeing in unison in full volume at a lively pace may be strange at first to those who are unaccustomed to this "new" form of group dynamics. The volume, the rhythm and the apparent "vain repetition of words" may be interpreted as "fanaticism" or "untempered zeal."

Lord Maitreya says that "the mere vain repetition of words is in itself completely ineffectual, as Jesus taught.[69] Therefore (since decrees are highly effectual), the wrong premise exists in the minds of those who assume that the giving of decrees is vainly repetitious."[70]

Many who for various reasons originally felt that they could not accept decreeing have changed their minds, once they have tested the efficacy of decrees for themselves. Those who thought that they were adversely affected by the "noise" have subsequently entered wholeheartedly into the giving of decrees with the accompanying visualizations and meditations upon the Presence after they once experienced the flow of energy that is released through decrees.

Because decrees are effective, many forces seek to discredit them. However, we must learn to value Truth wherever it is revealed, and we must love it even before we have made it our own. For Truth becomes ours when we test it, prove it and experience it.

The truth about decrees is not revealed merely by observing others decreeing or even by a half-hearted participation.

The truth can be learned only through understanding the scientific principles behind decrees, which are the very foundation of the creative power of the universe, and then through gradually mastering the art of giving decrees—for giving decrees is indeed an art even as it is a science.

Some who have discontinued their decrees after having developed a momentum over a certain period of time ask why they experience an inrush of unwanted conditions when they stop decreeing. Here is the explanation: the mass consciousness of mankind is composed largely of negative emotional energy, and this energy is in constant agitation outside one's own wall of Light (the tube of light).

This wall, which is built layer upon layer of one's devotions to God, acts as a dike to keep the waters of human emotion (energy in motion) from flowing into one's world. The decree patterns that the individual has used to build his wall of Light, while far more effective than the little boy with his finger in the dike, are the sole deterrent against the inflow of these forces.

When the little boy pulls his finger out of the dike—i.e., when the individual ceases to decree—the terrific pressures of the sea of the mass effluvia rush in to inundate his being, and he finds himself once again at "sea level."

"Pray Without Ceasing"

When Paul said, "Pray without ceasing,"[71] he did not mean that the disciples should be engaged in formal prayer every moment. His teaching was that we should be in a constant state of harmony (1) with ourselves, (2) with our fellow men and (3) with our God.

This trinity of harmonious living is prayer without ceasing, and whenever we break the thread of harmonious contact (communion) with any part of Life, we must seek to re-establish it by making formal application to God—through prayer, meditation or decrees—and to the flame of the Christ that is the connecting link between all hearts.

Jesus gives an understanding of how we may pray without ceasing: "Think on my words, 'He who seeks to save his life shall lose it.'[72] When you ponder the thought of unceasing prayer, consider those who fear to turn their consciousness to God lest they should miss something going on in the world around them. These seek to save their lives by involvement in the changing outer world. Those who lose (loose) their lives for my sake, by entering into the same communion with the Father that I did, truly find their life again; for only as God can live in man who exists in very Being itself, Life itself, does man really possess eternal Life....

"Blessed ones, it is unnecessary for you to strain or to struggle in order to achieve communion with God. He is not far from you; and as near as heartbeat or thought, he can flood you with a surge of his renewing strength. Each night when you enjoy restful sleep, you experience a recharging of your blessed bodies and minds with the purity of divine energy. The extroversion of human thought and its expenditure upon myriad trivia through the day take you away from the strength of your Source. Because your energy is then depleted and its levels have fallen, you do need to renovate your consciousness, which has passed through the turmoil of a busy day.

"How frequently I found during my own mission that by going up into the mountains to pray, getting away from the madding crowd, or curling up in one end of a ship, I was able to renew my strength and perform a greater ministry of service and healing.[73] All who would follow in my footsteps must understand that unless they are able to contact the great

Source of Life and continually renew their strength, their mission will not be carried forth in the manner desired by God. You cannot, as you say, 'burn the candle at both ends' and expect it to last. Yet when it is needed, there is a limitless flow of divine strength that can be acquired as you learn to use the charging methods of divine prayer during the busiest time of the day.

"Some of you are aware of the fact that the prince of this world[74] will often create a division in your mind by arranging two or more control points that clamor for your attention at the same time. In the rapid switching back and forth of your attention, your energy level drops dangerously; and when it is extremely low, that is just when the forces of negation rush in to trigger a sudden burst of anger or discouragement.[75]

"This is an entirely different situation from the natural two-way flow of consciousness that can be achieved through holy communion with God right while you carry on your activities in the world. In the former case, the attention is being jockeyed back and forth between centers of interest. In the latter, your attention is moving from the world to God and from God to the world.

"You need have no fear or distress that unceasing communion will disturb the efficiency of your tasks. I can truly tell you from experience that even when you are involved in difficult matters, if you carry your attention upward toward the Father and fear not the flow of his attention upon you, you can actually bathe the disquieted energies in your world with the harmony of God. And when your attention returns back into the world of form, it will no longer manifest the inharmony and imperfection that it formerly did....

"More things are indeed wrought by prayer than the world dreams of.[76] Yet ordinary prayer, strenuously engaged in, that cries out for emergency help in time of need is not to be

compared with that steadfast outreach for God that understands communion as a most fortunate means to the end of
personal freedom."[77]

No day should pass—and when you are under stress, no
hour should pass—without your freely offering your energies
to God that he might return them to you amplified by his love
and charged with his protection.

As water seeks its own level, so the flames of God that we
invoke on Earth—which descend from his heart as rays of
Light and spring up at our feet as flaming fire—rise to the
Source of Perfection from whence they came every twenty-four
hours. Therefore, unless we call forth the flames of God daily,
our momentum is not sustained and the fires on the hearth of
being "go out."

Be Ready for the Tests of Life

Saint Germain once gave this practical advice for maintaining our spiritual communion in the midst of the stresses of
life: "Sometimes when you suddenly feel a disturbance—you
are taken aback, you have a shock or a sudden reaction to
the actions of injustice of another—one of the reasons you
momentarily lose your balance is because the normal flow of
the aura has been disturbed, as though you would suddenly
agitate the waters.

"Now, your aura is your sanctuary, and it is the *sanctity* of
your God flame. Thus, before answering the demands of the
carnal mind—the questioning, the praying for favors, or whatever—reestablish yourself. Speak quietly, softly and slowly.
For in this way you will not engage into yourself the anger, the
impetuosity, the upsetness of anyone around you…. Be the
calm presence in a vortex of calamity and activity, beloved
hearts, and learn the way of the power, the immense power of

peace itself....

"Remember that anything that seeks to taunt you from the seat of the Buddha in the secret chamber of the heart must be noted as the enemy—not the person necessarily, for it is often a loved one, but the force attempting to use that one. Thus, it is your challenge to liberate that one as well as yourself from the human nonsense of the moment....

"Unless you center in the heart, which is the central sun of your being, you may find yourself tumbling on the periphery of the aura, which touches the world consciousness. That point, that outer circle of the aura, should always be a very intense blue—a blue fire of protection, which is also outside the tube of light. Now you visualize the violet flame in the very center of the tube of light.

"But I would make the point that when you are bristling with blue flame, this often antagonizes others because it is so powerful and brings out the worst in them. Thus, the better part of wisdom is to wear the kid glove—that is, to put another layer of violet flame outside the blue to be a calming effect, to consume that which may rub against the aura or come at you. And if it break through the violet flame, then you have the blue-flame wall, then you have the power of the tube of light. And if diplomacy does not work, there is always the strength of the shield of Archangel Michael!...

"Often it is a matter of stance. How do you hold yourself? Are you in readiness for the next delivery of God or thrust of the sinister force, or are you, as they say these days, 'laid-back'? If you slouch, if you are laid-back, wide open, lounging around—the TV set is on, the ads are bombarding their rock beat, the cat is meowing, the dog is barking, the children are screaming, the phone is ringing—how do you expect, then, to keep your cool? It is a setup, but you have allowed it.

"Now, you can maintain your calm in the midst of these

things but not with a laid-back attitude, for any moment the potatoes on the stove will burn and everyone will be in an argument and, if you don't watch out, yourself included. And then what have we accomplished?—a lost hour for Saint Germain and the vital work of Helios and Vesta; your own sense, 'I will never become a good chela. I will never master my life.'

"But, beloved ones, it's a matter of one, two, three, four, five—a few simple requirements: Do not allow the family to be bombarded from all directions. Do not allow all these things to be taking place at once. Strive for communion with the heart. Feed the cat, put out the dog, turn off the TV set, make sure all is safe on the stove, and enjoy that circle of communion with God-determination that each member of your family or household or friends shall have the opportunity, by your loving presence, to express something very important from the heart."[78]

Momentums of Light and Darkness

The sincere may well ask, "If decrees are not 'vainly' repetitious, then why are they repetitious at all?" Lord Maitreya answered this question by drawing an interesting analogy. He said:

"Now most of you are familiar with the construction of a simple electromagnet. You know that an iron core is wrapped with coils of wire through which a current is passed, enabling the magnetic field to be extended in concentrated lines of flux and to draw objects into close proximity to the coil. In a like manner, the vibration of fear (the energized coil) held, sustained or prolonged by an individual draws to him the fear of others.

"It must be recognized that each time man's consciousness revolves the idea of apprehension, fear as an unknown quantity is thereby strengthened. For the magnetism of fear is directly related to the number of times that the idea feared is wrapped around the core of being, just as each winding of the coil around the core of the electromagnet increases the number of turns through which the electrical current then passes, thereby strengthening the power of the magnet.

"By mankind's continual revolving of ideas of apprehension or fear, he is strengthening the magnetic field that draws the object of his fear into the orbit of his world. Thus Job declared, 'The thing which I greatly feared is come upon me, and that which I was afraid of is come unto me.'[79]

"What then of the vibratory action of countless years, days, hours, moments and lifetimes of wrong thinking and feeling? Often apprehensions have become galaxies of destruction within the universe of individual man. How can these best be removed? How can these best be contained? How can the vital energies of Life be withdrawn from them and be returned to the heart of the Creator for repolarization?...

"If the strength of fear is directly related to the number of times the object of one's fear has been revolved, then would it not be the part of wisdom to unwind each turn of the wire upon the pole of being? I ask you in God's name!

"Let us then recognize that through the power of the Holy Spirit and through the employment of thought and feeling in accordance with divine principles, man is able to sweep aside the imperfection of centuries and to set at naught those misqualified energies that were never of God's creation."[80]

Thus, each time a decree to the violet flame is given, the decreer is uncoiling a turn of the wire upon the pole of being. Whether it was a turn of fear, of hatred, of envy or of misconception, it does not matter, for the violet flame systematically transmutes man's undesirable creations line upon line, turn upon turn.

If he gives a decree thirty-three times lovingly, sincerely, humbly, with a spirit of forgiveness toward himself and all other parts of Life, he will be undoing thirty-three turns of the wire of his human creation. It is just that simple. And the momentum of Light gained through the transmutation of his dense, misqualified substance will propel his consciousness into a more rarefied plane of expression from whence he will be able to accelerate the undoing of his misdeeds and the doing of good deeds on behalf of all people. This is the magic of spiritual Alchemy!

Maitreya continues: "To give decrees, then, according to the divine plan is to produce a renewal of that momentum of perfection that God originally implanted in the human heart. Decrees mightily assist in reinforcing the power of Light, Life and Love that is within man."[81]

Decrees build a wall of Light not only around one's own forcefield but also around the place consecrated to communion with God and his Emissaries. The patterns of perfection that are invoked through the offering of prayers and meditations—some in the form of decrees powerfully spoken, some as decrees sung to the music of the spheres, and some as decrees offered reverently with deep feeling while listening to the spiritual music of the world's great composers—will erase the struggles of centuries and the long record of man's involvement with negation of every description. We would stress that this action occurs almost automatically, for inherent in the nature of Light itself is the power of God.

Light is self-luminous, intelligent energy imbued with the Creator's own omnipotence and his unfailing love. Light is indeed our manifest perfection of being.

Light is obedient to Father and Son,
Light fills the matrix that once was begun

By God when he spoke the mandate of Truth—
Let there be Light—and there was—'twas the proof.
It framed the world and all that is in it
So let us go forth to claim and to win it.

Light will release the fragrance of flower,
Light will bring comfort to man every hour.
For Light is a wall of energy filled,
The power of Truth, the Word that God willed.

Its essence contains the science of mind,
The substance unclean of our worlds to refine.
So remember, the proof of Creator's intent
Will always be found in the twig that is bent.

Wherever you plant the pattern of love
It will grow and conform to the pattern Above.
The Light is the key to the growing of man—
It will mold and transform him according to plan.

Layer upon layer the wall it will build
Round the one who decrees, his soul will be filled.
The pow'r to change 'tis automatic, you'll see,
For Light IS the alchemical key.

Transfiguring Affirmations
as Taught by Beloved Jesus the Christ to His Disciples

I AM that I AM

I AM the Open Door which no man can shut

I AM the Light which lighteth every man that cometh
into the world

I AM the Way

I AM the Truth

I AM the Life

I AM the Resurrection

I AM the Ascension in the Light

I AM the fulfillment of all my needs and requirements
of the hour

I AM abundant Supply poured out upon all Life

I AM perfect Sight and Hearing

I AM the manifest Perfection of Being

I AM the illimitable Light of God made manifest
everywhere

I AM the Light of the Holy of Holies

I AM a Son of God

I AM the Light in the Holy Mountain of God

Radiant Spiral Violet Flame

In the name of the beloved mighty victorious Presence of God, I AM in me, my very own beloved Holy Christ Self, beloved Lanello, the entire Spirit of the Great White Brotherhood and the World Mother, elemental life—fire, air, water, and earth! I decree:

Radiant spiral violet flame,
  Descend, now blaze through me!
Radiant spiral violet flame,
  Set free, set free, set free!

Radiant violet flame, O come,
  Drive and blaze thy Light through me!
Radiant violet flame, O come,
  Reveal God's power for all to see!
Radiant violet flame, O come,
  Awake the earth and set it free!

Radiance of the violet flame,
  Explode and boil through me!
Radiance of the violet flame,
  Expand for all to see!
Radiance of the violet flame,
  Establish mercy's outpost here!
Radiance of the violet flame,
  Come, transmute now all fear!

And in full faith I consciously accept this manifest, manifest, manifest! (3x) right here and now with full power, eternally sustained, all-powerfully active, ever expanding and world enfolding until all are wholly ascended in the Light and free!

Beloved I AM! Beloved I AM! Beloved I AM!

The Seven Rays

Ray	Color Magnetized on the Day of the Week	God-Qualities Amplified through Invocation to the Flame	Chakras Sustaining the Frequencies of the Rays in the Four Lower Bodies; Corresponding Body of Man
1	Blue Magnified on Tuesday	Will of God Omnipotence, perfection, protection, faith, desire to do the will of God through the power of the Father	Throat Etheric
2	Yellow Magnified on Sunday	Wisdom of God Omniscience, understanding, illumination, desire to know God through the mind of the Son	Crown I AM Presence
3	Pink Magnified on Monday	Love of God Omnipresence, compassion, charity, desire to be God in action through the love of the Holy Spirit	Heart Holy Christ Self
4	White Magnified on Friday	Purity of God Purity, wholeness, desire to know and be God through purity of body, mind and soul through the consciousness of the Divine Mother	Base of the Spine Physical
5	Green Magnified on Wednesday	Science of God Truth, healing, constancy, desire to precipitate the abundance of God through the immaculate concept of the Holy Virgin	Third Eye Causal Body
6	Purple and Gold Magnified on Thursday	Peace of God Ministration of the Christ, desire to be in the service of God and man through the mastery of the Christ	Solar Plexus Emotional
7	Violet Magnified on Saturday	Freedom of God Freedom, ritual, transmutation, transcendence, desire to make all things new through the application of the laws of alchemy	Seat of the Soul Mental

Chapter 2

Black Magic

*The kingdom of heaven
suffereth violence, and the
violent take it by force.*

GOSPEL OF MATTHEW

 # Black Magic

T HERE ARE THOSE WHO WOULD deny the existence of Evil; yet the effects of Evil in the world are self-evident. As proof of the Creator's existence is to be found in his mighty works, so do we know by the manifestation of unwholesome conditions that a force opposed to Good is operative on this planet.

The basis for the denial of Evil is to be found in cosmic law, the Law of the Christ that manifests the immaculate concept (the pure image) in every man, regardless of appearances to the contrary. This Law affirms for all time that God made man in his Image and Likeness and that God, Good, is omnipotent, omnipresent and omniscient. Truly, wherever Light is, Darkness is dispelled. Within the framework of absolute divine Reality, therefore, the denial of Evil is valid.

The Universal Presence of God

Standing on Mars' hill and viewing the altar of the unknown God, Paul declared:

Ye men of Athens, I perceive that in all things ye are too superstitious. For as I passed by and beheld your devotions, I found an altar with this inscription: TO THE UNKNOWN GOD. Whom therefore ye ignorantly worship, him declare I unto you.

God that made the world and all things therein, seeing that he is Lord of heaven and earth, dwelleth not in temples made with hands; neither is worshipped with men's hands, as though he needed any thing, seeing he giveth to all life, and breath, and all things; . . . though he be not far from every one of us: For in him we live, and move, and have our being.[1]

In his rebuke, Paul presented the case for the universal presence of God. If the nature of God is Good, and God is everywhere, where does Evil exist? Where, indeed!

If men were to deal in blacks and whites, the very thought of the presence of the unfailing Light of God everywhere would eliminate the blackness of negativity. On this basis, the existence of Evil could be emphatically denied right in the midst of life's most pressing problems. But there is one important fact that many do not take into account when pondering the question of Good and Evil, and it must not be overlooked.

In his present state of consciousness, man is imperfect; furthermore, he lives in an imperfect world. Yet from a base of imperfection, he strives to attain perfection. From the formless, he works to create form. Out of chaos he is able to define order, and his conscience reflects a higher morality than his own.

What sort of compulsion is this, which keeps him ever moving toward a receding standard whose inscription, "Come up higher!" is the greatest challenge to his soul? This compulsion is the fiery destiny of the sons and daughters of God. It is a compulsion that cannot be ignored. It beckons them on through joy and sorrow, through trial and triumph, all the days of their lives. It is God himself working in man, a portion of His Spirit to expand, that compels man's reach—and who can exceed His grasp?

If God were not living in man, man would not feel the magnetism that impels him toward that life that is Good because it is lived in God, nor would he feel the pull of his immortal destiny. Yet if the "law of sin"[2] were not warring in his members, man would not do the evil that he would not, as Paul lamented.[3] Somewhere between the dark and the daylight of man's belonging in this universe is a key to his personal being, and that key is relativity.

Relativity

When we say that man is relative to God, we mean that he is totally dependent upon God for his existence, even as the planets in their orbits are totally dependent upon the sun. Man exists only as an object of the Mind of God; he has no separate existence apart from this Mind, for man is an idea complete in the consciousness of his Creator. Thus we can see that man's existence, as the effect of Primal Cause, will always be relative to that First Cause.

Man, too, is a creator in his own domain. He asked for and received the gift of free will, and he was given the command to be fruitful and multiply and to take dominion over the earth.[4] Man's creations have ranged from the sublime to the ridiculous. He has emulated his Maker by bringing forth works noble and magnificent, and he has descended into the ignominy of total desecration of mind and soul.

In the nether world of mortal consciousness, Evil was born—"a liar from the beginning."[5] The existence of Evil, like that of all creation, is relative to the consciousness that created it. It has no independent ideology and no frame of reference outside the carnal mind, for it is the objectification of that mind and it is sustained by that mind. Therefore, when that mind shall cease to exist, Evil too shall cease to be. When the Mind of God, which was in Christ Jesus, is elevated in the consciousness of men to the place where it completely displaces the carnal mind, men will no longer propagate Evil. Then Evil, cut from the mother vine, will die of its own relativity.

Progress is the Law of God; hence it is native to the being of man. The ascending spiral of God's consciousness forms a pathway of Light that carries the evolving son into the realm of the Real. It is the nature of Good to transcend itself, and it is the nature of Evil to destroy itself. For inherent within Goodness are the seeds of expansion, and inherent within Evil are the seeds of destruction.

The growth process is observed from babyhood through childhood and adolescent years to maturity. Like the tides of the sea, the ebb and flow of the life of man follows the rhythm of the universe. Evolution is everywhere apparent. Man's ideas, his ethics, his faith and his love evolve as his consciousness is quickened by the Spirit of the LORD. His comprehension of Life is daily transformed; his understanding expands and is renewed; and in the light of a greater understanding, he walks toward the Light itself—the receding goal that beckons him onward to discover and to conquer more of himself.

The gradations of human consciousness that form the ladder of human existence indicate that life in the relative sense is a series of gray tones. It cannot be black and white because neither Absolute Good nor Absolute Evil can exist in a world of imperfect causal relations. Nevertheless, the human monad must have its blacks and whites. For the sake of preserving its own sanity, it must pigeonhole, categorize, classify and label anything and everything. It is either supremely happy or sorely vexed, totally confident or woefully incompetent, wildly ecstatic or in the depths of despair. Men either love or they hate; they laugh or they cry; either they think they know all things, knowing not that they are ignorant, or they acknowledge their ignorance, knowing not that they know.

The extremes of human consciousness are reflected in the contrast of tropic and polar climes. These exist side by side within the human personality, whereas Nature has distributed her cycles of relativity in more orderly fashion. In man, there often seems to be no middle ground. What a pity that he cannot learn to roll with the tides of life and to understand that each crest leads on to victory.

The Subtle Nature of Evil

The Ascended Master El Morya comments, "Actually, there are very few willfully Evil people upon Earth. Most individuals dwell in a state that we may unfortunately term the 'norm' of the mass human consciousness (for we hold for all men the concept of excellence)."[6]

In examining the problem of Evil, we should also note the simple words of the Master Jesus: "Father, forgive them; for they know not what they do."[7] If men were inherently Evil, they would know the Evil that they do, but because they are not Evil by intent, they do not understand the Evil that they do.

Evil is foreign to the very nature of the children of God, and this is precisely the reason that they are such unwitting victims of the ploys of the Evil forces. They do not understand the subtle nature of Evil, even though they have been warned: "Now the serpent was more subtil than any beast of the field."[8] Therefore, Jesus counseled his disciples whom he sent forth "as sheep in the midst of wolves: be ye therefore wise as serpents and harmless as doves."[9]

Men are wise in some of the ways of the world, and they are ignorant in others. To some, the fullness of the plan of Universal Law and Love has not been revealed. To others, it has been revealed but they have not accepted it. And so for lack of vision the people perish[10] in their ignorance not only of the things of this world but also of the things of the Spirit.

El Morya comments on this dilemma: "Religious and spiritual devotees are at times innocently unaware of some of the facts concerning the manifestation not only of God's Good but also of mortal man's Evils and how to protect themselves against untoward conditions. Jesus knew this aspect of human nature and pointed it out in the parable of the unjust steward: 'for the children of this world are in their generation wiser than the children of light.'[11]

"Some, like ostriches, thrust their heads in the sand and cry out, 'I cannot look.' The watchman upon the wall is not so, for he must guard the inhabitants of the city."[12]

We don't have to invent the concept of polarization of Light and Darkness. It is marching in front of our eyes. Yet some people are so indoctrinated by theology and psychology that they will not accept that Evil exists. And that state of mind is dangerous, because Evil is insidious and its identification can be difficult. And if you do not know that it exists, and if you do not know what its earmarks are, it can be extremely difficult to tie down, to isolate and to unmask.*

---

* One book that attempts to do this is *People of the Lie: The Hope for Healing Human Evil,* by M. Scott Peck. This book is an important study in the psychology of people who embody Evil, who have become the lie, written from the perspective of a Christian. He describes wrestling with people who are suffering from what could be described as the malignancy of Evil. These people are Evil in small ways, not in great ways; but the Evil they embody is horrendous because it destroys people around them.

Even the willingness to admit that what could be called simply a psychological condition is the embodiment of Evil is a tremendous advancement for the field of psychology. It is not unusual, perhaps, that this point of view would come from a Christian, but the author's analysis is so keen that it will appeal to those who do not happen to embrace any particular faith.

Origins of Evil

Throughout the entire creative drama, Evil is the mask of unreality and illusion, the shadow of the Real that is operative in the time-space continuum. Unfortunately, the mask is too frequently accepted as the Real. Men take their roles too seriously; they identify with qualities and conditions they are sent to expose as players on the stage of life. Identifying with the masquerade, they become hateful, fearful, avaricious, vindictive and full of lust. They become lovers of the mask, thinking it is their own. As Paul said, they are "proud, boasters, inventors of evil things."[13]

What is Evil? How did *Evil*—the energy *veil* that was spawned in the framework of relativity—come into existence in the first place? And how is it perpetuated?

On plate III, section V of "The Fall of Angels" taken from the Book of Life, which the Keeper of the Scrolls allowed us to see, we read the story of Peshu Alga, the first individual in this solar system to fall from the high state of the consciousness of Good.

Peshu Alga was a great and wise king and a graduate of the wisdom schools of the Brotherhood. But in a moment of grief over the death of his child, when God would not answer his pleas, he turned to the powers of Darkness to restore his child. Failing to ponder the Realities of immortality and the fact that the LORD's silence is often his most articulate answer, Peshu Alga lost his reason and his soul. In his mind, Evil was conceived.

And so it is written of him in the Book of Life: "And this man thwarted Reason; entering into a personal sense of loss, he justified his actions. He no longer cared for his universal responsibilities. He determined that the universe should meet his demands—and if it would not, he would take the law into

his own hands. His willful attempt to control the forces of
nature brought about the uniting of his energies with the
Luciferians."

The Luciferians, although they retained the concept of
God-Good, had become competitive and ambitious through
their misunderstanding of the transcendent nature of God,
whereby each part of Life competes with itself in order to
overcome and transcend its present level of accomplishment.
Their attempt to introduce rivalry within the framework of
God's consciousness was the beginning of the energy veil that
gradually separated them from their Creator.

In his negative frame of reference, Peshu Alga magnetized
and expanded the energy veil that was yet in embryo, a distant
cloud on the horizon of the Luciferians' consciousness. He
accused God of Evil—and alas, the Luciferians were the first
to take up his cry. Not satisfied to compete with one another,
they began to compete with the Almighty.

As we examine the record of this man's fall from grace,[14]
the lesson that we must apply diligently in our day-to-day confrontations with the energy veil becomes clear: the polarization
of our energies with Evil occurs through our sympathy with its
vibration. We cannot become caught in its downward spiral
unless we leave the pinnacle of our communion with the
Most High God. This occurs as we transfer the focus of our
attention from perfection to imperfection. Having seen as God
sees, we allow ourselves once again to see as mortals see.
Having compromised our consciousness of the Absolute, we
enter into the vibrational patterns of Evil.

This can happen so easily, often before we know it. Out of
sympathy for the pitiful state of someone's human consciousness, we compromise principle. Lowering our gaze, we
rationalize our behavior, which falls short of the high standard
maintained in the Holy of Holies of our own being.

Out of pity for the limitations that mortals have imposed upon themselves, we are moved to compromise the fulfillment of the Law through the power of love, which we know is the only permanent answer to mankind's need. We intervene and become "doers of good," instead of letting the Great Doer act through us to carry out his will according to his plan.

We depart from those moral standards that we know God has ordained to uphold our highest and noblest purposes. And we betray our own best interests because of our response to a sympathetic vibration—always a downward spiral—that pulls us lower and lower into the mire of the consciousness that has left the Presence of God to become a law unto itself, a cause apart from Primal Cause.

Thus, the Book of Life concludes: "Therefore, in the wisdom of the Chien, we must point out that Good must always beware lest it fall; for it exists at great height. When it becomes less than Good through sympathy, it no longer exists on the plane of the Absolute. And in its fall, it absorbs more of the energy veil of the limited and limiting qualities of the human created out of its vain imaginations. Therefore, Darkness is not just an absence of Light—it is a misqualification of Light."

The test given to Peshu Alga and to the Luciferians is given daily to everyone. We must all choose whether we will serve the God of very gods, or the human consciousness that operates within a framework of self-concern, self-interest and self-love.

The test is failed each time we decide in favor of the human and against the Divine. It is passed when we accelerate the momentum of our divinity in an upward spiral and accept nothing less than the perfection of the Godhead and the ritual of overcoming as the supreme Law of our being—no matter what the cost. Sympathy for the human—whether one's own or another's—is thus man's greatest enemy, whereas compassion for the Christ—whether in oneself or in others—is his greatest friend.

The great Master Jesus rebuked the consciousness that denied the Christ. He understood that Evil has its antecedent in the carnal mind and in the *devil* (the deified energy *veil*) that originated with Peshu Alga and became personified in Lucifer.

Jesus spoke harshly to those who claimed to be the children of Abraham and yet did not his works, saying, "Ye are of your father the devil, and the lusts of your father ye will do. He was a murderer from the beginning, and abode not in the truth, because there is no truth in him. When he speaketh a lie, he speaketh of his own: for he is a liar, and the father of it."[15]

Jesus knew that Evil (the mist that went up from the face of error) is perpetuated in the consciousness of those who, in denying the God in others, deny the God in themselves. These have no choice but to uphold the unreality of the night, to love Darkness because their deeds are Evil,[16] and to deify it within their personalities in order to perpetuate their own unreal existence.

There Is a Personal Devil

We always have the stumbling block of some people not believing in a personal devil. But Lucifer was a fallen angel; he was an Archangel. He fell through pride, and he took many angels with him. This is fact in cosmic history.

There came great darkness in the galaxy and in several galaxies through the fall of these individuals. We have experienced the personal confrontation of Lucifer challenging us and our Light. And his fallen angels are working very hard with him to take the Earth down, as we are working hard to raise the planet.

There has to be an embodied consciousness of Evil—not

necessarily physically embodied, but there have to be individuals ensouling Evil—in order to have the Evil we have on this planet. If there were no individuals consciously electing, by their free will, to do Evil, you would not see all the perversions of Divinity, all the actions of Antichrist that are happening on the Earth today.

And of course the best way that Lucifer and his lieutenants have of keeping their job an undercover one is to convince the intellectuals, in their intellectual pride, that it is fantasy to believe in a personal devil. The Pope has come forth with a very strong statement that there *is* a personal devil—this is part of Catholic theology.[17] But people who polarize mentally are fooled by their intellectual pride to look down upon people who have a basic fundamental understanding of Life and of the Hierarchies of heaven.

The Gift of Free Will

Central to the issue of Good and Evil is the concept of free will. If God created the universe, and he is only Good, how could Evil have been born? Saint Germain explains: "Each man must pass through the doorway of Light on his own. Understanding is the key that he must forge out of experience with life if he would unlock the door of the temple of Being and enter the kingdom of God.

"Perhaps you have mused upon the subject of the power of God long enough to realize that it would have been possible for God to have created man *without* bestowing upon him the gift of free will, making him instead subject wholly to His own will. The Creator could indeed have created man like unto a golden ball and thrust him into a groove so deep that he could not possibly alter his course; or he could have placed him, as one would a child, in a crib so high that he could not have climbed out. Yes, the Father could have confined the son insofar as his freedom to act and to create was concerned; and this would have been entirely within the prerogative of the divine will.

"But what of the primordial relationship of God and man as Creator and co-creator? Freedom and the power to create are man's greatest possessions. Obviously, then, the act of creating man without free will would have been completely contrary to the definition of God-freedom and to the very nature of the Creator. In one sense, man might see certain advantages to being what amounts to a puppet on a string. Certainly such a state would mean safety for the creature insofar as karma-making actions go. But as a puppet he would not be portraying the purposes of the Creator by choice, freely, lovingly.

"The infinite wisdom and love of God for his creation can be satisfied with nothing less than the full potential of Divine Selfhood—godlike, majestic, complete....

"It is this God-freedom within the soul of man that makes it possible for him to rise. That he has used it for error and for error's purposes is no fault of the Godhead. It can well be said that a calculated risk has been taken in bestowing upon man the gift of free will, yet the value in this risk is that it is the only means whereby the door of Light may be opened and the borders of God's kingdom expanded."[18]

The Departure from Perfection

Writing on behalf of the enlightenment of his disciples in this age, Jesus explains with simple logic the why and the wherefore of the presence of Evil within man and society:

"In a universe of absolute goodwill and perfection, it must be recognized that the freedom to choose, known as free will, has permitted mankind to depart from the perfection of God and to act as a creator in his own domain. Hence there have sprung into manifestation, along with the Good men are wont to do, myriad forms and concepts which utilize divine energy to spawn a shadowed veil of substance and thought which is distinctly Antichrist in nature.

"As the warning sounded forth of old to beware of the Antichrist, so mankind in this hour of trial must understand that the Earth has a very old residue comprising the energy records of past history. These have been sustained largely through custom, and they exist as a temporary force of Evil until challenged by the power of Light—for Evil has no permanent Reality except in the continuous misqualification by mankind of the pure energies of God released to all daily.

"The reactivation and revitalizing of ancient foci of Evil is accomplished, then, by contemporary man in most cases inadvertently, but in accord with a scheme perpetrated by the hordes of shadow, who have to the present hour refused to bend the knee and acknowledge the power of Light in their own beings or to confess the divinity of the Christ radiance as the divine Mediator between God and man."[19]

Black Magic Defined

Thus, having established the temporal nature of the serpentine lie and its prolongation in men's consciousness, it becomes obvious that all who have believed not the Truth have been damned by[20] (have suffered the condemnation of) the lie, because they have placed themselves outside of the consciousness of Reality.

Among these authors of nihilism are the "hordes of shadow" of whom Jesus often spoke, and their name is indeed "Legion."[21] They include fallen angels, black magicians and their astral creations—both man's entities and witches and astral entities, who have had to resort to the practice of black magic in order to perpetuate their nonexistent existence.

What, then, is black magic? Black magic is the scientific practice of Evil. It is a necessary function of Evil, for without it, Evil could not exist. Black magic involves the misuse of God's energies for any purpose that is inconsistent with the will of God. It is employed for (1) gaining ungodly control over the manifestations of God, and (2) securing for the finite self, by fraudulent manipulation of cosmic law, the things of this world and the next—money, fame, the power to manipulate men and nations, and the use of advantages gained to place obstacles in the pathway of those who aspire to do the will of God.

This comprehensive definition is by no means universally accepted—for people in general are not eager to admit that they, in their own hatred, fear, slander and disdain, are perpetuating the energy veil that, like a spider's web, snares innocent souls. This too is black magic—very much so.

One source defines black magic as "the use of supernatural knowledge for the purposes of evil, the invocation of diabolical and infernal powers that they may become the slaves and emissaries of man's will; in short, black magic is a perversion of legitimate mystic science. This art and its attendant practices can be traced from the time of the ancient Egyptians and Persians, from the Greeks and Hebrews to the period when it reached its apogee in the Middle Ages, thus forming an unbroken chain; for in mediaeval magic may be found the perpetuation of the popular rites of paganism—the ancient gods had become devils, their mysteries orgies, their worship sorcery."[22]

The reason people turn to black magic is that they want results without attainment, powers without grace, phenomena instead of communion with heaven. Not satisfied with simply being the beloved Son, they refuse to surrender the ego and want to control forces to be thought wise. They are too proud to see that their talents are not their own but the Creator's, which he has given and which he may take away.

White Magic

By contrast, white magic is the scientific practice of Good. It is the demonstration of Universal Law for the purposes of self-mastery and the precipitation of the attributes of God, including his abundant supply for the blessing of the creation and the expansion of the kingdom of God upon earth.

White magicians can and do practice for others, as well as for themselves; they assist men and women in their spiritual evolution. Jesus functioned as a true white magician in his mission of healing, teaching, raising the dead and multiplying the loaves and fishes in Jerusalem and Palestine. The seamless garment of his inner Light was a source of healing and compassion for the multitudes. All Ascended and unascended Masters are white magicians, and many of their devotees are accomplished in one or more aspects of this sacred science.*

Pallas Athena speaks of those emissaries of the false hierarchy who set themselves up as teachers: "These sinister overlords, who without our authority have set themselves up as teachers of men, are the brothers of the shadow, one-time pupils of the Ascended Masters. When they reached a certain degree of attainment, having already passed initiations that

---

* Nevertheless, it must be recognized that some who claim to be white magicians are, in fact, representatives of the false hierarchy. Evil is seldom self-proclaimed, and the dark ones often pretend to be working for the Good in order to lure the children of God to follow them. The false teacher will master the laws of white magic, master the laws of the uses of energy, but he will ignore the Christ. He will take that energy and use it to do whatever *he* wills with it. The true Teacher will always submit his use of energy to the will of God.

permitted them to be given advanced knowledge of the Law, they rebelled against the divine effort and the Creator's design. Taking full advantage of the spiritual advancement and power that had been given to them prior to their fall, these brothers have continued to practice the spiritual arts, but for selfish ends.

"It is at this point—where an adept uses the Laws of God to elevate his ego in direct opposition to the Creator's plan— that white magic becomes black magic."[23]

The Left-Handed Path

Today, black magicians learn their trade from other black magicians, who in turn learned from one-time disciples of the Ascended and unascended Masters of the Great White Brotherhood. These disciples learned to practice the Law as adepts of the occult.* But at some point in their training one of two things happened: (1) they failed in their disciplines and lacked either the humility or the staying power to take the grade over; or (2) they developed an inordinate desire, a secret burning ambition to use the knowledge they had received to glorify the ego rather than to glorify God through continued, and perhaps unsung, service to mankind. These, then, were not willing to complete their training program, but chose instead to practice without authorization before they had completed their novitiate.

Under previous dispensations, it was possible for such disciples to receive instruction in the inner mysteries and to make great advancement in the science of energy control before departing from the wisdom schools.† But because of

---

* *Occult:* hidden, concealed. The hidden spiritual knowledge that was not revealed to the world but only to students of the Masters.
† One example of such a disciple of the mysteries turning his knowledge to Darkness is Mainin, the high priest of Atlantis in *A Dweller on Two Planets,* by Phylos the Thibetan. Anakin Skywalker, a central character in George Lucas's *Star Wars* movies, portrays the same archetypal pattern in his transformation to Darth Vader.

such abuses, the Brotherhood evolved a system of initiations calculated to eliminate the undeserving before they reached the higher grades.

Today, those who retain the power to imprison elementals (nature spirits) and by secret keys and mantras force them to do their bidding are only pupils of the dark ones who originally betrayed the sacred mysteries. For the decree has gone forth that the divine gnosis shall be withheld from the profane, and no man shall enter the inner sanctum of the retreats unless the pride of the ego has been sacrificed in the Flame and a certain attainment has been won.

A Vampire Action Is Necessary to Perpetuate Evil

Once an individual sets his foot upon the left-handed path and turns from God, he cuts his supply line to the Great Source of Life. This act places him in the position of having to acquire his energy from a secondary source. Having taken the plunge into the astral sea, he is like a diver with a tank of oxygen on his back—he can go only as far as his limited supply will allow. When that runs out, he must either surface or tie into the supply of another diver.

Having spurned his contact with the Great Source, the black magician takes the alternative of "borrowing" energy from unsuspecting souls whose spiritual development must be less than that to which the black magician attained before his departure from grace—else they could not be deceived. He cunningly steals the misqualified energies of lesser evolved children of God, who are completely unaware that their very Life energies are being siphoned off at an alarming rate.

This vampire action, this astral bloodletting, will go on indefinitely until the children of God make up their minds that they will not allow their energies to be divided between God and mammon.[24] Only when they commit themselves whole-heartedly to God and to his Laws and approach the Masters in humility, desiring to be God-taught and to receive those initiations that will prepare them to meet and conquer the Adversary—only then will they be wholly free from the machinations of the evil ones who lie in wait to steal the very lifeblood of the holy innocents.

Needless to say, invoking the protection of Archangel Michael and his legions, putting on the tube of light and maintaining the state of listening grace will assure one's safety under the aegis of the Brotherhood, even before one has mastered one's own energies and environment.

Those who are black magicians, knowing that they themselves can never become one with God so long as they remain committed to the vanities of the ego and to the practice of the black arts, must keep others from reaching God in order to keep open the supply lines of their lifeblood. This they accomplish by enslaving the children of the Light to their vibrations and forcefields and by victimizing those who, once caught in their energy fields, continue to misqualify God's energy according to their computerized patterns.

Their goal is nothing less than the annihilation of the souls of men and of this planet. For they know that the tremendous quantity of energy that would be released through terror and agony as millions perished in cataclysmic action or atomic holocaust would give them enough misqualified energy to corrupt other worlds and other solar systems and ultimately to destroy them as well—all for the perpetuation of their own ego-centered vampire existence.

Black magicians operating from the astral plane and entities who serve as their willing tools (for they too have been cut off from the Source) attach themselves to the astral (emotional) bodies of men like common bloodsuckers. But to gain entrance to the consciousness of men, they must first precipitate an incident of discord—one that will cause the individual to let down his guard and in so doing to rend the garment of his harmony, the one dependable source of protection whereby he maintains exclusive oneness with his God Presence.*

Only when the individual's harmonious attunement with Life is broken can the door to his consciousness be opened. Then they ride in on the havoc they have caused, the individual's attention upon discord being the red carpet for their grand entrance into his world.

Black magicians have quite a bag of tricks,[25] which they use most effectively to trigger in mankind all forms of emotion (*e-motion*, or *energy in motion*), causing them to spill their cup of Light down the drain of the astral world. God's energy that has thus been misappropriated through human emotion is hoarded in pools of darkness, where all who have been cut off from the God Source may come for a transfusion. Thus by their constant harassment of the children of God, they assure themselves a form of "immortality" and the wherewithal to pursue their Evil work.

The black magicians have such a field day in operating among men because of the general low level of the mass consciousness. Most people are self-centered and totally involved in their environments, in their families, in their futures and in concerns that are not conducive to the search for the Divinity in their lives—except in time of need when they feel that the Deity can help them and deliver them out of their sea of troubles. Thus, the very selfishness of human nature causes men, in their self-centeredness, to be subject to a host of

---

* These entities and their methods of operation are described in detail in book 7 of the Climb the Highest Mountain series, *The Path to Immortality.*

negative forces that perpetuate their negative standards of conduct among men.

Commenting on these activities of the black magicians, the Goddess of Truth says: "There is more than one serious drawback to the left-handed path. Aside from the prospect of being cast into outer darkness and losing one's soul, the rebellious sons must come to grips with the fact that the moment they turn from the Light, they are cut off from the Divine Source. They can no longer call to the Presence of God for protection, power or energy in any form. Faced with the dilemma of requiring energy and not being able to invoke it from on high, the black brotherhood devised a system of vampire activities whereby they steal the energies of mankind to perpetuate their existence and their nefarious deeds.

"But here they are also limited, for it is impossible for one committed to Evil to usurp Good—Darkness cannot overcome Light. Therefore, the black magicians can take from mankind only those energies that they have misqualified with discord, doubt and fear, whereas that which mankind hold in harmony, purity and Truth can never be taken from them. Considering the tremendous amount of God's energy that is being misqualified daily by mankind through feelings of hatred, greed, treachery and every imperfect vibration to which the race is heir, it is easy to see how the false hierarchy rule *in tempus** in the footstool kingdom of the psychic realm.

"Because all knowledge begins with God and because the black magicians took their training from the Brothers in White, in some cases apparent benefits are derived by the students of their techniques. However, without realizing it, their pupils do take in, along with some questionable outer benefits, the vibratory action of deceit and betrayal of the will of God.

---

* Latin: for a time, temporarily.

"We are aware of the fact that it is often most difficult for some students, by reason of a lack of previous training, to discern that which is Truth and that which is error. These must not only beware of the mingling of Truth and error in the presentations of the charlatans and the deceivers, but also they must remember that the errors postulated in the name of Truth by these most clever masters of deceit are so subtle that they are easily taken for Truth by those whose zeal for attainment is greater than their developed discrimination.[26]

"You see, precious ones, it is not difficult for them to secure any of our writings that we put forth for the dissemination of God's Word among men. It requires but a little ink and paper to prepare a discourse that did not emanate from our realm—and even less effort for those who are without moral scruples to affix our name either below or above it.[27] Some among the students of Truth have the vantage point of longer service on the Path; these are able to discern the LORD's body of holy Truth and to detect a vibration of error in a more sure manner. Nevertheless, you would be amazed to find just how many advanced students are fooled by such misrepresentations.[28]

"Some would-be teachers believe themselves to be our messengers when actually they are taking psychic dictations from those who pose in our stead. The members of the false hierarchy make it a point to counterfeit our every move. Many times, before we have even released to the students the announcement of a certain victory of an inner action of Light, they bring forth a dictation to 'steal the show,' as you would put it. There are many false activities that exist solely on the credulity of the members who, after years of study, do not believe they could be fooled by a lie. And yet they are deceived.

"I am certain that our students and all students of Truth will recognize the great pity of it all. On the surface, it seems unjust that those who seek the very living Word of God should be subjected to a barrage of psychic forces and disturbances. But certainly a moment's thought will show you that the one place where the sinister force desires to prevail is at the point where Truth passes from God to man. For the sure word of prophecy has always been the means by which heaven has contacted unascended mankind and helped them on their Homeward way.

"From the beginning, the recorded word has assisted mankind in his search for God; and without the spoken and printed word, I am certain that mankind would be far behind in their comprehension of Life and that civilization would be far from its present level of advancement."[29]

The Need to Decree for the Removal of Black Magicians

Early in the twentieth century, the Karmic Board released the dispensation whereby great numbers of discarnate entities and black magicians were removed from the planet. Some students were and still are under the impression that since these beings were taken, there was and is no longer any need to be alert to the practices of black magic, witchcraft or variance. Neither do they perceive the present need to decree for the removal of discarnates from the planet.

Mother Mary explains why the threat of black magic is still present and why vigilance is needed: "When the entities and black magicians were brought under control and taken from the planet through the power of the Light, this dispensation applied (where the entities were concerned) to the then current hour.

"With each passing hour, new souls, released into the Earth's atmosphere, become trapped in the psychic and astral regions. In the case of black magic, while the so-called mighty or great black magicians were indeed removed and controlled, their pupils continued to exist and expand to some degree of adeptship in those arcane arts that were calculated to exalt the individual and give him some form of control over lesser men. Likewise, many of the writings and formulas used by them [by the black magicians who were taken] were left behind for the unscrupulous to employ or experiment with.

"The peril of so-called black magic continues to exist today and requires the vigilance of the elect so as to counteract all such forms of necromancy by unyielding attention to the Light of God that never fails. There is only one way to overcome Evil, and that is with Good.

"Through alertness, the sincere student will learn the art of challenging all intrusions upon his happiness with the command 'Show me your Light!' and the firm decree 'I AM the only power that can act!' This affirmation gives the individual some concept of the fact that only God can act in his world and that all that is less than the perfection of God must come to naught.

"Some schools desire to inform their students that black magic does not exist, but I am one who witnessed the feigned power of the mass consciousness seeking the destruction of the Christ Light within the heart of her son! I beheld the darkness over the face of the land while my son hung between heaven and earth until the veil in the temple was rent in twain.[30]

"I recall that in that black hour, I perceived, by contrast, the wonders of Light's triumph over every outer condition. His cry 'It is finished'[31] *seemed* momentarily to spell my own end; yet I lived to witness his triumphant ascension into heaven!

"Many little ones today all around the world are, innocently enough, it is true, practicing a form of black magic when they seek to interfere with the free will of their fellow men or to influence lifestreams by asserting some form of control over them. The very fact that spiritually minded people sometimes fall prey to this habit without being aware of it makes it vital that we call it to men's attention today.

"It is never wrong, when invited, to visualize Good coming forth for others and to see them held within a circle of blazing Light. But to seek to force them to bend to your will without the benefit of their own blessed response to reason or wisdom is ever an ominous karmic responsibility that has launched many enduring ties that have not had the blessing of attendant happiness.

"The practice of *spiritual* magic, the art of calling forth exaltations and blessings for mankind, is not practiced nearly enough; let me make this clear. But the selfishness of humanity and their fears of the morrow have caused them to take thought in a manner that has only resulted in needless complications without giving them any permanent deliverance.

"The struggle for world domination goes on, spearheaded by the most nefarious and sinister mass, and yet the students must exhibit and have no fear of these conditions. Rather, consecrate yourselves to such areas of service coupled with devotion to the Holy Cause that there is no room in the inn of your being for aught else but the purity and love of God.

"We do not desire to see the sincere students of the Great White Brotherhood be babes in the woods where the abuses of the Great Law are concerned, yet we do not want any of our chelas to be brought under the power of aught else except love and the divine intent....

"Secure yourselves, then, behind the bastions of your own God-design, but be aware, as was my Son, of the need to be elastic, rising to fit the occasion and yielding to no impulse save the moving impulse of love alone."[32]

Perfection Has Its Own Natural Protection

In each outburst of anger, fear, derision, discord or unbridled conduct of any kind, energy is released. Usually it passes through more than one lifestream, reacting, reverberating and being reamplified. The vampire agencies of the astral quickly seize this energy and use it to perpetuate their life span and their activities. They are experts in the use of mob psychology, and wherever they can cause many individuals to respond simultaneously in emotional outbursts, violence, raw emotion or sorrow, they have that much more energy to draw upon.

The mass media coverage of war, crime, death and rioting thus serves to perpetuate these social disorders rather than to arrest them. For many who tune in to these events tie up their own energies in their concern, while others imitate what they see.

This is possible because the crystal cord of each lifestream is connected directly with his own individualized God Presence. The energy he draws daily and hourly from the Presence is constantly being qualified by his thoughts and feelings. As long as the qualification of energy is affinitized with the purity of God and the right conduct of his Christ, God's Light cannot be stolen by the negative forces of the world. For perfection has its own natural protection.

However, when the white-fire core of the atom and the tiny electrons that flow from the heart of God become overlaid with negative qualification, densification occurs—that is, the vibratory rate of one's energy no longer has the speed of Light. It is no longer "too hot to handle" but becomes a readily assimilable source of energy for the negative powers of the world. Thus by one's own discordant conduct, thought or feeling that slows down the God-given rate of the vibration of his own electrons, he affinitizes his energy world (whirl) with the common denominator of the mass consciousness and mass confusion.

Jesus referenced this action of transforming Light into Darkness when he said, "If the light that is in thee be darkness, how great is that darkness!"[33] Either we retain our Light in the ration of perfection in which it was originally released, or by our free will we step it down to the fractions of division, disloyalty and deceit. By the flow of our energy, we ally ourselves either with Light or with Darkness. Either we are in the LORD's camp or we are in the swamps of the enemy.

Because loyalties are defined by vibration rather than by profession, they are not always easily discerned, especially where there exist spiritual wickedness in high places and demons often masquerading as angels of Light.[34] The allegiance of one's energies is never a matter of argument but clearly one of cosmic record, for the vibratory rate of one's energy cannot be high and low at the same time.

As the records of infamy and treason are unmistakable, so the activities of the black magicians can be read and known for what they are by the wise disciples of the Brotherhood. Jesus said, "No man can serve two masters: for either he will hate the one and love the other, or else he will hold to the one and despise the other. Ye cannot serve God and mammon."[35] The scientific explanation of this statement is that energy cannot vibrate at opposite poles at the same time. Either we serve the Light or we serve Darkness, and by our fruits we are known.[36]

The old saying "Birds of a feather flock together," which is true of spiritually minded people, is also true of carnally minded people. There is both an outer and an inner tie among practitioners of Evil, which causes them to function at times as a single unit or entity. When Jesus approached the man who had a spirit of an unclean devil, the demon cried out on behalf of the legions that were allied with him, saying, "Let us alone; what have we to do with thee, thou Jesus of Nazareth? art thou come to destroy us? I know thee who thou art: the Holy One of God."[37] The name "Jesus of Nazareth" was known by the dark forces throughout the world as that of one who had power and used it to cast out demons from the consciousness of embodied men.

Witchcraft—A Form of Black Magic

There exist today throughout the world numberless witches' covens whose members follow the religious code (if it can be called that) of the witches. These strange practices of witchcraft—forms of black magic—are carried on daily by people whose outer appearance would never indicate this degrading activity of the Antichrist.

There is no question that witchcraft has a definite attraction for those who seek power over others, self-aggrandizement and various forms of sensuality. We refer to the power to control mortal minds and forms by invisible forces, the power to influence the motives and acts of others by hypnotic suggestions and the power to invoke various spirit forces, entities and even elemental beings to carry out their spells and schemes.

El Morya writes on the subject of witchcraft, as discussed in an address by the God Meru:

"He spoke on witchcraft, not only as it was practiced in past civilizations but also as it has continued to be practiced through the centuries and is extant to the present day in many parts of Africa, the Caribbean, England and even America, particular infestations occurring in and around parts of

Louisiana. All such negative foci contribute much to disturbances not only upon the planet itself but also in the hearts of its people. Incalculable damage has been done to the Christ Image through the practice of this discordant human art....

"God Meru emphasized ... that the name 'witchcraft' and its practice have no power (except that which men give to it). [This word] is derived from the words *wit* and *craft*, indicating that witchcraft is nothing more than the craftiness of the human wit or intellect. Never could it originate in nor derive power from the Divine Mind.

"He defined it as man's cleverness or 'wit' in manipulating the forces of the mind and the human psyche and the projecting to distant points of a vibratory action of fear and domination over others. He emphasized the terrible karmic penalties involved, but particularly desired to alert the students of the greater Light to these continuing negative practices and the resulting emanations, in order that they might effect the proper safeguards at this present hour.

"There are, of course, individuals who feel that by merely denying the existence of such forces, they are able to negate their influence. I do not question the fact that to deny is to remove much power from such conditions. For my statements are not at all in affirmation of the power of the human 'wit' to successfully compete with the permanent Realities of Being. Nay, I am hereby offering to those willing to receive it the wisdom that will enable men to stand the guard in their own world and in the world of others against all forces not derived from the consent of the Holy Spirit and the purity of heaven.

"It is not that men themselves desire to give power unto the 'world's wits' or to those who would presume to be manipulators of others. It is that the power of negation is often unwittingly assumed over others without their knowledge and without their recognition of the source of influence that attempts to defraud them of the great blessings God intends man to have.

"Let me compare this to the incident of a legacy that a relative in a distant city bequeaths to a loved one. He entrusts it unknowingly to an unscrupulous attorney who, through manipulating the law, does not give proper notice to the heir at the passing of the relative and secures for himself an appointment as trustee, thereby gaining control of the fortune himself. This defrauds the heir either in part or in toto, who is thus unaware of the total good that should have befallen him....

"We affirm that all men are children of God in that they were originally endowed with a threefold flame and were intended to inherit God's kingdom. But the fact remains that those who at the present hour desecrate the divine intent by the practice of witchcraft are not only hindering themselves, but they are also hindering the planet through the emanations of negation that they release.

Self-Condemnation

"Now, self-condemnation is one of the factors that governs the amount of negative radiation that men take in. The Christian Church, in its mission of saving men's souls, has frequently emphasized the nature of 'sin' in the human psyche, and thereby many have been burdened with feelings of guilt that they have inadvertently accepted in place of the joy of their own individual Christ-identity.

"Those who desire to have dominion over the consciousness of others may seek to achieve it through the imposition of intense feelings of self-condemnation upon their victims, who, in their resultant state of self-delusion, are easy prey to those Evil designs that the malpractitioner then masquerades as

Good....

"Condemnation, then, which is actually a frontal attack against the Christ-good in man, is one of the most insidious types of witchcraft because it opens the door to the disorientation of personality and a great deal of unhappiness. In addition to the more obvious and direct attempts to depreciate the manifestation of God, there are projected into the subconscious recesses of the human psyche animal forms and astral distortions that would be enough to unhinge the most balanced of minds if they were aware of them.*

"The dissonant lines of force emanating from these projections cut across the beautiful soul-regenerating powers of the Christ, which would ordinarily flow unimpeded down through the whole lifestream from the great Source of Life, the individualized mighty I AM Presence. Eventually these distortions reach the surface of men's conscious awareness, there to manifest as even more complex lies of insecurity, remorse and shame. Thus men's hopes are dashed by these treacherous thieves, which have entered the night of his subconscious mind, and he, cast down before his own eyes, is unable to rise and behold the love of God that flows forth from the fount of Life to free him."[38]

The Reinforcement of Darkness

The fallen ones work their Darkness directly and also through those in embodiment who are their tools. Astral forces of black magicians are gathered around every enemy of the Light, and this is the source of their power. When you see individuals who seem to move with extraordinary Darkness and an extraordinary protection of Darkness, when you see

---

* An outer manifestation of the projection of these forms into the subconscious occurs in movies that use such forms as focuses of fear or horror.

things going from bad to worse and yet the people through whom these things are happening seem to be unaware—they have a certain amount of magnetism and maya around them, but they're not gods themselves, they're not geniuses, and they do not have the total awareness of the strategies of Darkness— these are tools managed and controlled by the false hierarchy, the anti-hierarchy of the Great White Brotherhood.

Cadres of black magicians on the astral plane form rings of protection and direction around the enemies of the Light, and the enemies of the Light actually take their orders from these black magicians and receive dictations from them. Sometimes it is directly through a false hierarch and sometimes it is actually through a type of astral computer tape—where you can hear individuals talking in a certain monotone, a certain absence of mind, and if you are sensitive to the vibration, you can hear the voice of a computer speaking through an individual.

There are also forces that surround the enemies of the Light that are half demon and half elemental—imprisoned elemental forces that behave in an elemental way. These forces add to their seeming charisma or magnetism. They are the antithesis of guardian angels, and they form what might be called a "rubber-tire ring" around individuals. They insulate these fallen ones, and karma bounces off of them because of this reinforcement of very unsavory creatures that are not of the Light. They are like barking dogs or wolves baying or coyotes barking—almost in the category of familiars.

The Use of Familiars

A familiar is a being of any sort that a black magician uses as an anchor point in Matter. Whenever you have electricity, you need the positive and negative for a current to flow. Wherever you have a Guru-chela relationship, you need Alpha and Omega for the completion of the circle. Your soul is the negative polarity of your Christ Self, and you are complete in that wholeness as an instrument of God.

The black magician has polarized himself in the perversion of the Spirit, or the Alpha, current. He has perverted the energies of heaven* (the energies of the upper chakras) and the Light of the people to work his black magic. But in order to complete the circuit, he must have an anchor point in Matter that constitutes the negative, or Omega, polarity, and this is called a *familiar.*

Familiars may be discarnate entities, they may be demons, they may be people, or they may be imprisoned elementals or animal forms on the astral plane. They may also be physical animals—like the black cats, toads or other animals that are often depicted accompanying witches. In the film *Snow White and the Seven Dwarfs,* the witch had a raven. A raven is a very key familiar on this planet; in fact, the raven, as a bird, is the representative of the Brotherhood of the Black Raven, to which all betrayers of the Light belong.

The raven was associated with the "Hapsburg curse." According to the legend, every misfortune happening to the House of Hapsburg was associated with the appearance of a raven. The day before the assassination of Elisabeth of Austria, she was in the mountains around Lake Geneva and a black raven brushed her forehead with the tip of its wing. Knowing the legend, her companion became extremely disturbed and agitated. She said not to be concerned because it was not the raven or the curse, but the will of God that determined life and death, and where she was to be today or the next day was not of her concern. Nevertheless, she was assassinated, and the raven was the bearer of that sign.[39] The

---

* Jesus said, "The kingdom of heaven suffereth violence, and the violent take it by force" (Matt. 11:12).

Brotherhood of the Black Raven, the curse of the black raven, is something that we can also name when we gives decrees or invocations on black magic and witchcraft.

The Difference between the Christ and Black Magicians

Those who practice the black arts always aver that their work is, in reality, good and that many benefits accrue to individuals and society as a result of their group efforts. But how can this be, when the magnificent power of the living Christ is readily available to assist all men in the winning of their immortal freedom?

The power of the living Christ bears testimony in the heart of every child of God that he embodies none of the aspects of witchcraft or psychism. Jesus never employed witchcraft or black magic to heal the sick, to raise the dead, to cast out demons or to win his own victory. On the contrary, his every act refuted the tenets of necromancy, demonology and wizardry.

The Maha Chohan speaks to those who claim to use these practices for good: "Children of the Light, in your own expression I say, wise up, wise up! Understand that you are not alone in this forcefield of initiation and of the testing. There are forces of Light and forces of Darkness vying for the very existence of your soul. Wise up and recognize that your soul can be lost by wrong choices, by entering into the black arts, even unwittingly, practicing those practices that are called witchcraft that are truly not of the Light.

"I say, come out from among them. Forsake these perversions of the Mother flame and of the Holy Spirit. Understand that these are the archdeceivers of mankind who tell you that witchcraft is of the Great White Brotherhood. I say it is not.

And I denounce it as the practice of the dark ones usurping the Light of the Father-Mother God in the cities of the twin flames and the cloven tongues of fire.*

"There is no such thing as a white witch. Who gave you that word? Who told you that you could go by that name? You are a child of the Light. Claim the Light and practice the Teachings of the Great White Brotherhood. Shun Evil and forsake the manipulators who are manipulating your soul to its utter corrosion. Understand, then, that the term 'witchcraft' has nothing in it of the Light, but only of Darkness. This is not the teaching of the Brotherhood. Therefore, if you would do Good, forsake even the word that implies the turning around of the Light into Darkness.

"Be followers of the Christ within your heart. Forsake all that is less than the Christ-perfection that God has given you. Understand that these archdeceivers are abroad in the land, and they have sought to manipulate those who have the greatest Light to turn that Light into Darkness until it is spoken of you, 'How great is that darkness!' "[40]

When Jesus was touched by the woman who sought to be healed, he said, "Who touched me?" The disciples were surprised that he should ask such a question, and they said, "Thou seest the multitude thronging thee, and sayest thou, Who touched me?" And he said, "Somebody hath touched me: for I perceive that virtue is gone out of me."[41] His consciousness was aware of his own energy levels; therefore, he recognized the momentary loss of that energy.

Men and women today must also become sensitive to their own energy levels, for they do not realize the tremendous amount of energy that goes out of them in unnecessary conversation, in gossip, in downgrading others and in asserting their

---

* This dictation was delivered in Minneapolis, Minnesota. Minneapolis and Saint Paul are known as the twin cities.

own egos. They are involved in senseless activities, and they are playing with the law of no return. For such energy cast upon the waters of human emotion does not return to them except for redemption. Believe it or not, in most cases the cause of physical death is linked directly with the huge energy losses that mankind suffer daily. For the energy men throw away is their very life. When it is spent and the sands run out, they have no impetus to sustain their forms.

When the first men and women dwelled upon the planet and their habits were not oriented around the fashions of the times, which have been in and out of vogue for centuries, men preserved their energy and invested it as a wise broker would the proceeds of an estate. Hence the return of that energy continually renewed their bodies, minds and beings. Their life spans were measured in terms of hundreds of years rather than the brief threescore and ten we moderns have come to accept as the norm.

Many people have no emotional or mental control over their worlds, and they ally themselves unthinkingly with the negative forces of the planet, seeking to shape their own ends and designs at the expense of society, profiting from the labors of others, exploiting the credulity of the masses and manipulating whole power blocs to their wicked schemes.

The bitter struggle for human fortune that occurred early in America's history showed the crushing effect of human greed upon all who toiled in its grip. Fortunes were made and lost. Broken bodies, families and friendships were strewn across the deserts of human hope, ruthlessly crushed by the mania of desire to possess that which was not rightfully earned. This trait is the mark of the black magician and of his philosophy, but it has also become the identifying factor of many souls who refuse to contain their lusts for material possessions.

Many nations have taken the same route, and black

magicians have been at the helm of their ship of state. The late Adolph Hitler was himself a black magician who allied himself with the negative forces of the world. Such individuals must first of all convince themselves that they are great and that the end result of what they do will be a blessing in disguise to mankind. Their method of achieving their ends does not seem to them to be as important as the fact that they succeed.

The difference between the Christ and the black magician is expressed in these two opposing statements: "Do unto others as you would have them do unto you" and "Outsmart your brother before he outsmarts you."

Inroads of Black Magic in the World

The violations of cosmic law are legion. Black magic has invaded the Church from its beginning, for there were many, like the Emperor Constantine, who joined the Church because they could not defeat it from without. These pagans carried over ancient and perverted rituals from an unholy pantheism, which were incorporated either privately or doctrinally into the teachings of the Church, without the authorization of the Christ. There have always been black magicians among the religious leaders of the world, and their infiltration is effective to the present hour.

We dare not withhold this Truth from men. On the other hand, we do not propose to initiate a witch-hunt for "Evil forces." Our motive is to protect the life of seekers for Truth from the nefarious influences of black magic that are being directed against them daily.

We recommend as a countermeasure that individuals direct their attention to their own divinity—to the divinity that shapes their ends, bearing in mind that whatever else may be happening, they are the targets of the arrows of divine love that are released from the bow of the Infinite Archer.

Those who would lead men through the long night of chaos must warn of lurking danger as well as pointing to the star of Christ-victory—for all that hinders man's ascension must be reckoned with before the day of victory. Our desire is to teach the children of the Light how to protect themselves from the subtle traps of the negative forces.

The Signs of Witchcraft and the Cycles of the Moon

We are in a battle today, and the battle is being waged within our consciousness. Most people do not even realize that the enemy has placed upon them a consciousness of condemnation. It is as a pall. It is a forcefield of belittlement and of criticism.

It is very important to understand that witchcraft is practiced daily and hourly against the students of the Light. It is the condemnation of the Christ within you and a condemnation of the Feminine Ray. The signs of witchcraft practiced against you are irritation in your feelings, the breaking of things, accidents, nervousness, an irritability that even comes to a point of explosion, anger, and just a general feeling that you are not yourself. It affects your mind as self-belittlement, self-condemnation and the acceptance of limitation.

It is very wise to watch the cycles of the moon. Whenever there is a full moon, you can be certain that the misqualified or astral energies of the moon, the emotional substance, is being drawn into these witches' covens and then directed against all focuses of the Christ and of the Light. Even if you are not known personally or directly by specific witches, you can be certain that they attack all that is of the Light, because they are not of the Light.

How to Counter Witchcraft and Condemnation

There are very few among mankind who at one time or another or in one embodiment or another have not had a cursing against their lifestream. These curses last until they are challenged. They may be curses of a limitation of consciousness, a limitation of illumination or a general feeling of encasement, almost in a mold of darkness. You have to break the back of the lie. You have to draw the sword of the World Mother and plunge it into the cause and core. You may use these words:

> In the name of my mighty I AM Presence, I draw the sword of the World Mother, and I plunge it into the cause and core of all mortal cursings, criticism, condemnation and judgment that have ever passed through the nexus of my consciousness from within or without, directed against me or the Light for which I stand, or directed by me against anyone else upon this planetary home. And I call for the freedom of my consciousness and of all others that I may have ever harmed. In the name of Jesus the Christ, I accept it done this hour in full power. Amen.

That is a very important invocation. If you have a matrix of witchcraft projected upon you, it must be broken. A matrix can be a geometric form, a warp such as you see in modern art or in pornography. It can be simply a distortion of the Christ Image.

It is very important that you understand, then, that you will be attacked by witchcraft and that you must counter it. When you begin to invoke the Light, you have a lot of Light in your aura. But if your aura is not purified and your chakras are not purified, this Light may then come through as an amplification of bad habits or desires. You must recognize that you have to undo this pattern. Whether a witch has put it on you, whether it is a cursing or whether it is your own consciousness, it doesn't matter. The Light is flowing through it, and you must break the pattern and replace it with a perfect mold so that the Light can resurrect in you the Christ Mind. It is very important to deconstruct imperfect matrices in your consciousness.

Raising the Sex Cone: Perversion of the Ascension Spiral

Witchcraft is based entirely on the perversion of the Life force, of the sacred fire, or of sex energy. One means by which this is done is through the raising of what is known as a *sex cone*. This cone is a spiral of energy that rises from the ground, built in the shape of a cone. It is a direct perversion of the ascension spiral.

The sex cone that is used by witchcraft is formed by the misqualification of energies through the chakras below the heart by the use of incantations, formulas, dancing in a circle, blood-letting and other means. When the matrix is completed, it is directed to a specific purpose, perhaps directed against individuals or groups or used to imprison elementals in matrices of Darkness.*

What is your defense? You may say the following:

In the name of Almighty God, in the name of Jesus the Christ, I demand the shattering of the sex cones, of the incantations and the forcefields of all witches and witches' covens, and all energy directed against me or

---

* One example of the manifestation of energies that are misused in this way is in the hurricanes that originate off the coast of Africa, move through the Caribbean and strike the southern coasts of the United States. All three areas are centers where witchcraft, voodoo and black magic are practiced.

the Light for which I stand. In the name of Almighty God, I demand that that energy be seized and drawn into the circle and sword of blue flame of mighty Astrea and transmuted. Let it be done in the name of the living God and according to his will. Amen.

Then you may give the decree to Astrea (page 127) or the decree for the reversing of the tide (page 253). Visualize the legions of Light reversing this tide of Darkness sent against you and reversing it right back to the source from whence it came. This is cosmic justice.

The ascension spiral is something that all of us must build in order to transmute all of the energies below the heart. This is part of the ascension process, and we build this in the center of the square of our own pyramid of Life. Serapis Bey lectures on this subject to us when we go to his retreat while our bodies sleep at night.[42] We can make the call to be taken to the Ascension Temple to learn how to raise the ascension cone for our immortal victory. The use of the resurrection flame helps to raise this ascension cone.

Consciousness Must Be Guarded

Since witchcraft is based on the perversion of the energy at the base of the spine, when it is directed against you and you have a large amount of Light in your aura that the witches or black magicians are trying to take from you, they will try to amplify in you a feeling of desire. It could be a desire for food, for sex or some form of indulgence. If you give in to this indulgence, you allow the Light that you invoke to flow into old patterns, into old molds and to go down into the forcefields of the sex cone that the witches have projected around you.

They do this through condemnation. They try to belittle

you through these vibrations, telling you that you are unworthy to serve the Light, that you have these desire patterns, that you can never overcome them, that this is the way you are. And you get more and more and more belittled until you feel totally unworthy even to lift up a decree book and raise your head to God in praise of the Light within you.

You simply call to the Elohim Astrea: "I demand in the name of Almighty God the raising of the Light!" You visualize the Light rising up your spine just like a thermometer—just going straight up. And where is it anchored? It is anchored in the heart. And there your Holy Christ Self uses that energy to extend love to the world and to counteract this condemnation of the Divine Mother and the Divine Manchild.

It is the total perversion of the Feminine Ray and of the Christ that the forces of witchcraft and black magic are using to tear down our civilization. All the ills in society today are based upon this principle of trying to take man and make him into an animal by taking the Light from his Presence, taking it below the heart and then making him channel it out through the lower chakras in anger and all types of passion, in the dancing that is done today and in rock music. This is all the release of energy through the lower chakras. That very beat of the rock music will draw your energy down. And if you are in the presence of it, unless you are almost an unascended master, it is very difficult for that energy not to flow, because these matrices have been implanted in your subconscious.[43]

So you must guard your total consciousness. Let us be free of condemnation of ourselves for our past mistakes and for our weaknesses and let us realize that right now today is the rebirth, is the resurrection.

Whenever you are criticizing, judging or condemning other lifestreams or yourself you are, in effect, practicing witchcraft, you are practicing black magic. You are annihilating yourself when you condemn yourself, and you are annihilating other people when you condemn them; and you will bear the karma for it one day in your physical body.

You may see Evil, you may see injustice, you may see wrong; but you don't have to condemn it. You have to heal it! When you see faults in people, you can say: "Mighty I AM Presence, I commend them into your care and I magnify the Christ. I call to their Holy Christ Self to rise up and take command." You can point out Evil and you can call for it to be encircled by Astrea; you can know that it's wrong and you can demand the Light through it. But you must not go around with the feeling in your heart of condemnation, hatred, judgment or pointing the finger.

This does not mean that you don't have discrimination. If you are functioning from the center of the Christ consciousness, you are always dividing Good from Evil, Light from Darkness. You are making this discrimination hourly in deciding what you will or won't do, what you will or won't allow to act in your own consciousness; but this does not involve condemning one's fellow man or oneself.

The World of Advertising

The use of black magic is prevalent upon the planet, although it is often disguised, sugarcoated and legitimized by the most ingenious minds and methods. Aligned with the forces of Evil are momentums of human greed that have become centered through various institutions. These institutions have become a necessary and integral part of our civilized world. Some were founded by the Brotherhood upon the principle of the Golden Rule taught by Avatars, but have largely become instruments of darkness.

For example, black magic in various forms has even

invaded the advertising world, often without the knowledge of the top executives. Through the perversion of pure art forms and the inversion of the symbols used in white magic, men are being taught to control the minds of others and the markets of the people.

Advertising agencies have become agencies of control, employing artists and creative people who are masters in mind manipulation. Almost all advertising contains elements of hypnosis. The training of the eye on key images that engage the attention involves the flow of energy of the viewer and thereby sets up automatic reflexes in the brain, causing the victims to carry out predetermined acts (namely, the purchase of the advertised product) without the correct use of his free will.[44]

There is no question that in our generation the use of liquor and tobacco (both of which impede the flow of Light to the brain, not to mention that they may cause lung cancer, heart disease and other deleterious side effects) and the display of evocative and partially or wholly nude figures in motion pictures have taken a frightful toll upon the energies of our youth. All of the contact media—radio, television, national magazines, newspapers, books and motion pictures—have been linked in a vast network to spread abroad the poison of crass materialism and sensuality.

All of this is the work of the black magicians to steal the Light of the youth and to keep them forever bound to the rounds of karma-making experiences (hence reembodiment) and to the Darkness of this world. For the soul who is imprisoned is the soul whose Light can be stolen. The soul who is free is of no use to the brothers of the shadow. Her Light is a menace to their existence.

The apathy of many of the churches of the world in opposing this Evil has caused them to lose members rather than gain converts, by their utter failure to meet the spiritual needs of the people. Some churches today hold no position that is separate from the world, save in name only.

All of these controls and influences in society, in politics, in government and religion stem from no one individual or even from one fallen angel. The total plot has been well organized in the inner councils of the dark powers that be. They employ every human agency they can get into their clutches to perpetuate dark concepts upon mankind. This they accomplish by blackmail and bribe, which few have the courage to withstand. Let it never be forgotten that they thrive on the fattening of men's egos, and by flattery or intimidation, they get them to do their bidding.

The Master Plan of the Evil Forces

Let no one suffer from the illusion that there is no master plan of the evil forces. For there *is* such a plan, and it is perpetrated upon an unsuspecting humanity by the black magicians and their tools and focuses of darkness. What happens in the world today is no accident. It is planned.

We say to the children of God: Awake! and cease your slumber. Realize that there is only one defense against the monstrous plot, and that is in Christ himself, in the God Presence of each individual and in the Spiritual Hierarchy, the Brotherhood of Light, their legions of angels, and the all-embracing love of God for his creation.

Turn away, then, from darkness and all within thyself that would gain thee the world and cause thee to lose thy soul.[45] There is no higher religion than Truth. The Law of Love will eventually balance in the scales of cosmic justice every activity that has ever been perpetrated against mankind or that they themselves have practiced against one another as they have mimicked their overlords in a fantastic spiritual genocide.

Let us remember that every person and every organization that seeks to uphold the living Christ will of necessity experience the attack of the black magicians (the Antichrist). Whether or not these attacks are successful, and to what degree, is determined by many factors.

Black magicians often employ individuals who are allied with religious endeavors and get them to engage in what seems to be harmless gossip or character assassination of the leaders or pillars of various faiths. They then attempt to vilify these individuals, to trap them in compromising situations or to prove them guilty of some man-made law, to create schisms between spiritual organizations and to amplify the divisive nature of man that has prevented his unification.

Their motto is "Divide and conquer." Therefore, we must unite with the Eternal One and with his living Truth in daily life. This is our best and only sure defense.

Daily decrees to one's God Presence, to Archangel Michael and to Mighty Astrea are a sure defense against all that is not of the Light (known or unknown) that would attempt to alter or interfere with the true disciple's course of Truth.

Because we are the authority in our world, the Law requires that someone on this plane, in this octave, make the call to the Ascended Masters to transmute and remove unwanted conditions. The Masters do not have the authority to step into any of our four lower bodies or the earth unless they are called into action by someone in embodiment.

Let none think that we are giving undue attention to the veil of Evil that will one day fade as a mist in the sunlight of Truth. Rather let all understand that by the law of polarities, those who aspire to the highest Truth are subject to the attacks of the lowest forms of error. They must seek, therefore, to find a place in the arms of God, in the citadel of his strength, where they can be cloistered from those tragic occurrences that have for centuries robbed the planet of its birthright.

There is no purpose in shielding the seeker for divine Truth from the exigencies of the hour or from the plots of the dark forces that have caused civilizations to fall, continents to sink and men to lose their souls. To put one's head in the sand as an ostrich and to refuse to recognize the existence of organized Evil is utterly ridiculous. Those who do so in the name of Christ or Christian metaphysics are victims of the very forces whose existence they deny. For the easiest way for the evil powers to have free rein in the world (as they seem to have today) is for them to have a group of religionists who affirm that they do not exist!

If these affirmations were effective in stopping nefarious activities, we could endorse them, but the fact remains that they are not. We must, therefore, take countermeasures, being wise as serpents and harmless as doves.[46] However, we must not beat the air in a frenzy like Don Quixote and his wind-mills, thereby neglecting to establish within our own domain pillars of cosmic wisdom and bastions of strength against the fury of phantom foes.

Men must seek to hold themselves in the consciousness of God and his Christ. They must recognize that the power that overcomes the world is in the Christ, who cast out demons and gave to them that believe the power to cast out devils in his name.[47]

The Knowledge of Good and Evil

Saint Germain explains how we may transcend this realm of relative Good and Evil and reclaim our immortal birthright: "It is difficult for individuals who contemplate the existence of Evil to understand that it is the one consciousness of God that,

in its fluidic nature, flows into the individualized consciousness of man (into the spiritual as well as the human monad)
and conveys to it sentient power that enables man to create
through free will not only after the likeness of God but also
after the energy veil called Evil.

"The miracle of the spiritual senses, and of the five
physical senses as well, is born of God's own Self-awareness;
in knowing Himself he gave to man the like faculty of
knowing himself. In fact, God commanded self-knowledge to
all in whom he placed the flame of identity. But the knowledge
of Good and Evil, the yin and yang of world thought, was
forbidden and foreseen as unnecessary to the evolution of the
soul.

"In discovering the self, man is in reality discovering the
God Self. But he is borrowing the consciousness of the Eternal
One in order to reach the ultimate goal of becoming wholly
unified with God, thereby meriting the full possession of His
spiritual faculties. Only God is in full possession of the divine
attributes. And although he freely lends them to all who will
be just stewards, only those who have become wholly one with
him in the ever-ascending spirals of Being are awarded like
possession of the Law. Mankind cannot rightfully claim any
virtue or achievement as his own until he ascends to become
one with God, for God alone is worthy of being God.

"Whatever mankind choose to imagine within their hearts,
it is often possible for them to create. While a God-idea has
the full potential of God-expansion, an Evil concept has the
potential that unascended mankind give to it through the
misuse of their creative faculties. Mankind often believe that
Evil is something apart from God, and indeed it is; however,
all externalizations, whether they be of Good or Evil, are
comprised of the same energy, which is borrowed by man
from his Creator.

"Destined to be a co-creator, man was given experimental use of energy through the gift of free will. Understandably, through the misuse of that free will, he might use God's energy to create all manner of wickedness and distorted forms. Therefore, it was decreed that not until such a time as he should prove his mastery, by demonstrating the willingness and the humility to choose always the Good, could man himself win the crown of becoming one with God as a Creator-Son.

"I quote now the words from the Book of Genesis: 'And God saw that the wickedness of man was great in the earth, and that every imagination of the thoughts of his heart was only evil.'[48] Adam and Eve were privileged to live in the Garden, a place set apart from the rest of the world where God himself manifested through the sacred-fire essences of the Tree of Life. It was the secret place of the Most High[49] wherein lesser mortals had not yet earned the right to walk. The Tree of Life in the center of the Garden was for the nourishing of the outer as well as the inner man with the vital Light essences. It was a tangible manifestation of the mighty I AM Presence, to which all men have access but which few, in reality, now see, prior to their ascension.

"When Adam and Eve partook of the tree of the knowledge of good and evil in violation of the divine plan, they broke the covenant that had established their haven of Paradise. Thus man was driven from his home in the Garden to till the soil as other men, 'lest he put forth his hand, and take also of the tree of life, and eat, and live forever.'[50] Subsequently, Adam and Eve were given the opportunity to reestablish the state of grace that they had lost through unwitting disobedience. They were required to pass the same tests they had failed in the Garden, but under much more difficult conditions.

"And so you have an example of the fact that the one firm

foundation of heaven that cannot be broken is the law of protection of the Immaculate Image—the design of God— which abides behind the doorway of Light. This radiant Light Image, in all of its great power, wisdom and love, could never permit itself to be so desecrated in the holy place of God's own Being as to be brought under the bondage of the outer creation and made subject to its laws. For the LORD hath also set the bounds of his own habitation, and no man durst commit the sin of mortality while standing in the Holy of Holies.

"Consider for a moment what a frightful thing it would have been—how self-annihilating and productive of shadow or 'not-being'—if Evil had been permitted to usurp the place of Good. 'But when ye shall see the abomination of desolation, spoken of by Daniel the prophet, standing where it ought not, (let him that readeth understand,) then let them that be in Judaea flee to the mountains.'[51]

"I am well aware of the fact that in the mysteries of the Earth itself, and deep within the heart thereof, in the manifold evolutions of this planet, and even in solar and galactic evolutions, there are many layers and conditions that do not bring the happiness and delight of the divine plan fulfilled to the Being of God. How these conditions came about and what the ultimate end of them will be perhaps for the average student are best left untouched, at least at this stage of our instruction....

"In order for unascended man to take the hand of the Christ, to pass through the door of Light and to enter the Holy of Holies, he must be wholly purified, having utterly committed himself to the way of divine obedience and perfection. Unless this ritual of purification is completed and the vow taken, he, like those who sojourned in the Garden of Paradise, will be expelled until the dawn of deeper consecration floods his being with the desire to 'try' again.

"Opportunity is the Mother of the infinite cycles of Being afforded man to work out his salvation.

Rise to the Sun of Being

"Awareness of the meaning of Life must come about through a gradual spiritual evolution that infuses the seeker with an inner proof of Truth and godly vibration, although he and his companions may not necessarily have full awareness of the transformation that is taking place within his total consciousness. It is true that the fashions of mankind change from generation to generation, but the spiritual fashion of the Creator's intent changeth not. The outer man judges after the signs and fashions of the times, and these seldom point to the individual's inner mastery. (It required the assistance of an informant to ascertain Jesus' identity in the Garden of Gethsemane.)

"We would, therefore, direct the attention of men back to the original design. Discover the power that lies within your hand when you commit yourself wholly unto Him. Your mighty I AM Presence is the fullness of all discovery; there is no lack, no limitation imposed upon your Divine Presence. But in the holy name of mercy, I say to all: It is well that God has imposed his Laws and some necessary restraint upon mankind in their present unascended state and upon the use that men make of universal substance.

"There are many perils that surround mankind in his search for Selfhood. The closer he draws to the doorway of Light, the more the hordes of shadow plot to turn him from the Path and to steal from him the little Light that he already has aglimmering in the lamp of Being. As thou gainest in spiritual stature, expand thy humility, for the armour of humility becomes increasingly important as spiritual victories

are won. Let no man steal thy crown,[52] especially not the
enemy within thy gates, the carnal mind of the untransmuted
world.

"Strangely enough, precious ones, we often find that with
the attainment of spiritual power, individuals are sorely
tempted to forsake their humble ways. Among the esoteric
groups in existence throughout the world, there are many
whose members have become supercilious. There is often a
tendency on the part of the adherents of these groups to, in
your words, 'lord it over one another' in spiritual matters. The
very statement of God recorded in letters of living fire, 'God
resisteth the proud, but giveth grace to the humble,'[53] should
move these would-be followers of God to exorcise the spirit of
pride from their midst....

"Now, the doorway of Light is opened by various means:
by prayer, by decrees, by attunement and meditation, by
affirmations of Truth, by awareness of the true Reality of
Being, by obedience, by chasteness of soul, and with the
assistance of the mighty I AM Presence, the Holy Christ Self,
the Ascended Masters, the angelic hosts, Cosmic Beings and
elemental builders of form....

"Men have by nature carried over from higher octaves a
great desire for speed in the manipulation of substance. Many
people deplore lethargy in any of its forms, and even in
spiritual matters they seek to obtain swift improvement of
their lot. The powers of heaven and the powers of freedom are
ever joyous to convey Truth to mankind with the speed of
lightning and to give every assistance that the Great Law will
permit. But the students must realize that there is no one
supreme formula that will lift them directly through the door
of Light into heavenly octaves without effort, without patience
and without obedience....

"I would to God that a greater measure of perspective

could be engendered in our students. Your world may be the size of an acorn or of a dazzling sun. Your mind may lie dormant as a dry seed or burst with fervent heat like popping corn. Your consciousness may be the size of a microbe or of a spiral nebula. Whatever your stature in a relative universe, it is secondary to the great measuring rod of souls: how you make use of free will. For He who has the power to expand or diminish all things at will cherishes the judgments of men made in His own favor.

"Therefore, faith is most precious in the eyes of God. If you would have greater soul progress, believe in God and in his capacity to reward those who diligently seek him. See the future, whether you are in the body or out of the body, as a scroll held in the hands of God. Consider your opportunity here and now as most precious, a gift whereby you may enter the doorway to Light. Seal, then, the door where Evil dwells— the dens of iniquity, the caves of materiality—and pierce the cobwebs of spidered thought! Leave the cocoon of mortal ignorance and rise on wings of Light to the Sun of Being....

"Seal the Door Where Evil Dwells"

"Man is in reality a being of Light, but his own natural resources remain untapped. Not only do the subterranean levels of the subconscious hold their secrets—but also the magnificent universal knowledge of the Godhead, unrevealed, untouched by human hands, remains sealed behind the door where Light dwells. The fiat went forth: 'Seal the door where Evil dwells,' and it has been well said; but unfortunately for the aspirant, many have sealed, or attempted to seal, the doorway to Evil without ever opening the doorway to Light.

"Thus has mankind found himself trapped as in a vacuum in the corridor between two ways of life: the human and the

Divine. Through one doorway, he hears the bawdy players on the stages of the world. Through the other, angelic choirs proclaim the unity of heaven. No longer oriented around the human personality, he dare not go back to the old way of life, and so he stands before the doorway of Light, awaiting the mighty revelation of Being.

"Content for a time to stand in anticipation of gaining entrance, he finds it difficult to long abide in the sovereign aloneness of the inner search. Sometimes the way has become arduous, the wait monotonous; in despondency he has gravitated once again toward the human forcefield. The planes of Sodom have seemed more immediately satisfying and accessible than the heights of the mountain route of escape. At times like these, it is well to remember, precious ones, that heaven and the Ascended Masters' way of Life are closer at hand than the golden sunlight and the crystal dew, that the summits of Truth are easier to scale than the echelons of society with all of its false values and goals.

"If men, then, would determine to open the doorway to Light by shutting out of consciousness all that is less than the Divine Image, their faith in the Good, the enduring and the True would sustain them until the necessary soul advancement had been made. Such advancement is a prerequisite to their being made acceptable in the sight of God, fit to dwell in his Presence, and therefore worthy of being given the golden key of Truth that will finally unlock the door to the kingdom.

"The initial vow made by unascended mankind to return to the Paradise way, to walk humbly with God and to express all that God has intended for him, does not automatically make him fit to receive the golden chain around his neck and the promise of Paradise. God requires proof that the disciple will remain constant to his word through all of the tests and trials attendant upon one who is gaining self-mastery, especially during the reaping of the harvest of all that he has sown. When all is in order, his debts to life balanced and his consciousness wholly purified, the disciple steps upon the threshold of True Being and the door of Light is opened.

" 'Whither shall I go from thy spirit? or whither shall I flee from thy presence? If I ascend up into heaven, thou art there: if I make my bed in hell, behold, thou art there. If I take the wings of the morning, and dwell in the uttermost parts of the sea; even there shall thy hand lead me, and thy right hand shall hold me.'[54] This cry, uttered of old by the psalmist, signifies to the present hour that everywhere that man can be, God already is and will forever be. There is no place where God is not, for he is All in all. Where consciousness is, there God is. Where Life is, God is indwelling. Where love is, God is expanding the nature of True Being. Where Truth is expressed, God is revealing his Laws and the nature of Reality."[55]

The Blue Lightning of the Sword of Astrea

We conclude this chapter with two very effective calls that may be given by all who are willing to give this method of invocation a try, and at the same time will give the Heavenly Hosts the opportunity to enter their worlds and to prove— even to those who may doubt their existence or scoff at the idea of divine intercession—that God will send his emissaries to man to defend him against all enemies. The call compels the answer!

Astrea is the feminine complement of the Elohim Purity. Their twin flames focus a cosmic momentum of the action of white fire and blue lightning for the binding of the hordes of darkness and the demons that torment the possessed. Astrea's whirling circle of blue flame locks around vortices of negative energy, shatters matrices of Evil and draws the misqualified substance of the mass consciousness into the sacred fire for transmutation. In answer to the calls of mankind, she strikes her sword of blue flame into the cause and core of all that opposes the freedom of mankind and their victory in the Light.

The circle of blue fire invoked from the heart of Astrea is a dazzling blue-white fire that oscillates as two concentric rings of fire—the blue of Astrea, the white of Purity—interchanging frequencies at such a rapid rate so as to appear as the action of blue-white lightning flashing around souls, planets, solar systems, galaxies—wherever there is a need for the reinforcement of the will of God in the divine blueprint held in the white-fire core of Being. Whenever and wherever you invoke the circle and sword of blue flame from the heart of Purity and Astrea, you can know with absolute certainty that an action of cosmic momentum is taking place.

Whenever and wherever there is discord in any form, in any of its aspects, you should call in the name of the Christ to the Elohim Astrea: "Lock your cosmic circle and sword of blue flame around the cause and core of that condition." Then see this circle of the sacred fire lock around the individual at the waist, around entire groups of individuals, around buildings, around entire cities, states, nations and even around the Earth at the equator. See this in your mind's eye as a ring of regular, almost geometric fire cutting away, like a buzz saw, layers and layers of discord and density.

Then visualize the sword of blue flame as a pillar of blue fire perpendicular to the circle of blue flame, breaking the matrices of Darkness, shattering forcefields of disease, decay and death. And above all, see the Elohim standing over each individual for whom you are praying, holding the sword of blue flame two inches from the spine and parallel to it. This is the action whereby the Elohim demagnetize the being and consciousness of the individual of all darkness, all sinister strategies of the fallen ones, and the serpentine energies of the carnal mind. The blue-lightning ray cuts through psychic effluvia, etheric records of the past and calcinations of the mental body.

The action of the blue-lightning ray, when invoked in the name of the God Presence from the heart of beloved Astrea, works effectively to clear the patterns of human creation that have been accumulated by individuals through hundreds of embodiments. Students on the path of the ascension have no single greater need than that of being cut free from their own personal densities as well as the astral contamination of the mass consciousness. Not until these old records and momentums are consumed is the individual aspirant free to move forward into the initiations of the Great White Brotherhood. The freer he is from his past and his human personality with its insatiable desires, the more immediate will be his transformation in the Light until there will be no limit to the possibilities of Christly manifestation in his world.

Having exchanged the human patterns for the Divine, he then knows the meaning of the exclamation "Heaven and earth are full of thy glory!" for he will have drawn down into the chalice of his four lower bodies, now become purified vessels for the Holy Spirit, the glories of God's kingdom. This can be accomplished only when the room in the inn of being is swept clean in preparation for the coming of the Christ.

Decree to Beloved Mighty Astrea

In the name of the beloved mighty victorious Presence of God, I AM in me, mighty I AM Presence and Holy Christ Selves of Keepers of the Flame, Lightbearers of the world and all who are to ascend in this life, by and through the magnetic power of the sacred fire vested in the threefold flame burning within my heart, I call to beloved Mighty Astrea and Purity, Archangel Gabriel and Hope, beloved Serapis Bey and the Seraphim and Cherubim of God, beloved Lanello, the entire Spirit of the Great White Brotherhood and the World Mother, elemental life—fire, air, water and earth! to lock your cosmic circles and swords of blue flame in, through and around my four lower bodies, my electronic belt, my heart chakra and all of my chakras, my entire consciousness, being and world.

[You may include here calls for specific circumstances or conditions for which you are requesting assistance.]

Cut me loose and set me free (3x) from all that is less than God's perfection and my own divine plan fulfilled.

1. O beloved Astrea, may God Purity
   Manifest here for all to see,
   God's divine will shining through
   Circle and sword of brightest blue.

First chorus: Come now answer this my call
   Lock thy circle round us all.
   Circle and sword of brightest blue,
   Blaze now, raise now, shine right through!

2. Cutting life free from patterns unwise,
   Burdens fall off while souls arise
   Into thine arms of infinite love,
   Merciful shining from heaven above.

3. Circle and sword of Astrea now shine,
   Blazing blue-white my being refine,

> Stripping away all doubt and fear,
> Faith and goodwill patterns appear.

Second chorus: Come now answer this my call,
Lock thy circle round us all.
Circle and sword of brightest blue,
Raise our youth now, blaze right through!

Third chorus: Come now answer this my call,
Lock thy circle round us all.
Circle and sword of brightest blue,
Raise mankind now, shine right through!

And in full faith I consciously accept this manifest, manifest, manifest! (3x) right here and now with full power, eternally sustained, all powerfully active, ever expanding and world enfolding until all are wholly ascended in the Light and free!

Beloved I AM! Beloved I AM! Beloved I AM!

[Give each verse, followed by the first chorus; repeat the verses, using the second chorus; then give the verses a third time, using the third chorus.]

Lord Michael, Cut Me Free!

In the name of the beloved mighty victorious Presence of God, I AM in me, my very own beloved Holy Christ Self, Holy Christ Selves of all mankind, beloved Archangel Michael, beloved Lanello, the entire Spirit of the Great White Brotherhood and the World Mother, elemental life—fire, air, water and earth! I decree:

1. Lord Michael, Lord Michael,
    I call unto thee
   Wield thy sword of blue flame
    And now cut me free!

Refrain: Blaze God-power, protection
    Now into my world,
   Thy banner of faith
    Above me unfurl!
   Transcendent blue lightning
    Now flash through my soul,
   I AM by God's mercy
    Made radiant and whole!

2. Lord Michael, Lord Michael,
    I love thee, I do
   With all thy great faith
    My being imbue!

3. Lord Michael, Lord Michael
    And legions of blue
   Come seal me, now keep me
    Faithful and true!

Coda: I AM with thy blue flame
    Now full charged and blest,
   I AM now in Michael's
    Blue-flame armour dressed! (3x)

And in full faith ...

Chapter 3

Antichrist

*Who is a liar but he that
denieth that Jesus is the Christ?
He is antichrist, that denieth
the Father and the Son.*

EPISTLE OF JOHN

Antichrist

The False Hierarchy

IT MUST EVER BE RECOGNIZED THAT the Real and the counterfeit have been with humanity for a long time. Whenever God has blessed men with Truth, its counterfeit (or Antichrist) has also asserted itself. Each attempt for Good is usually inverted and the opposite end of the axis brought to the fore in the attempt to alienate the allegiance of men from their highest Selfhood.

John the Beloved warned: "Little children, it is the last time: and as ye have heard that antichrist shall come, even now are there many antichrists; whereby we know that it is the last time."[1] Many have misunderstood his warning, and just as many have misapplied it. Let us clarify the concept of Antichrist so the admonishment that was intended may be known by the children of God to whom it was addressed. For it was the intention of the disciple to teach the followers of Christ the art of divine discrimination and how to avoid unnecessary entanglements[2] with the psychic, which corrode the soul and consciousness.

Who Is Antichrist?

The Antichrist is one who denies or opposes Christ. Some believe that in the last days a great antagonist will appear to deliver the world into the hands of the wicked. These believers expect that the antagonist will be overcome by Christ upon his Second Coming. However, the Reality is not so simple.

The term *Antichrist* symbolizes all that would enthrone the human ego and dethrone the Holy Christ Self, and all that would create division or dissension between peoples—whereas all that affirms the Truth of the manifestation of Father and Son, individualized as the I AM Presence and Holy Christ Self of every man, all that unites man with his God Source and the blessed Mediator and all that establishes true brotherhood and respect for the Laws of God is of the living Christ.

The Christ has coexisted with God since the living Word went forth to do his will in the world of form. Declaring the infinite nature of the Christ, Jesus said, "Before Abraham was, I AM."[3] The Christ is the Lamb of God who was slain from the foundation of the world.[4] Therefore, it should be clear that opposition to the Christ did not begin with the birth of Jesus, nor did it end with his ascension. The carnal mind always opposes the manifestation of the Christ in every child of God. The carnal mind is enmity with Christ, because the death of Evil and the consciousness that gave it birth is brought about in the victory of the Christ.

Thus the history of Antichrist begins with the mists of error that attempted to obscure the very first rays of the Son-Sun—but, as always, the warmth of His love dissolved their nebulous forms.

Imitation of the Divine Creation

We remember the story of Moses and Aaron at the court of Pharaoh in Egypt. When Moses, that great servant of God, directed Aaron to cast down his rod, it became a serpent. Then Pharaoh called the magicians of his court, who cast down their rods. Their rods, too, became serpents—but Aaron's rod swallowed up their rods.[5]

Here we see an example of white and black magic practiced side by side. Aaron, the white magician, was initiated in the retreats of the Brotherhood. Pharaoh's sorcerers learned their enchantments from black magicians, who perhaps were once trained by the Brotherhood but subsequently chose the left-handed path.

Aaron's knowledge of white magic was greater than their knowledge of black magic. Nevertheless, it was not Aaron's understanding alone that saved the day but the presence of the living God and his Christ, which consumes on contact all that is opposed to the Light.

The imitation of the divine creation is the forte of black magicians. They are not of God-Good, they cannot become God-Good and they cannot create Good. They can only imitate God's creation, and they offer a poor imitation at best.

This they do to confuse the central issues of Reality and unreality, of Truth and error. Their goal is to gain the allegiance of those who are weak in discrimination and easily lured by the glamour of illusion. Without the assistance of their Holy Christ Self, these people lack the power to distinguish the Real from the unreal.

The Black Brotherhood

The imitations of the black magicians extend not only into the practice of black magic and the falsification of the

Teachings of the Christ, but also into the organization of the hierarchy itself. The false hierarchy is composed of a group of unascended adepts dwelling in the astral plane, organized to impersonate the true Brotherhood of Ascended Masters who comprise the governing Hierarchy of the Earth—the Great White Brotherhood.

The false hierarchy is also known as the black brotherhood. Its members practice the black arts, or black magic—a system of the misuse of God's power to exert control over others, thus depriving them of the immediate direction of their own mighty I AM Presence and Holy Christ Self.

In the eleventh chapter of his second epistle to the Corinthians, Paul speaks of these false brethren: "For such are false apostles, deceitful workers, transforming themselves into the apostles of Christ. And no marvel; for Satan himself is transformed into an angel of light. Therefore it is no great thing if his ministers also be transformed as the ministers of righteousness; whose end shall be according to their works."[6]

The members of the false hierarchy consist of the fallen Luciferian angels and those who were once pupils of the Ascended Masters who elected to use the knowledge of the sacred fire vouchsafed unto them for self-glorification rather than for the glory of God and the expansion of his kingdom. This is known as taking the left-handed path.[7] The tools of the false hierarchy cooperating from astral levels include disembodied witches, discarnate entities and mass forms or entities of human creation.

The tools of the false hierarchy dwelling among mankind in physical embodiment are those who, like themselves, are dedicated to the destruction of all that is of God. Included in their ranks are the fallen angels, the laggards, the godless creation, witches, practitioners of voodoo and other forms of jungle magic, and those among the children of God who remain uncommitted to living the life of the Christ and can therefore be manipulated to carry out the schemes of the black brotherhood in many circumstances.

All of these forces work together as the "legion"[8] that opposes man's spiritual progress. They work zealously to preserve the entrenchment of social systems that enslave the race to a ceaseless round of economic drudgery, making materialism the goal of existence and justifying it by the philosophy of dialectical materialism. All the while they attempt to strike from the memory the soul's knowledge of her origin in God, Good, and her ultimate return to the Father through the ritual of the ascension.

The most skilled among the false hierarchy who abide on the astral plane appear regularly to receptive channels in embodiment. They impersonate the Ascended Masters with such cunning that many sincere seekers have been fooled. Thinking they were in the presence of one or more of the Ascended Masters, they have dedicated themselves unwittingly to the cause of Darkness and chained their energies to the wiles of the masters of deceit.

It is the policy of the false hierarchy to trap mankind by imitating the dictations of the Ascended Masters. This they accomplish by parroting truisms. When they have lulled their listeners into a state of false peace and utter self-satisfaction, they introduce bits of doctrine that are in absolute contradiction to cosmic law.[9] These deviations from basic Truth are couched in glowing terms and rationalized to the ego by appeals to pride and the desire to be thought wise among men and superior to others who do not have contact with the invisible world.

Seekers for Truth must ever be mindful that curiosity, pride, desire for attention to the personal ego and hunger for strange phenomena open the door to psychic intrusions. Once these psychic intrusions are "turned on," as the sorcerer's apprentice discovered, they are difficult to turn off.

On the other hand, unswerving devotion to the Presence of God in all Life, dedication to the immaculate concept, and a thorough, ready knowledge of Ascended Master Law are spiritual bulwarks of defense that provide infinite protection from all that would oppose man's individual self-mastery and his ultimate ascension in the Light.

In most cases, the defamation of the Christ by the Antichrist in this manner is not accomplished by a deliberate or blatantly fraudulent distortion of Christ Truth, but by minute distortions. (However, we have seen examples in which the entire context of the material is more or less a distortion. Such material is designed to take advantage of those who are by nature rebelling against a current system and are ready to throw out the good and the bad all at once.) These distortions are intended to disturb men and spread confusion and unrighteousness among mankind. Those who promote these distortions are primarily interested in discouraging people and making them feel a keen sense of frustration that there is no hope that the Christ will win the battle for the minds of men.

Some activities go all out to spread delusion wholesale. In such cases, gross distortions occur that may seek to defame the character of one or more of the Ascended Masters. We know of one such case in which a woman spread statements attacking the Master El Morya across certain areas of the United States. She painted him as black and satanic and attempted to discredit him in the eyes of his own disciples. By the power of an outspoken personality and a form of psychic dominance over people, she succeeded in subverting some individuals to her tenets, in a limited way. The Lords of Karma will, of course, correctly judge and assess her case, as they will each one individually. For all who purvey any form of deceit or untruths against the Laws of God or the great Masters of Wisdom will ultimately themselves come to naught.

Antichrist is always that which seeks to attack the mouth of God. In every age where progressive revelation rather than rigid dogma is enshrined, the negative forces seek to attack the person or character of the individual prophet.

After all, individuals do tend to reject the words or works of those whose character or person they cannot accept. The truth from a Christ could be accepted; from a pirate it would be questioned. Thus the false hierarchy directs its tools to spread malicious lies and subtle statements against all true Messengers of God. These statements may take the form of hints that perhaps the Messenger is not receiving his material directly from the Ascended Masters or that it is being received in some form of psychic trance.

At other times, those who are also doing spiritual work or appearing to do so may completely misinterpret the character of the chosen Messenger of God. This is often based upon subtle jealousies, which some of these individuals may not be aware of themselves. They could honestly recognize that in the world with its manifold varieties of religious activities, very few agree completely, but there is a real need for all to work together for the good of humanity. Instead, these individuals seem to feel the need to protect their own organizations by downgrading others.

There is no doubt that many individuals working for the Antichrist are themselves unaware of just what they are doing. They may be acting in ignorance and in some cases even sincerely. The whole concept becomes more understandable if we recognize that we must separate the person from his work. All men upon the planet have at some time or another made a mistake. As one of the great Indian yogis, Sri Yukteswar, said, "The vanished lives of all men are dark with many shames."[10]

There is indeed "none righteous, no, not one,"[11] as Saint Paul said. Yet all men can simply claim their kinship with God, accept the divine Law according to His holy will, and work out their perfection to the best of their ability.

If men were already perfect (any among mankind) they would not be here to work out their salvation—they would now be Ascended Masters. Nor would they need to work out their salvation if the crucifixion of Christ itself and its acceptance were enough to complete their course of righteousness.

"Try the Spirits"

Impersonal observation is important. Men's works should always be recognized according to their own merit. But when men gossip or talk about another, tending to assassinate his character (whether the person they are attacking is a Messenger of God or just the sweeper on the street), the very act of carrying tales or bearing judgment against another is an ungodly act. This act is punishable according to cosmic law by the Great Lawgiver himself, who has often said, "Judge not, lest ye be judged."[12]

Yet the Christ clearly indicated (in the person of his apostles and followers) that it is just and proper that men should "try the spirits" to see whether they are of God. "Every spirit," John says, "that confesseth that Jesus Christ is come in the flesh is of God. And every spirit that confesseth not that Jesus Christ is come in the flesh is not of God."[13]

The simple explanation of this is that every spirit that confesses not that Jesus Christ is come in the individual flesh of any monad, any spirit that states that Christ is unique and cannot come into the flesh of man to assist him to attain his own divine Sonship, is not of God.

But every spirit that confesses that Jesus the Christ is come in the flesh of every individual who will receive him, that he can be received and assimilated by them (hence, "ye must drink my blood and eat my flesh"[14]) understands that the coming of the Christ into anyone's being raises him in the course of time and by proper acceptance and obedience to the place where he can become one with the Universal Christ and actually become, as Jesus did, the "Only Begotten of the Father,"[15] thus following Christ in the regeneration. Such a spirit that confesses this, is of God, for he establishes the equality of the whole creation in its right to progress and be counted as a prodigal son[16] who truly returns to the Father. There is not one prodigal son, but many, and all may return. This is Christ Truth.

The Activities of Antichrist in Political and Social Fields

The spirit of Antichrist, in reality, is not only engaged in religious activity of a negative sort, but at times makes positive postulations that appear benign but also invade the political and social fields. Thus God's plans for man are often thwarted.

The apostles and teachers in the early Church discussed both the kingdom of God and the kingdom of heaven. The kingdom of God was spoken of as being "within you,"[17] whereas the kingdom of heaven, which was the intent of the Father for all life manifesting upon Earth, was referred to separately. Thus the kingdom of heaven could be made manifest upon Earth.

In the great family of nations, the tenets of all religions that seek to promote peace, harmony, love, brotherhood, diplomacy and illumination are honored by the lips of men. But their codes of conduct and their deeds are often far from the lip service they have given to the cause of man's immortal freedom.

Every little child, whether aware of it or not, has a right to expect to receive the blessings of the kingdom of heaven upon Earth. This means not only food, clothing, housing and education, for each child also has a right to expect to receive guidance and Truth from his compeers and to expect that that guidance will be correct—or at least as correct as possible. Unfortunately, however, the world today, with all of its scientific progress, is, politically and geographically speaking, divided and conquered by its own avariciousness.

In Proverbs we find the remark "With all thy getting get understanding."[18] Jesus followed this by saying, "Father, forgive them; for they know not what they do."[19] In this supposedly wisest of ages, men still know not what they do. In fact, the divisive nature of nations, religions and man is everywhere accentuated to the hurt of the world order. Defamation of the purposes of Christ (the bringing in of the kingdom of God into the world) and the defamation of the Christ by denying man the kingdom of heaven, the Golden Age of Righteousness, and so forth, is continually being accomplished by any manifestation that divides and conquers man. With their lips men say that they love, but their deeds seek continually to divide and to express condemnation and criticism of one another's opinions.

Men are, and should be, entitled to their honest opinions, whether or not they agree with one another perfectly. This is how men expand their consciousness and obtain spiritual growth, and all men are entitled to the freedom of their own thought. But there must be a universal ideal that provides for the best interests of the "allness" of humanity. This ideal is to be found in the Christ, in the Light, in the idea of the universality of the Son.

Just as God found it possible to accept and to love Jesus, so God accepts and loves all who will come to him. There is no room in the kingdom of God in the heart of the Father for the fraudulent monolith men have raised to Christ by which they do hurt to one another. The Master himself said, "Inasmuch as ye have done it unto one of the least of these my brethren, ye have done it unto me."[20] If humanity is to be considered guilty, then, of doing acts unto Christ that they do to "the least of these my brethren," would the Father make such a law and apply it to humanity and not to himself? Would he, himself, render inequitable judgment, have a favorite Son and then deny the Light to all others?

The guidance of God toward a distraught humanity has been manifest in so many ages. Even in the marvelous story of Moses leading the children of Israel out of Egypt and across the Red Sea, it was God who parted the water, it was his pillar of fire and pillar of cloud[21] that enabled them to see a tangible grace that accompanied them on their journey.

In contrast, the religions of the world have often failed to take their place as exponents of righteousness. Corruption of morals and ideals has occurred among the leadership, and the "getting" of individual groups has often taken precedence over their "givingness." In every age, the hungers of man have gone unsatisfied. These hungers have been very great, and no greater hunger has ever occurred than the yearning of the soul and man to know the Truth that he may be truly free. For men and women to make merchandise of one another concerning knowledge of God's sacred Laws is the greatest travesty that has ever been practiced upon humanity. Men are driven by the winds of their own emotion. Becoming extremists, they move from positions of virtue to positions of vice, and vice versa.

The Divinity of the Christ

What is needed in the world is the balancing action of the Christ himself. The Christ acts as Mediator and as a buffer between the great fiery spiritual energies of God embodied in the divine I AM Presence and the coiled spring of the serpent that has been nurtured in the human breast by wrong acts down through the ages. The Christ has ascended into heaven and sitteth on the right hand of God.[22] The Christ has been one with the Father[23]—yet the Christ has also been one with man.

The divinity of the Christ must be honored and upheld. But the divinity of the Christ can also be drawn close to the human figure. No mere symbolical or imaginative concept is this, but a drawing down of the vital, spiritual, magnetic energies of the eternal Creator.

"By him were all things made"[24] means that the individualized Divine Presence has released from his heart the magnificent Christ Self of each individual. This Christ Self acts as the guardian Higher Mental Body of that individual to fashion all the parts of the manifesting and emerging ego according to the divine pattern.

As the ego turns from the depressions and doldrums of self toward the mountain peaks of spiritual illumination—as Moses lifted up the serpent, so shall the son of man be lifted up.[25] The serpent signifies vital energies and redemption and the buffering action depicted in Genesis: "And I will put enmity between thee and the woman, and between thy seed and her seed; it shall bruise thy head, and thou shalt bruise his heel."[26]

Antichrist Has Come

Antichrist has come, indeed, and is in the world—working particularly wherever there are uplift groups, either political or religious, that seek to improve the lot of men. Antichrist seeks to create dissension and, where possible, warfare and blood-shed. Antichrist persists in dividing and conquering men. To do this he first subverts one or more groups through black magic, through the false allegiance to the ego and through the power complex that was spoken of in the saying, "Power corrupts, and absolute power corrupts absolutely."[27]

The representatives of Antichrist persist in dividing and conquering, turning the blacks against the whites, the whites against the blacks, capital against labor, labor against capital —and seeking to bring all under the domination of social control or communism. They have held the world in the icy grip of a fate worse than death.

This plot of Antichrist is an ancient one. Let us see what the records of history can tell us of its origins.

The Nephilim and the Power Elite

OUR SEARCH FOR WHO WE ARE, where we came from and where we are going takes us into the distant past, beyond the reckoning of historians—back to the lost continents of Atlantis and Lemuria, back to the time when people from other worlds arrived on Earth in spacecraft.

The records and artifacts of ancient Sumer, Egypt, India and even the Incan civilization bear witness to these visitors from distant planets. They arrived here with superior technology some 450,000 years ago. The aliens were not benevolent, and they manipulated the evolutions of Earth. They practiced genetic engineering and taught men the arts of war.

They were followed here by people from Maldek, a planet that at one time was in our solar system but was destroyed by warring factions. All that remains of Maldek is the asteroid belt between Mars and Jupiter. When the Maldekians began to incarnate on Earth, they too brought an advanced science and a warlike nature.

The Mahabharata, an ancient Hindu text, talks about great battles, flying war chariots and advanced weapons of mass destruction. It all sounds like something out of George Lucas' *Star Wars*. But it is a vision of the past, not the future.

Earth has become a crossroads in the galaxy. She has many different evolutions—people who have their origins here, others who started out on other systems of worlds. Some are of the Light. Some have committed themselves to Darkness. Some are men, some are fallen angels who have taken embodiment, and some are angels of Light. It is a complex tapestry.

Origins of Western Civilization

For a long time Western man has believed that his civilization was built on the foundation of Greece and Rome. The similarities between their civilizations and ours would certainly support that belief. But what was the source of Roman and Greek philosophy and technological advances? How did the Greeks and Romans develop language and art? Who taught them the arts of war and international diplomacy? The discoveries in 1845 of ancient cuneiform tablets and the uncovering of a civilization lost and nearly forgotten gives us a clear look at our past and a stern warning for the future. A drama that unfolded thousands of years ago affects all of our lives today.

Ecclesiastes said, "There is no remembrance of former things; neither shall there be any remembrance of things that are to come with those that shall come after."[1] Because there is no remembrance, we do not have the facts of ancient history that we need to know today to deal with the oppressors of God's people. If we are to anticipate the challenges of the future, we need to understand our history. We need to examine a civilization on whose shoulders sat Rome and

Greece and that predated and animated Egypt, Babylonia, Assyria, China and India. We turn to the records of Sumer.

By 3000 B.C. a high civilization was already in full bloom along the Tigris and Euphrates Rivers in Sumer (modern-day Iraq). The lowlands of Sumer were located in what was later called the Fertile Crescent. Sumerian medical schools trained brain surgeons. The Sumerian ruler could not send his armies marching at will; he had to first submit his request to both chambers of congress. Sumerian cities were bustling with activity: ancient recipes for "coq au vin" inspired poems of praise. Sumerian songs, based on the seven-tone musical scale we use today, contained familiar sentiments. They calculated the planetary positions for every planet in our solar system including Pluto, which was not rediscovered in modern times until 1930. Unbelievably, they knew the Earth was tilted on its axis and had calculated its slow 25,800-year backward precession. Ancient texts and drawings show that they had weapons like lasers, practiced germ warfare and population control, and were capable of space travel.

To this day, scholars are baffled by the Sumerians and cannot say for sure exactly who they were, where they came from, or what sparked their remarkable civilization. Its appearance was so sudden that scholars have called it "astonishing," "extraordinary," "a flame which blazed up so suddenly."[2]

Our morals, our laws, our sense of justice, our architecture, our civilization are rooted in Sumer. That civilization began 3800 B.C. Did evolving man have extraordinarily good luck? What caused the transformation that catapulted primitive nomadic hunters and food gatherers into the builders of an advanced civilization of cities, mathematicians, astronomers, merchants, engineers and priests?

The Sumerians had a simple answer: "Whatever seems beautiful we made by the grace of the gods."[3] The question remains and must be answered by us today: Who are these gods?

The Gods of Sumer

Ancient tablets reveal the names of a pantheon of hundreds of gods governed by an assembly of deities, all related to one another. They were immensely powerful, capable of extraordinary feats. But they looked like humans and acted like humans in almost every way.

By comparing the Old Testament in its original Hebrew against Sumerian, Babylonian, Assyrian and other ancient texts, linguist and archaeological researcher Zecharia Sitchin has evolved a unique theory about the origin of these gods.* He describes them as "a divine family, closely related yet bitterly divided."[4] They were led by the god Anu, whose abode was not on the Earth, and his son, Enlil, who carried out the gods' decrees. Enlil selected kings to rule over man, not as sovereigns but as servants of the gods. Hammurabi prefaced his codes of law stating that "Anu and Enlil named me to promote the welfare of the people ... to cause justice to prevail in the land."[5]

Enlil's brother Enki was the third great god of Sumer. He was their chief scientist and a master engineer. Enki and Enlil and their sons were continually battling for positions of power and authority. The gods were ferocious in war and amorous in love. Sumerian texts repeatedly show the gods seducing or raping one another, practicing incest and intermarrying to a rather extraordinary degree.

The Sumerian texts often refer to them as gods of heaven

---

* Sitchin's theories are controversial, and we cannot endorse all of them. However, they do provide additional insight into certain revelations of the Ascended Masters regarding Earth's ancient past and the forces of Light and Darkness that we face today.

and earth. In the Bible they are referred to as the Nephilim.[6] They are the people of the *shem*.

"Shem" is usually translated as "name," which accounts for the verse in the Bible that describes them as "men of renown."[7] However, the etymology of the word *shem*, according to Sitchin, can be traced back to the root word *shamah*, "that which is highward," thus suggesting that *shem* should be translated as "sky vehicle" and the people of the shem as "the people of the rocket ships."[8] Sculptures showing the gods inside rocket-shaped chambers and artwork with cruising missiles and rockets mounted on launch pads corroborate the linguistic evidence.

The term "Nephilim" is normally translated into English as "giant." However, its Semitic root means "to be cast down." According to Sitchin, the gods of Sumer were those who were cast down upon Earth—cast down in their spaceships.[9]

The Nephilim

Zecharia Sitchin believes that Sumerian texts and artifacts and the Bible reveal an alien race of fallen ones descended to Earth. In 1978 he published his theories in a book called *The Twelfth Planet*. His thesis is that the early Sumerians believed that there were twelve major celestial bodies in our solar system: the sun, the moon and ten planets. But our solar system has nine known planets. Adding the sun and the moon brings the total to only eleven bodies—eleven planets, in the broad sense of the word. Why, then, did the Sumerians count twelve? Sitchin's answer: There is a twelfth planet, the home planet of the Nephilim, which they called Marduk.

According to Sitchin, 450,000 years ago the Nephilim arrived on planet Earth in their spaceships to exploit Earth's resources. Enki, the Lord of Mining, pioneered the first base.

The Nephilim landed in Sumer to take advantage of the temperate weather and abundant petroleum resources necessary to support society and smelt ores. But Sumer had relatively little in terms of mineral resources. Therefore, the Nephilim traveled to the area of South Africa and other mineral-rich lands in the southern hemisphere to mine gold and other ores. Artifacts found in southern Africa reveal mining activities dating back at least fifty thousand years.[10]

Using advanced technology, the Nephilim mined gold, platinum, uranium and cobalt. But despite their technology, mining was still hard work. This heavy labor caused a strike by the mine workers. The Nephilim were on the horns of a dilemma; they wanted those minerals, but the chief gods were not about to roll up their own sleeves and work. Enki quickly offered a welcome solution—why not create a primitive worker, a slave? The vote of the gods was unanimous; they said, "Man shall be his name."[11]

Sitchin's texts describe how the creation of a worker caused a flurry of excitement among the Nephilim. They summoned the birth goddess who would carry out their plan. She in turn needed assistance from Enki, chief scientist of the gods. After a series of experiments, he took *Homo erectus* and mixed its genes with those of a Nephilim donor. In a hospital-like place, Enki helped the mother goddess prepare a mixture out of which she fashioned man. Then over and over again, she repeated incantations. Suddenly she shouted, "I have created! My hands have made it!" With that fiat, the primitive proletarian was created.[12]

The ancient terms used for man illustrated his status and purpose. He was a primitive worker, created to be servant of the gods. The deity was lord, sovereign, king, ruler and master. The commonly used word for "worship" meant "work."[13]

Man Begins to Multiply

The creation of mechanization man solved an internal dispute among the gods, but it wasn't long before they were fighting again, this time over who would get to use the workers. But dark and threatening clouds were gathering on the horizon, clouds that signaled an event recorded in no less than eighty thousand different accounts and seventy-two languages—the Great Flood.[14] It is recorded in Genesis that because "God saw that the wickedness of man was great in the earth, and that every imagination of the thoughts of his heart was only evil continually"[15] that he decided to bring a flood of waters upon the Earth.

According to Sitchin, this biblical account concerning the wickedness of man is an edited version of the earlier Sumerian record and compresses into one story the rivalry of the Nephilim. He explains that the original Hebrew text suggests that the evil of men's hearts and thoughts was of a fleshly or sexual nature. Yet the lusty Nephilim would hardly condemn man for practicing the same sexual behavior as they did. Or would they? A second condition of antediluvian man helps clarify this problem. It says in Genesis 6:

> And it came to pass, when men began to multiply on the face of the earth, and daughters were born unto them, that the sons of God saw the daughters of men that they were fair; and they took them wives of all which they chose.[16]

"Men began to multiply" is the key here—the man whom the Nephilim had created began to multiply. Why was this a problem for the Nephilim?

Sitchin believes that their genetic creation was originally sterile and had to be mass produced, until Enki made it possible for them to reproduce themselves sexually.[17] Henceforth, like the Nephilim, mechanization man could then reproduce themselves and therefore control their own lives. In this sense they were "in the know." Therefore, the Nephilim gods were very angry that their mechanization man discovered sexual reproduction.

We find that because of this confusion, through this biblical account we have hanging over our heads the theory that original sin is sex, which is always difficult for us to understand. How can God, who placed us upon this Earth as children of the Light to "be fruitful and multiply,"[18] expect us not to use the normal means of sexual reproduction? How can we suffer from this "sin" when our own God has made us, so to speak, the victims of it?

The enormous guilt that has overshadowed this area of our lives is partly a result of a misunderstanding of this account of what really happened with the Nephilim and their mechaniza- tion man. In the eyes of the Nephilim, it was a sin for their creation to know reproduction because they would populate the Earth and become so numerous that they would rise up and overtake their own creators.

Enki's actions of introducing this knowledge to them had consequences of virtually catastrophic importance. What happened is that the Nephilim themselves, in their degenerate consciousness, began to interbreed with their own mechaniza- tion man. As a result, their robots lost the exact genetic code necessary to maintain the primitive workers as a slave race. Even worse, their rapid population growth—the first known population explosion—threatened to overwhelm the Nephilim with an inferior race as well as the dilution of their own genetic strain. That is the meaning of Genesis 6.

However, the biblical account takes into consideration the purposes of God as well as the Nephilim—and they were not always in one accord. The problem was different for the children of God. Not only were the Nephilim intermarrying with their mechanical creation, but they were intermarrying with the children of God as well—a condition that could not continue, for God himself would not allow it.

Now we understand why there is the tradition among the Jews not to intermarry with those who are not Jews. That comes because surrounding the Israelites in biblical times were the Nephilim creation and mechanization man. And God forbade that the children of Light should intermarry with them and therefore dilute their seed of Light, and in intermarrying, give to mechanization man that seed wherewith he would perpetuate his own existence in a more powerful sense. Mechanization man never had that seed, because the Nephilim could not endow him with it. So intermarriage became a great sin.

God's decree against intermarriage does not concern itself, however, with the intermarrying of the Jews with other nations today, because there are now children of God and children of Light in every race and nation. But the forbidden interchange of Lightbearers with the fallen ones is the meaning of the original warning.

According to Sitchin, in the Sumerian account of the Flood, the gods met in their councils and formally decided to destroy their own mechanical creation. What the Sumerian text does not disclose is that the populace contained more than the Nephilim and their mass-produced man become sorcerer's apprentice. It contained, as we have said, the sons of God and the children of God as well.

The Nephilim used technologies familiar to military planners of today to carry out their war against man in yet another Nephilim first—genocide. Enlil ordered that a disease be spread. Because of the great suffering caused by this germ warfare, the Babylonian Noah, Utnapishtim, appealed to Enki for help. In defiance of the gods, Enki provided the remedy.

Enlil, upon learning that something has foiled his plan, complained bitterly to the gods. "The people have not diminished; they are now more numerous than before!"[19] According to Sitchin, soon Enlil was at it again. This time he modified the weather so that rain was held back and the irrigation failed. This produced a famine so great that cannibalism became rampant. And just when mankind were about to be destroyed, Enki again foiled Enlil and saved them.

Finally, in a meeting of the gods, Enlil pointed out there was still a way to destroy mankind, but the plan required absolute secrecy. And Enlil didn't trust Enki to keep quiet. Too many times he had broken the rule and rescued man from the jaws of death.

The Flood

According to Sitchin, for some time the Nephilim had known that there would be a killing Flood. This predictable yet unavoidable catastrophe was the result of a chain of natural events. His theory is that the Flood occurred about thirteen thousand years ago, when the last ice age ended and our present mild climate began, and that the pivotal event that marked the changeover between the two climatic epochs was the breaking off of the ice sheet from the continent of Antarctica.[20] He proposes that it was passage of the Twelfth Planet that triggered the ice sheet to break loose from its base.[21]

With this in mind, Enlil proposed to the council a policy of not benign, but malignant neglect. The Nephilim would keep the expected Flood a secret from man. Note that the Nephilim could not create the Flood nor could they stop it. It was the work of a hand mightier than their own. They could only exploit the natural flow of events to their own ends.

Recognizing that Enki might again rescue man, Enlil and

the council of Nephilim took an oath of secrecy and forced Enki to join them. But Enki was something of a strategist and a conniver. In short order he found a method to keep his oath and reveal his great secret to man.

As he chose to interpret it, the oath bound him not to reveal the secret of the coming deluge to mankind—but did that prevent him from telling it to a screen? And if an exceedingly wise earthling happened to be standing behind the screen and overheard him, would he be guilty of breaking his oath?

Thus, Utnapishtim learned of the oncoming Flood while Enki poured out his heart to a screen, knowing full well who was behind it. Enki advised his servant to build a water-borne vessel and provided him with precise instructions. It was an ark—one able to navigate under water. It was a submarine.

According to Sitchin, the Nephilim intended to escape the Flood in their spaceships. Their departure was to be the signal to Noah to board the ark. The Babylonian Noah entered the ark as the deluge began.[22]

What prompted Enki to act in such an apparently laudable fashion? Was it because he had a hand in the creation of man? Did he have a genuinely soft heart?

No. Archetypical of the fallen ones, he had a hidden motive. According to Sitchin, Enki's defiance was aimed primarily at frustrating the decisions and plans of his brother and archrival, Enlil. He had a burning jealousy of Enlil, who had been appointed Lord of the Earth by Anu. Enki believed it should have been none other than himself who should have received this honor.[23] Whenever Enki espoused a good cause or performed seemingly noble deeds, he had ulterior motives—power and glory. First and foremost, the Nephilim are for themselves. They are of assistance to man only when it enhances their own struggles for power. This characteristic of the power elite is true to the present hour.

The ancient texts record that even though they knew it was coming, the Flood was a frightening experience for the Nephilim. The noise of the deluge set the gods trembling. While in their spaceships the gods cowered like dogs, crouched against the outer walls. God's power overwhelmed them. The texts recorded that the gods, all humbled, sat and wept, their lips drawn tight one and all. The mother goddess, the great gods and the birth goddess wept for the loss of the land. The mother goddess lamented the loss of her creatures who "filled the river like dragonflies." The gods were cramped with hunger and "thirsted for beer."[24]

The loss of the good life hit them. They did not want to ascend back to the Twelfth Planet. They liked the Earth. They liked having their slaves on the Earth. The Nephilim had become attached to Earth and to its inhabitants. According to Sitchin, the gods might not have been so mournful if they had known Enki's plan. But Enki, Sitchin believes, must have been in another spacecraft.

Enki had done more than just save some of mankind. The evidence suggests he arranged a rendezvous—Mount Ararat. When the ark landed, Noah slaughtered and roasted some animals on a fire. The gods, exhausted and hungry, "gathered like flies over the offering."[25] Suddenly the Nephilim realized that man, the food he grew and the cattle he raised, were essential. The texts record that when Enlil saw the ark, he was wroth, but then the logic of the situation prevailed. Frightened, exhausted and hungry, the Nephilim realized that the Earth was still habitable, and if they were going to live on it, they needed man. Enlil proved himself every bit as willing as Enki to sacrifice principles for the practical political arrangements. First things first. Nephilim first, comfort second, man last.

Nearly all men were destroyed in the Flood, and it was obvious that they would need men to do the work. The Nephilim decision to let them "be fruitful and multiply"[26] was ever so practical.

According to Sitchin, faced with their own dire conditions, the Nephilim lost no time in imparting to man the arts of growing crops and raising cattle. It was a "new deal"; mankind would get to survive.

Yet the Nephilim were not about to take men in as equal partners. They would still need to remember who were the rulers and who were the ruled. The dynastic rule of the gods was adapted to the new conditions. The Nephilim established kingships, appointed rulers who would act as intermediaries between themselves and the masses. Nevertheless, it was the same old Nephilim power elite that monopolized political, social and economic power.

The rivalry continued between the Nephilim Enlil and Enki, the fierce struggles for supremacy. They divided lands and jurisdictions among their heirs. Thousands of years later, the kings of Assyria still went to war at "the command of my god."[27] The gods, then, through human intermediaries, retained the powers of conducting foreign affairs.

The descendants of the Nephilim—their children's children and also themselves reembodied—are still in a state of rivalry. And today, the children of God still go to war and die in battle to settle rivalries between one group of Nephilim and another, perched in the high offices of seemingly belligerent nations.

These archrivalries are present today in some of the rulers of the nations of the Earth. They're holding hostage the peoples of the nations. They engage them in wars. They engage in genocide when it suits their convenience. They continue to try to reduce the population of the Earth through war, chemicals in food, abortion and other forms of population control, pollution of the environment and nuclear fallout.

In civilization after civilization, the Nephilim have arisen to form national and international power elites in order to divide and rule over the people—the children of God as well as their mechanization man. They use people for the continuity of their own life, already cut off from God.

The Creation of Soulless Beings: Mechanization Man

What truly happened when the Nephilim combined their genes with *Homo erectus*?

When the fallen ones rebelled against God, they were cut off from the Source; that is the price of rebellion. They were cut off from God, and the Word was no longer in them. They no longer received the continual flow of Light from God because they had rebelled against his Presence. Though they walked the Earth as gods, they were in effect the living dead. Jesus spoke of them and he said, "Ye are like unto whited sepulchres which indeed appear beautiful outward, but are within full of dead men's bones."[28]

The living dead cannot regain the throne of grace. In the end they will be judged, and they know it. Thus they are unscrupulous because they have nothing to live for except to eat, drink and put off that tomorrow wherein they shall surely die. Their motive, besides putting off the day of their judgment and establishing a synthetic kingdom in the interim, is to strike out at God in vengeance. And since the fallen ones can't reach God, they try to destroy the souls of God's children by enticing them with the good life and telling them that they "shall not surely die"[29] if they sin against God's Laws.

The fallen ones cannot endow their artificial creation with a soul. Mechanizing the production with biological techniques only mass-produces a mechanization man. Mechanization man is a robot, or a computer, or a political animal, but not a child of God, not the offspring of the Most High—much less a son of God.

Sons of God

A son of God is one in whom the Spirit of the living God dwells. Paul said, reminding the children of God of their truly divine origin: "Know ye not that ye are the temple of God, and that the Spirit of God dwelleth in you?"[30] Moses, who knew all about the Nephilim, gave an intense rebuke with the fierceness of the Holy Spirit to the children of Israel. He said to them, "I have said, Ye are gods; and all of you are children of the most High. But ye shall die like men, and fall like one of the princes."[31]

Moses was angry because the children of Israel wanted to pattern their lives after the idolatrous cult of these fallen ones and their mechanization man. He had rescued them out of their civilization in Egypt. He had brought them to a place where they could fulfill their divine destiny. Yet they hankered after this society of the Nephilim. And so he rebuked them and reminded them that every one of them were gods—gods in the sense that the spark of Life was in them and to realize its fullest potential would make them One with Almighty God himself.

This is our destiny and this is our evolution. And all of the Avatars and Christed Ones of East and West have come to remind us of this, century after century. They have come to expose the fallen ones. They have rebuked the Liar and the father of lies, the murderer from the beginning.[32] And yet the children of the Light have abandoned their Avatars in the hour of their persecution and crucifixion, and they have sided in with a popular way of the cult of death of these fallen ones. This is the disease that besets America today, and this, we must understand, comes forth from this ancient Armageddon.

What is the nature of consciousness? What is the nature of those who would enslave us to a culture of death? Who are the true ones who would liberate us by the culture of Light and Life of the Word?

When we can answer these questions and discover our own inner identity in God, then we will have the confidence and a sense of self-worth—and above all the sense of the power of God to go forth and meet the challenges that beset us as a nation. And so Moses was saying, if you are going to behave like them, you are going to die like them, and you're going to fall like the princes of the Nephilim.

Those who have come to deliver us, those who are here to deliver us today through the power of the Holy Spirit have always said, as Joshua the Son of God said, "Come apart and be a separate people."[33] Separate yourselves out from this false hierarchy, this false civilization, this mechanization, this materialism. Separate yourself from the false gods and the idolaters, their own creation, their own mechanization man.

The condition that was prevalent in the Old and New Testament and still prevails today is that the children of God have forgotten that they are a distinct people, apart and separate from these. They have forgotten that the Nephilim and the power elite are not their true leaders, but their true leaders are the Sons of God.

Who are the Sons of God? They are true shepherds of the people, appointed by God to be the leaders and teachers of God's children. But some of them forsook their mission. They were also influenced. They left off from the initiations of the Cosmic Christ given in that Mystery School called the Garden of Eden.[34] As a result, they also became temporarily subservient to the Nephilim and to their mechanical culture. Because these Nephilim were formerly with the Archangel Lucifer, so bright as to be called the son of the morning,[35] the Nephilim even appeared to some of the sons of God to be the true interpreters of God's Law, his universe, his hierarchical order and his divine plan.

Archaeology reveals the history strictly of the fallen ones and their mechanization man. We have to go the retreats of the Great White Brotherhood to realize that we are not this creation but that we have beating within our hearts an eternal flame that makes us an eternal part of God. That there are two types of evolution upon the planet is becoming evident every day as we look around and try to understand what kind of people would do the things in society that are being perpetrated against innocent people by governments and nations, banking houses and multinational corporations.

The Nephilim did not create life on Earth. They did not create the sons of God or the children of God. What they did was to take a primitive man, *Homo erectus,* and drastically alter his capabilities by implanting in him their own image and likeness.

Saint Germain says: "I pinpoint, therefore, the conspiracy of fallen angels known as the Nephilim gods and as the Watchers. I pinpoint their conspiracy to control the populations of the worlds, where they have spawned their experimental creation, their mechanization man. And therefore, in order to control their laboratory experiment, they have used all manner of devices.

"Now, therefore, other nefarious powers moving against the evolution of life everywhere have seen fit to use mechanization man, computerized man—plastic man, if you will— as trend-setters, jet-setters climbing after the gods and the fallen angels to tempt, to taunt and to hypnotize the seed of the Ancient of Days, the seed of Christ in embodiment.

"Their end is manifold but it centers on the desire to steal the Light of the threefold flame, to draw the Lightbearers down into the valleys of the pit itself where they would engage in the practices of Darkness. And therefore, there are available fallen angels in embodiment to demonstrate the 'way that seemeth right'[36]—to provide the drugs, to direct the processing, and to draw mechanization man into the entire conspiracy as they are set up as storefront manikins to be copied by the children of the Light.

"Thus, those who are the glamorous and those who comprise the multitudes of the mass consciousness exert a momentum that is planetary in scope to magnetize the Light-bearers into their practices of drugs and perverted rock and nefarious deeds—and therefore karmically ally and align these Lightbearers with the darkest forces of the pits of hell to draw these into the alliances, sexual in nature, that result in the bringing forth of life—life that is of darkness and of the pit which, when combining with the seed of Christ, gains a transfusion of Light otherwise not obtainable.

"Thus, by the serpent philosophy of the egalitarian way of all equality among all evolutions,* you find that the Light-bearers have no sense of their worth or mission or of their God-determination at inner levels to lead all people out of the control of the fallen angels. Therefore, they are lured into these alliances at various levels of crime and sympathetic entanglements, and the seed of Light is diluted: it is overcome, it is betrayed. And we will discover, as we see in my trans-mission to you this day of a necessary knowledge, that this does result in the watering down of the total planetary Christ consciousness and the betrayal, one by one, of the

---

* The Ascended Masters teach that all are created equal in the Beginning but by the exercise of the original gift of free will, each one has forged a God-identity or none.

Lightbearers who ought to and *must* take their stand in Life in this very century so that the true foundations of the age of Aquarius can be laid."[37]

Fallen Angels: Rebellion in Heaven

Jewish writings of the time of the second temple recognized in the verses of the Bible describing the Nephilim the echoes of the ancient perditions of fallen angels. Going back to the archives of the Great White Brotherhood that contain millions of years of spiritual/material evolution of solar systems and galaxies, we find that these fallen ones were a part of the original angelic and Archangelic bands created even before the sons of God were created.

The angels occupy a position in the panoply of the kingdoms of God as servants of the sons of God. Thus, like nursemaids or teachers and protectors, they came first to prepare for the incarnation of the Word, the incarnation of Christ—not in one son of God but in many sons and daughters of God throughout the universes.

There are Archangels with whom we are familiar today—Archangel Michael, Archangel Gabriel—and there are many others. But there was one who was called Lucifer, an Archangel of great stature who rebelled against the LORD God. His rebellion was against becoming a servant of the offspring of the Most High. He was too powerful, had too much glory, was with God in the very creation of His offspring. Now he would not bend the knee and bow before the Light of the offspring of the Most High.[38]

This was the actual cause for the rebellion and for the war in heaven that is recorded in the Book of Revelation. And so we understand why it is written in Isaiah,

How art thou fallen from heaven, O Lucifer, son of the morning! how art thou cut down to the ground, which didst weaken the nations!

For thou hast said in thine heart, I will ascend into heaven, I will exalt my throne above the stars [above the sons] of God: I will sit also upon the mount of the congregation, in the sides of the north: I will ascend above the heights of the clouds [above the very Shekinah glory]; I will be like the most High. Yet thou shalt be brought down to hell, to the sides of the pit.[39]

Who are these Nephilim that are exposed in this very hour? They are the very same ones, the fallen ones referred to collectively as the Dragon in Saint John's vision of the Apocalypse.[40]

Many people think that the Apocalypse of Revelation is about to occur. But in fact, many of its scenarios have already occurred and are being outplayed in the great drama of tens of thousands of years of history that we have all experienced. There is a veil that descends, a loss of memory, as we take incarnation again and again so that we do not recall the experiences we have had—and yet our curiosity about them is not quenched. We go to science fiction movies, we read science fiction books, searching for clues to that memory and record that is just below the surface of our present awareness.

And so John wrote, in his Book of Revelation, which was given to him by an angel of the Lord Jesus Christ as a dictation:

And there was war in heaven: Michael and his angels fought against the dragon; and the dragon fought and his angels, and prevailed not; neither was their place found any more in heaven.

And the great dragon was cast out, that old serpent, called the Devil, and Satan, which deceiveth the whole world: he was cast out into the earth, and his angels were cast out with him.[41]

What is heaven and what is earth? They are but frequencies of vibration. These rebels against God could no longer occupy the higher frequencies, and therefore they were cast down in a deceleration spiral into bodies of the "earth, earthy"[42]—which we ourselves now occupy. These souls that we are occupy the temples that we wear. Our bodies are not our identity; they are vehicles of consciousness for a temporary sojourn on Earth. The only problem is, this temporary sojourn has been going on for hundreds of thousands of years because we have never come to grips with the problem of the Nephilim, the fallen ones.

We have forgotten this scenario, but it looms in the subconscious and we cannot get away from it. That is why we were intrigued when we were children with Western movies with the white hats and the black hats, and now with the forces of Good and Evil translated into the skies in science fiction. We have an ongoing desire to watch the outcome of this interplay of forces of Light and Darkness.

Thus, the Archangel and the third of angels that followed with him, as it is written in the Book of Revelation,[43] were cast down into the Earth to move no more as angels and as gods but as men—as mortal men confined, then, to bodies of clay—having no longer the immense power they had before their rebellion. They were given a time to outplay their existence of time, times and a half a time. We read about these in Daniel and the Book of Revelation.[44] These refer to cycles, not years—some of them tens of thousands of years comprising a single cycle. This is opportunity that comes from Almighty God for the individual being who was once with him in heaven to repent, to confess the Light that lighteth every son of God that cometh into the world as the true Word, the true Light, as

God himself, and to bow before that Light.

Is it so hard to bow before the Light of God that lights our temple? I can bow before the Light of God within each and every one of you. I can bow before the spark of creation. Who are these high and mighty ones who will never say die, who will not bend the knee and confess that the noble creation of Almighty God has one purpose and one purpose alone—to embody that true Light, that Word; yea, to be the incarnation of the Word.

Were they to acknowledge this, this power elite would lose their stronghold. For them to elevate and recognize God in the children of the Light upon Earth would mean that they would acknowledge them as superior to themselves. They would have to relinquish their positions of power nation by nation and acknowledge that the true government should be upon the shoulders of the Lord Christ[45] who lives in every one of the children of the Most High God.

These Nephilim have usurped the thrones of the sons of God nation by nation and even planet by planet. And they have been doing it a long, long time. This is the hour for the turning around—for the revolution of Lightbearers. But there are certain understandings of history and conceptualizations of our individual identity that we must have firmly within ourselves if we are to meet this enemy as David met the giant Nephilim, Goliath.[46]

Thus, these angels fell from the grace of their reason for being—service to the Father in the Son. They were cast out of heaven to the planes of Matter by Archangel Michael and his hosts. And the warning is written:

> Woe to the inhabiters of the earth and of the sea! for the devil is come down unto you, having great wrath, because he knoweth that he hath but a short time.[47]

The "woe" that is upon the people of Earth is that these fallen ones with their superior science and technology and evolution are in a position to outsmart the children of God. Therefore, great woe is come upon this planet, and we see it today in every form of manipulation of the people nation by nation. It is not confined to communism or capitalism; it is across the board an international power elite bent on their ambitions of power and the control of the Earth and the control of Earth's people.

Ever since the Nephilim were cast down into the Earth they have been trying to preserve their waning identity as gods. They are no longer gods except we elevate them as gods and enter into their idolatrous cult. They have been surrounding themselves with material trappings as a substitute for the spiritual kingdom they once knew. They have created a kind of "kingdom of heaven" on Earth. And to do this, they have used their technology and Earth's natural resources wherever they could find them to fashion and sustain their kingdom—with mankind, with their mechanical creation and with the children of God as their slaves.

Parallel Accounts in the Bible

When Sitchin looks at the writings in Genesis, he considers that the god who is referred to there is one of the Nephilim. He does not touch upon Jehovah or the LORD God Almighty, or the God revealed to Abraham as El Shaddai or the I AM THAT I AM who appeared to Moses. However, in Genesis and throughout the Bible, there are parallel accounts. Intertwined in the writings of sacred scripture is the account of the Nephilim gods on the one hand and the one God, the one LORD of Israel, and the Ascended Masters on the other.

We see towering figures of pure Sons of God who have

come forth in the descent from Abraham. We see them leading children of Light away from the idolatry of their neighbors in the Canaanite civilization. We realize, then, that there is more than meets the eye in the accounts of scripture, and scripture is more than just a transfer of Sumerian text to sacred writings. The records in the retreats of the Brotherhood reveal the coming of the sons of God to Earth with the great Guru, Sanat Kumara, who is known as the Ancient of Days.

Daniel, the Son of God, communed with the Ancient of Days and saw him face-to-face.[48] The prophets experienced the Presence of God. And we have our own internal witness, you and I, that God is able to contact us and we are able to contact him, and this God is Light and exalts his own Light within us and leads us into paths of righteousness.

Ancient Golden Ages

Prior to this history of the Nephilim, thousands and hundreds of thousands of years before, there were Golden Ages upon Earth, when the people of Earth knew who they were, knew that they were of the Light and of God. They had immense powers in the use of the science of the spoken Word. These civilizations predated Lemuria, which sank beneath the Pacific, and Atlantis, which is very recent by comparison. They existed on the African continent, in Asia, in South America and in other areas of the Earth that are now beneath the oceans or desert sands. These past Golden Ages are a faint memory that antedates our memory of Armageddon and the warfare of Good and Evil and the more recent Fall of the Archangel.

In these Golden Ages, individuals came forth from God, had transparent bodies of Light. People understood the incarnation of the Word in every Son and Daughter of God. They used the Word to precipitate Golden Age civilizations, magnificent structures, art and science. They lived hundreds of years in the same body, and they did not experience death, disease or discord. This is why we are always reaching for a way of perfection and a higher way of Life—we know it is possible because it has already existed.

There came a time when certain of the more recent Golden Age civilizations began to decline because the people left off from acknowledging and giving adoration and glory to God for every accomplishment. When individuals are endowed with limitless power (as Christ said before his ascension, "All power is given unto me in heaven and earth"[49]) it is easy to forget that "I of mine own self can do nothing, it is the Father in me who doeth the work."[50]

Lucifer forgot that, and so did some of these Golden Age civilizations. Through that forgetfulness and the misuse of the science of the spoken Word, there was a rapid decline. The great Hierarchs of Light withdrew into higher octaves, and major cataclysms occurred. The sinking of the continent of Lemuria is one such cataclysm.

The Rescue Mission of Sanat Kumara

Due to the absence of adoration of the Flame of Life, there was a rapid decline in consciousness, and hence in outer appearance. Bodies became more dense and more gross until they descended to the level of the ape. That is where the Nephilim found Earth when they came. They came on the scene at the time of *Homo erectus*. That is also the time when Sanat Kumara, who is acknowledged in ancient Eastern writings as the original and first Guru of the entire planet, stood before the councils of Almighty God and his Sons and pleaded for another opportunity for this fallen evolution of the children of God upon Earth to return to their Source. He volunteered to come to Earth, and there were many others who volunteered to come with him.

These sons of God who volunteered recognized that they would have to embody in dense bodies and work their way through a very dense evolution. They realized that because of their betrayal of his divine plan, God's children were vulnerable to these evolutions of the Nephilim—because in themselves they had similar qualities of ignoring God's Laws. This is how the children of God were reduced to this low, low estate. This is why the laggards were allowed to come.[51] This is why the Nephilim could penetrate this planetary home.

Sanat Kumara, then, figures as the great archetype of Light, as the Father principle in the major texts of the world's religions East and West. He is known by many names. *Karttikeya* is one such name in the Indian tradition.[52] He came leading sons of Light who took embodiment. But by and by, after centuries of being embodied in this dense evolution and lifewave, some of these sons of God forgot their Source, their reason for being and the purpose of their mission. Therefore, the Nephilim became the ones who began to rule the Earth and take over, and even cause the sons of God, whom they were created to serve, to be subservient to them.

This masquerade has been ongoing for thousands of years. Today and in this hour, the sons of God are waking up to their ancient memory, to their realization of who is the Ancient of Days, and to the specific purpose of why we are here on this rescue mission—to give back to the children of the Light that threefold flame of their Divine Identity, which they lost because they left off from the adoration of God as the Light, God as the Almighty in his universe, God as the Light and the flame that beats men's hearts.

Jesus Christ, Avatar of Pisces

Now we can understand the words and the mission of Jesus Christ, Avatar of the Piscean age. This Son of God came with a great message. We read that God sent his Son into the world, "not to condemn the world"—not to condemn the children of the Light for going after the false gods of the Nephilim—"but that the world through him might be saved."[53] And it is written that whosoever should believe on his name, he had the power to make them sons of God.[54] The power this Avatar was given was to transfer back to the children of Light that original spark of Light they had lost when they went downhill in their rebellion against God.

Jesus Christ is the great initiator of your and my individual Christ consciousness, to give back to us the Flame and the Light. Gautama Buddha came with a similar mission. So also did Zarathustra and many whose names are not known to us because they came in such ancient times of the past. Thus we realize that in every nation, in every race, in every civilization, there have been the Sons of God who have come with this message.

The same evolutions are present with us today as at the time of Noah—the sons of God, the children of God, the Nephilim gods and their mechanization man—evolving side by side on planet Earth.

How do you tell them apart? Jesus said, "By their fruits ye shall know them"[55]—by their consciousness, which is reflected in their works. The Great Divine Director has said that he advocates no witch hunt for these fallen ones,[56] because the only lawful means for dealing with them is transmutation. Transmutation is by the sacred fire of the Holy Ghost, and it comes forth by our intoning of the Word.

Beginning with the Word and the sacred AUM, we draw forth that Light, and it begins to accelerate our own individual vibrations until our very bodies, atoms and cells and molecules begin to contain more and more Light of the creative Word itself. We become lighter; we are not so dense; we are starting to live in higher planes of consciousness even while yet moving about in these physical vehicles.

The self-transcending process that has been taught by the Gurus of East and West, the liberating power of the Word, is what is needed. When the evolution of Lightbearers determines that we will come apart and be a separate people and accelerate, we will find that we will accelerate out of the dimensions of the dense ones, those who are the living dead and those who are the mechanical creation.

But what about this mechanical creation who had no say in their creation? It is even written that if they will confess the name of the Avatar, of the LORD God Almighty, that they, too, will be saved—that the Avatars who periodically come into Earth as the Word Incarnate have the power to convey even to mechanization man a Flame of Life. And that spark of Life is essentially the only difference between a robot created by ancient scientists and a child of God.

Therefore, even those individuals who are in the situation of having been created as a slave race, who now perhaps have intermarried and their descendants form a part of every race upon Earth—even they have the opportunity of contacting that Word Incarnate, that Saviour, and receiving the gift of eternal Life. The price is simply obedience to the Laws of Almighty God and the living flame of love.

An Increment of Light from the Holy Kumaras

The sudden flare-up of creativity and technical advancement at the time of Sumer did not come exclusively from the fallen ones descending in their spaceships. Sumer may trace part of its glory to the Nephilim, but not all of it. The Sons of God also survived that Great Flood and returned to Sumer. Their purpose was to elevate and illumine mankind as well as to teach them the arts and sciences of culture.

God did not entrust the intellectual development of his evolving creation solely to the fallen ones, but to those identified by Helena Blavatsky in *The Secret Doctrine* as the givers of intelligence and consciousness to man. They are known by many names; we know them as the Seven Holy Kumaras. Sanat Kumara, the Great Guru, is one of seven.

These seven are the sponsors of the progressive enlightenment of the children of the Light. Not by genetic engineering but by initiation, they have transferred Light to increase the potential of the mind and to accelerate the evolution of the body. This explains the acceleration of the evolution of the life-waves of Earth.

It is not merely by genetic engineering of *Homo erectus* that man's evolution advanced. While the Nephilim were busy accelerating that evolution, the Holy Kumaras gave to the children of Light who had descended from their Golden Age civilizations a new opportunity to turn and serve the living God. They gave an initiation that is an increment of Light that accelerates the crown chakra and causes the brain and its functions to accelerate.[57]

The brain is the outer effect of the inner cause. The inner cause is the Light retained in the crown chakra. When we learn to raise the Light in the physical temple and to use the Light of the heart to expand the seven chakras, we can contain more Light in the body; and therefore, the body itself evolves into higher consciousness.

We are facing the decisions today whether we are going to pursue these false gods and genetic engineering or we are going to choose to go with the great initiators of the race, those appointed by God himself, who are the Ascended Masters, who are truly Christed ones, who have the love in their hearts and the compassion to engender the true qualities of God as well as the ability to master our environment. Their sponsorship, then, assists the children of God to learn the arts and sciences brought forth by representatives of the Brotherhood who work behind the scenes at inner levels as well as through representatives in physical embodiment.

There are many people on Earth who serve the Ascended Masters who have no idea that they are in touch with the Great White Brotherhood. They are compassionate, loving, humble people, whatever their field of endeavor. They are serving to set life free, and the flame of freedom is more important to them than a peace without honor. Whether in the sciences or religion or humanitarian endeavors, there are souls all over the planet who are actually tied to the real and living Sons of God through this communion of saints, and all they need is the outer reminder so that the outer mind realizes the inner soul connection. And these people are the great innovators of Good in every walk of life.

We Must Understand Embodied Evil

We have to get off the track of our previous concepts of devils running around with tails and pitchforks. We have to realize that the devils are only fallen angels who have misused the science of the spoken Word and elevated their energy veil, their entire creation of mechanization man and materialism.

The angels who never fell are seeking to exalt God's children to a higher way of Life, a higher Light, a higher acceleration, the spiritual universe. But the fallen angels want to entrap the children of God into a perpetuation of a quasi-life in the material universe. As long as they can keep the children of the Light reincarnating in these dense earth bodies, they can daily milk them of their Light, their supply, their money, their talents, their consciousness, and thus sustain this endless, unreal materialism on which they thrive.

Indeed, genetic monsters loom in our midst undetected as the Nephilim themselves and their robot creation, who terrorize entire nations with their murders, sabotage and wholesale slaughter of millions of innocent victims—whether in two world wars, the Communist takeover of Russia, Eastern Europe and China, the Nazi holocaust or modern-day abortion, whether by chemicals, pesticides or nuclear fallout and waste, or by a nuclear disaster at Three Mile Island or Chernobyl—always carried out with characteristic insensitivity towards life and endless ambition and drives for power.

"Fear Not Them Who Kill the Body…"

In the few short years they have left, the fallen ones, the original Nephilim themselves, are bent on destroying the souls of the children of God. It is the souls of God's people they would destroy. And therefore, Jesus said, "Fear not them who kill the body, but those who are able to destroy the soul in hell."[58]

How can your soul be destroyed in hell? It can be destroyed if you abandon your true reason for being in God and follow the false gods, and give away piece by piece the precious seed atom, the core identity of Life that persists embodiment after embodiment. Your real identity is a gift of God to you; it is your gift to give back to him. If you choose to give it to the fallen angels, they will chew you up and they will spit you out.

Inasmuch as we have seen the repeated incarnation of the Word, we have likewise seen the reincarnation of the Nephilim. The fierce gods of Sumer reincarnated and swarmed over the Earth like Genghis Khan with his hordes of mechanization man or Hitler with his robot armies and crazed chiefs of staff, insane in their extermination of the Jews—a classic example of the Nephilim councils of war employing robots to wipe out millions of God's children.

What is the characteristic you note about those warlords who went to the trials at Nuremberg? An insane ego, an insane pride, the ability to totally deny what they have done, the ability to murder millions and millions of God's children.

We must understand that there are two kinds of people living on Earth. And until we do, we will never get on with bringing this Earth into a Golden Age. This Teaching is the missing link in your individual path, your own career, the life you will live, how you will raise your family, how you will bring forth children and how you will educate them. It is more than religion; it is the science of universal Life.

The Tares and the Wheat

Hitler and his crazed chiefs of staff are easy to identify, but when the Nephilim become the benign benefactors and we see them doing nothing but taking tax dollars and giving them away in order to get a good reputation, it becomes difficult for us to define who is on the right and who is on the left, who is of the Light and who is not. It is by your own heart and soul and the Word within you that you must know them by their fruits.[59]

The children of Light have not always recognized who are the oppressors. They do not realize that the destroyers of the people are also the deliverers, and the game goes back and forth. And in order to keep a good name, you've got to pose as the deliverer right while you are destroying the very people you would conquer. Wherever murders in cold blood occur en masse, there we find behind them the manipulation and the bloodthirsty designs of people who are somehow not people, not quite like the rest of us.

Jesus carefully explained the difference between the tares and the wheat. He said the wheat were the children of the Light and the tares were the seed of the wicked one that the enemy had come and sown. He said that they would not be separated until the last days when the angels would come and bind the tares into bundles and burn them as chaff, and the children of the Light would be free.[60]

Somehow that message of Jesus Christ has not gotten through—and most of all, it doesn't appear to be relevant to today. But it is very relevant. And so the tares grow side by side with the wheat, and you never know until the final judgment itself whether an individual is living on the borrowed Light of the sons of God or whether he is a source of Light and truly one with God. Therefore, Jesus warned us, "Judge not, that ye be not judged."[61] But an absence of judging does not mean that we should not have Christ-discrimination and discernment to see what we will see and to choose our representatives well.

People today are simply not willing to face the facts and figures at hand. The Nephilim and their godless creation are alive and well on planet Earth. They are the spiritually wicked in high places of Church and State, government and economics, education, the arts, the media and in the forefront of the scientific manipulation of the future.[62] They are the ones who say, "We are the gods and the future belongs to us." They stand unchallenged. Now it is up to us to say, "Nay. The future is to the Word. The future is to the Word Incarnate. And I elect by free will to be that Word."

God has given that option to us. Paul said it. We can elect to be joint heirs of the universal Christ consciousness that Jesus embodied,[63] that Gautama embodied, that the saints of East and West have had. The words and works of the sons of God set them apart from the Nephilim.

The Karma of Atlantis

We are living now approximately twelve thousand years after that last Flood. Twelve thousand years is a unique cycle. It represents a period of initiation to the evolutions of Earth.

We have come full circle. We have come back to everything that was being done on Atlantis in terms of genetic engineering and manipulation. We are back to that point where we must exercise free will and take command of our history, our era, our nation and the nations of the Earth. Because if the same events are repeated, if the ungodly creations come out of the test tubes of the laboratories and Earth becomes infested once again with more and more wickedness and greater and greater burdens upon the people, we can only foresee that this absence of the harmony of God in life on Earth will precipitate another major cataclysm.

Of all of the evils that caused the judgment of the LORD God to descend in the sinking of Atlantis, in the opening of the floods of the deep, it was genetic manipulation resulting in the artificial creation of godless life-forms that was the greatest and the worst.[64] This is reemerging at a fantastic pace. Therefore, we are on the brink of facing those tests as to whether or not we will allow this manipulation of the Life that is God to go on to our own self-destruction.

Therefore, as Atlantean genetic engineering rises above the plateau of traditional science, ask yourself what kind of people are behind it and who will use genetic engineering for what purpose. Then ask yourself if you feel secure that we will pass through the dark night of the reemergence of Atlantean culture without a cataclysm. The very rumblings of that cataclysm are already being felt in earthquake, in extreme weather conditions, and there is a general fear on the planetary body that we will be faced with an intense cataclysm in the coming years.

God has told us by his Holy Spirit that this can be stayed.

How? By the power of the Word, by the invocation of the Word, by you so meditating upon that Word and speaking that Word and loving that Word with your life that you become one with it; hence you become the Word Incarnate.

It is to this end that you were born. You were born to blend your soul with that moving stream of the Word—the universal Word that was in the beginning with God, without whom was not anything made that was made.[65] We were not made without that Word in us, and therefore, to that Word we return. It is the key, because what creates can uncreate. And the Word can uncreate the entire destructive mechanization of the fallen ones that is worldwide.

The prophet tells us that the Hosts of the LORD are encamped on the hillsides. The leader of the battle, the leader of the armies of heaven who figures in the Book of Revelation, is none other than Sanat Kumara.[66] There are supporting Archangels and Sons of God, and they are there ready to deliver the Earth into the hands of the children of the Light. But we have to make the call. We are required to use the spoken Word to invoke God to manifest on Earth. There is a very important Law: the legions of Light cannot come in to this earth plane unless we invoke them, because God gave us dominion in the Earth and free will.

It's our Earth. It doesn't belong to the Nephilim. It doesn't belong to their godless creation. It belongs to the children of Light and the sons of God. If we want divine intervention, we have to ask for it. And that means prayer, dynamic decrees, meditation—using every single day the Science of the Spoken Word to invoke God's presence, to say "God, come down to Earth. Take over! Judge the fallen ones and bring this Earth to the victory."

The Enemy Within

IN THESE LATTER DAYS, MANY PEOPLE are taken up with the idea that one single figure, Antichrist, is about to appear. Many books have been written on this subject, and everyone looks for *the* Antichrist.

However, the teaching of the Brotherhood is that it is not so important that they should prophesy who this Antichrist is, when he should appear, in what form and in what country. Rather is it important to teach the people of God on Earth to be prepared to meet that Antichrist in whatever form it should manifest.

The Antichrist that is most dangerous to the individual is the Antichrist that lodges within his own mind. This anti-Self is known as the carnal mind. This anti-Self is the synthetic self or the unreal self, and it consists of momentums of karma and momentums of creation that have accumulated over many, many centuries and thousands of years of living on planet Earth or other systems of worlds.

El Morya says, "Let none deny that there is an Antichrist. For the Antichrist is every force within and without the psyche of man that would put down that true and living God within you. Realize that this is not of necessity a person who will appear at a certain time, but it is the decision on the part of many to embody the destructive forces of the universe to put out the Light of freedom, nation by nation."[1] "Antichrist is both a person and a state of consciousness. Antichrist permeates where there is weakness, where there are no moral foundations, where society crumbles."[2]

The greatest Antichrist that you are facing right now is the enemy within. Who is threatening you from without? Who is taking your Christhood from you right now? Only the enemy within.

If you are searching the planet for Antichrist, you have missed him. If you imagine it is someone like Nostradamus' Blue-Turbaned One of the East[3] or some very evil person who it going to come along, you never come to grips with the enemy within.

The Dweller-on-the-Threshold: The Enemy Within

Dweller-on-the-threshold is a term sometimes used to designate the anti-self, the not-self, the synthetic self, the antithesis of the Real Self, the conglomerate of the self-created ego, ill-conceived through the inordinate use of the gift of free will, consisting of the carnal mind and a constellation of misqualified energies, forcefields, focuses, animal magnetism comprising the subconscious mind.

Man's contact with the reptilian anti-magnetic self—that is the enemy of God and his Christ and the soul's reunion with that Christ—is through the desire body, or astral body, and through the solar-plexus chakra. The dweller-on-the-threshold is therefore the nucleus of a vortex of energy that forms the "electronic belt," shaped like a kettledrum and surrounding the four lower bodies from the waist down.

The serpent head of the dweller is sometimes seen emerging from the black pool of the unconscious. This electronic belt does contain the cause, effect, record and memory of human karma in its negative aspect. Positive karma, as deeds done through the divine consciousness, registers in the Causal Body and is sealed in the electronic fire-rings surrounding each one's own I AM Presence.

When the sleeping serpent of the dweller is awakened by the presence of Christ, the soul must make the freewill decision to slay, by the power of the I AM Presence, this self-willed personal anti-Christ and become the defender of the Real Self until the soul is fully reunited with Him who is the righteous Lord, The Lord Our Righteousness,[4] the True Self of every lifestream on the path of initiation.

The dweller appears to the soul on the threshold of conscious awareness where it knocks to gain entrance into the "legitimate" realm of self-acknowledged selfhood. The dweller would enter to become the master of the house. But it is Christ and only Christ whose knock you must answer—him only must you bid enter.

The most serious initiation on the path of the disciple of Christ is the confrontation with the not-self. For if it is not slain by the soul who is one in the Christ Mind, it will emerge to devour that soul in the full-vented rage of its hatred for the Light. The necessity for the Teacher on the Path and for the Guru Sanat Kumara with us, physically manifest in the Messenger of Maitreya, is to hold the balance both spiritually and in the physical octave for each individual initiate on the Path as he approaches the initiation of the encounter—face-to-face with the dweller-on-the-threshold. The planetary dweller-on-the-threshold is personified in the forces of Antichrist.

Christ and the Dweller

The Ascended Master Kuthumi, our divine psychologist, comes to teach us about the war that must be waged between Christ and the dweller right within our four lower bodies:

"It is difficult to become a dragon-slayer when the age of chivalry has long passed. Some find it a bit unpleasant to take up sword and slay the not-self. But in the meantime, while their stomachs are in too delicate a condition (and their egos as well) to perform this act, they themselves are being devoured by the dweller—dallying, marking time and often drifting backwards with no realization. For in relativity, it sometimes appears one is going forward when one is standing still or moving backward....

"'What does it mean,' you have said, 'this slaying of the dweller-on-the-threshold?'...

"Beloved, by free will all have forged action, word, desire. Some of these, as vibration, have been pure and perfect, building individual Christhood and the mantle, the seamless garment. Through ignorance, absence of tutoring, forgetfulness of First Cause and origin in the higher spheres, others of these vibrations emanating from actions and words and desires have fallen; for they had not the balance of flight of Alpha and Omega. They have fallen and begun to form a spiral like a solar system around the solar plexus, the 'place of the sun.'

"Momentums, then, of lifetimes for many thousands of years have builded the antithesis of Self, sometimes entirely unbeknownst to the outer mind who thought itself so sincere and desirous of doing right that in the very desire to do right there has been the mistaken conclusion that the desire should make all things right. Nevertheless, the Law perceives that there is right action, there is wrong action, and the proof is in the Causal Body—the pure vessel of Light of all good deeds and acts in Matter—and in this electronic belt.

"Now, in the eye of that vortex of misqualified energy—in the very eye of the vortex—there is the point of consciousness and identity that emerges as the collective consciousness of all misdeeds. Each time a decision is made that registers as the unreal, a portion of the unreal mind must be used to make it. Thus, the collection of actions has a collective consciousness, and the dweller is the collective manifestation of all that has been in error. It emerges as an identity, a figment, you might say, but a momentum that wields human power to a grave and great extent.

"This identity is the impostor of the soul and of the Christ Self. A portion of the soul by free will is invested in the impostor, and a portion of the soul is invested in the Christ. Thus, the battleground and Armageddon is of the soul, which, as you know, can be lost.

"Now cometh the Christ and the Ascended Masters and their chelas to woo the soul away from unreality, to prove to the soul what is Real, what is Light, what is the eternal Goal. This is your office as shepherds and ministering servants and students of the World Teachers. When the soul is enlightened and quickened and gains awareness through Christ, she begins to be able to see on her own through that Christ intelligence what is unreal.

"But seeing is not necessarily believing. Seeing, then, is the first step; believing, the second.

"The action to deny that which is unreal is fraught with the burdens of the individual's psychology. And thus, sometimes hard lessons—burning in the trial by fire,[5] pain in this world—must convince the soul that Life is more important and therefore that one must let go of certain situations and conditions and beliefs and comfortabilities.

"We move the soul as close to the precipice of knowledge of Absolute Good and Absolute Evil as is possible, at the same time to preserve the integrity of the soul and not to cause that one too much fear, too much awareness of the great Darkness within that opposes the great Light.

"Thus, beloved hearts, the slaying of the dweller—not all at once but little by little. And this is something you should be aware of, though you have been told before. Each day, according to the cosmic cycles, a little bit of the head of the dweller emerges above this dark pool of the electronic belt. It is a still darkness, and one can see perhaps the head or the ear or the eye or the nose of this dweller, this self-created monster. You see this, then, in your own actions and reactions. You see it in the musings of the mind—sometimes only a telltale ripple on the surface or perhaps the tail when the beast has dived to the bottom.

"Thus, you must listen and watch what is lurking. And as soon as you find a tendency to fear, to be jealous, to become angry or whatever, go after it as the tip of the iceberg! Work at it! This work is truly a profound work of the Spirit. It is not easy always to be on the path of confrontation.

The Path of Accommodation of the Dweller

"I come with the message of Maitreya and to amplify his previous messages. For he has spoken of the path of accommodation* whereby, instead of slaying the dweller, you find

---

* *accommodation* (fr. Latin *ad* + *commodare*, to make fit, give, lend): adaptation; adjustment; functional adjustment of an organism to its environment through modification of its habits.

ways to go around this side and around that side.⁶ And thus, you begin to build the tower of Light—you build a great momentum of decrees and service, trusting that somehow, in some way, this terrifying encounter will go away. But it will not go away. And the day you discover once again that all of that goodness is not the acceptable offering is the day when, in the presence of Maitreya, you once again encounter face to face that dweller-on-the-threshold.

"You may go far and wide and keep a wide berth from the Messenger and never notice the dweller and build a positive human momentum in those outer attainments, whether through yoga or decrees or this or that discipline. And you may be very happy with yourself, and others may be exceedingly happy with you. Of course, this is not the question.

"The question is whether your I AM Presence and Christ Self are happy and whether your Teachers will tell you that in the light of cosmic initiation your offering is acceptable. Thus, beloved, to avoid the Masters or to avoid the instrument whereby we may speak to you is to avoid the Day of Reckoning of your karmic accountability that has been called, in biblical terms, the day of vengeance of our God.⁷…

Rebellion and Disobedience

"Understand, then, the accommodation of the aspect of the beast known as rebellion against the Guru and disobedience to the LORD God. Understand that that core rebellion has been the undoing of many chelas, some who were not calculated by us to make it in the first place.

"Although we held the immaculate concept, the record of the past was before us. We gave the opportunity in purest hope, in support and with the full momentum of our Electronic Presence. Yet, beloved, others who have not made it have lost in the race simply for want of this very instruction from Lord Maitreya, which, because it has helped so many, I give to you again.

"The accommodation, then, of rebellion, going to the right and to the left of it, becoming as it were, a workaholic, performing many good human deeds and social deeds, or the performance of ritual and prayer and yoga, the assiduous following of perhaps asceticism or personal discipline or diet— all of these things may be a careful accumulation of human virtue by the individual to avoid (subconsciously, at least) what is *the* most important step that must be taken: the step of the encounter with that satellite orbiting in the electronic belt that has come between the soul and her I AM Presence— namely, the rebellion against Lord Maitreya or Sanat Kumara or against the Law itself because it was spoken, perhaps, by a very imperfect vessel. This rebellion, then, becomes a block self-perpetuating, for it is set in orbit by free will and it cannot be removed from orbit without free will.

"When you place planets in orbit in this electronic belt, you create your personal subconscious astrology and psychology, which are one and the same—focuses of your karma. Now, when you think of the solar system you inhabit and you consider the weight, the volume and the magnitude of the planets, you can learn the lesson that it is far easier to set a planet in motion than to call it back—even as the words that proceed from your mouths cannot be called back, no matter how great the regret, else it is by the violet flame.

The Necessity for the Master-Disciple Relationship

"Thus, to remove the planet of rebellion, you must have a oneness with the Central Sun of your being—the I AM

Presence, the Christ Self and the externalized attainment of the heart chakra. This is why we preach on the Sacred Heart. This is why there is a union of religion East and West through the path of the heart; for all who have ever attained have done so by this sacred fire.

"Listen well, then. To recall the planet of rebellion in the electronic belt, you must have an equal and greater force of Light and sacred fire manifest in the heart to counteract it and dissolve it, else you must be holding the hand of the Master or the Guru who has that development and can transmit to you the Light that can keep you above the waves when you would sink as Peter did.[8]

"Thus, the necessity of the Master-disciple relationship. For there is not one among you or those upon Earth today (save those who are already in our inner retreats) who can make it alone, who has not in his electronic belt something that requires reinforcement of the Masters who have gone before to remove—to remove, I say, in a timely manner, for we do not have a million years for you to sit and give the violet flame and to pursue these disciplines....

"Cycles must not be lost. Tests must not be postponed. And when you see it, call it and move on. Beloved ones, when the aspect of the dweller of rebellion is not challenged and bound and cast out—and these are steps; for that planet may be bound before it is ultimately cast out, which means it is in submission to your free will and to your Christhood but not entirely eliminated—when it remains, therefore, and you are in the twilight zone of not having slain the dweller and not having entered into complete union with Christ, these are treacherous waters....

The Acceptable Offering
Is Christ-Good

"When you are in that twilight zone, scurrying about like frightened mice to pile up good karma, yet not facing the problem—the offering of human righteousness and human goodness is *not* the acceptable offering. If the individual is not willing to take this teaching to heart and to change, then, you see, he will become angry, as Cain was angry when his offering was not accepted.[9] He demanded of Maitreya that his human goodness be received as a substitute for Christ-goodness—that the Law be changed for him and, instead of his fulfillment of that Law, that all of this grandiose human goodness should suffice.

"And individuals do this again and again, and their schemes and their deeds become more and more grandiose, sometimes encompassing the Earth. And they say, 'Surely this great good deed, this great endowment, this great act I have done that has blessed millions should be the acceptable offering!'

"It is only the acceptable offering when it is Christ-good. What is Christ-good? It is the soul united with Christ who has slain the dweller through that Christ and therefore can say, 'This I have done to the glory of God and not as an accommodation for my rebellion, not as a substitute for my surrender, not as my demand that God should take me according to *my* path instead of according to His.'

"Now when the offering that is not Christ-good is rejected, as it always is and shall be, there is an anger that occurs at the subconscious level, which on the surface may manifest as depression. Beware depression and moodiness, for it is a sign of severe problems. Depression is that state of the twilight zone where the individual has neither slain the dweller nor entered fully into the heart of Christ. It is the most dangerous situation of the soul in this octave of the Matter universe. Therefore, you desire to quickly remove yourself from that place of jeopardy.

"Some of you have recurrent dreams of walking over very insecure bridges, over deep chasms or through narrow passageways, or of being confined in a box. You may wake up in a cold sweat, you may experience terror in the night. And thus, a lesson is coming through from your Higher Mental Body that tells you that you have placed yourself in a condition that is dangerous, that you must pass through it, you must make a move, you cannot go back and you cannot stand still: you must move forward.

Enter the False Gurus Offering Souls False Fruits

"For here the tempter may come, here you may be vulnerable to those who are offering you wares and fruits that are not the initiatic fruits of Maitreya.

"Thus enter the false gurus to take advantage of souls who have refused to pass through the initiation of challenging that core rebellion. Now they find a false guru, now they satisfy themselves that all is well. They may keep their rebellion, for the false guru is the embodiment of the dweller-on-the-threshold of rebellion against Maitreya. And they will follow the false teachers lifetime after lifetime, totally suppressing all other awareness of the Light of Christ.

"For that awareness would demand and force them once again to the point of the encounter and the point of the choice. Thus, they have a system of knowledge, of education, of academia—all these things to confirm and hold together a system of civilization based upon pride and the development of the human ego, situation ethics, the modification of behavior, and all that occurs in the molding of the human animal.

"Now understand how the individual who ten thousand or twelve thousand years ago in rejecting Maitreya made the conscious decision to keep the dweller of rebellion, does react in this hour or in any century when the representatives of Maitreya and the Great White Brotherhood come forth with the true Teaching and the true requirements of the Law. Now the anger that is subconscious, that used to manifest outwardly as depression, inverts and is on the surface in an all-out campaign to destroy the society or the organization or the orifice of the true Light.

The Soul Holds the Balance of Right Choice, Fortified by Prayer and Meditation

"Blessed ones, to a greater or lesser extent, now and then the dweller within you rebels against your own Christhood. But the soul may choose. For the soul ultimately, though she hangs in the balance, holds the balance of right choice. Thus, when you do not know the way to go or the right hand from the left hand, pray—pray for attunement and oneness with us.

"Learn the steps of prayer and meditation we have taught in our release[10] that you might also be fortified by prayer and meditation as the right hand and the left hand of the presence of the Bodhisattvas who come to reinforce your desire to be all that God intended you to be.

"Thus, you see, depression then begets inefficiency, more rebellion, disobedience, until finally there is a clamoring and a clanking in the electronic belt and in the four lower bodies. And unless that individual swiftly choose the Light of his own mighty I AM Presence and choose to align himself with us, the helpers who can help, that individual must surely make the choice to run for the hills or for the canyons of the big cities where he may lose himself and place himself at the farthest possible distance from the one who can help—if not ourselves, then the Messenger.

"Realize, then, beloved hearts, that all who do this must have an excuse, and their excuse must be based on some sense of injustice, some offense, or some real or imagined fault of our witness or our chelas or our organization. It is a pity, beloved hearts, that personal offense based on a core rebellion should unseat the rider, should unhorse the knight and he thereby lose such a grand opportunity. This work of the ages is a joyous work when you have one another, when you have community and such joy unlimited that is possible in this circumstance with which you are blessed, having this center with all that it portends for your lifestream."[11]

The Anti-Buddha Force on Planet Earth

The betrayal of the Light of the Son of God by the not-self in each one of us is a link to the planetary force of anti-Buddha, anti-Christ. It can be seen in the electronic belt at the level of the seat-of-the-soul chakra manifesting as a black suncenter—a literal vortex of Darkness swallowing up the soul's Light as it spins in a counter-motion to the rotation of the Great Causal Body. Unless bound and cast out by the fiat of Almighty God himself, this dweller will not stop agitating for the enslavement of the soul.

Jesus has given us a new and wondrous decree for this very purpose—the binding and the casting out of the dweller-on-the-threshold of this anti-Buddha force in all of its ramifications. When we give the decree for the binding and the casting out of the dweller, we are getting at the core of the human creation that is in opposition to the Divine. We are getting at the nucleus of the anti-God, or the anti-Self, and demanding that it be bound.

This decree, "I Cast Out the Dweller-on-the-Threshold!" (page 242), is a step-up from the first judgment call dictated by beloved Jesus ("They Shall Not Pass!" page 240). The latter involves the judgment of words and deeds, the judgment of actions, step by step. It may bring the judgment of returning karma to the individual for a single act, for a single embodiment, for a single momentum; whereas the decree on the dweller is for the binding and casting out of the entire conglomerate of the carnal mind coiled in the center of the electronic belt. It is the original seed of Evil at its inception that has grown to the present hour from the point of its beginning anytime—millions of years ago, a hundred thousand years ago, five years ago.

The dweller-on-the-threshold is the focal point of the consciousness behind the human creation—the mind behind the manifestation. This term has been adopted by the Brotherhood because it conveys the meaning that it sits at the threshold of self-awareness where the elements of the subconscious cross the line from the unconscious to the conscious world of the individual, and the unknown not-self becomes the known. Once surfaced, the dweller has entered the realm of the conscious will where, through the decision-making faculties of mind and heart, the soul may choose to "ensoul" or to slay the components of this antithesis of her Real Self.

The dweller is right there ready to come through the door of consciousness, but at that threshold, at the line separating the planes of awareness, the guardian action of the Christ Mind, the holy angels and one's free will stand to prevent the dweller from actually surfacing and moving into action in our world.

Now, there are individuals, of course, who do not stand guard; and therefore they become suddenly and ferociously the instrument of a monster that is out of control. And so the more people become psychologically disturbed and have divisions in the four lower bodies, the more they are apt to manifest aberrations by which the dweller may gain entrance to their world through the lever of the conscious mind.

They may be schizophrenic, they may be subject to hearing voices and carrying out anything from mayhem to ridiculous little pastimes that they repeat all day long—all of this being the surfacing of the dweller, mocking and taunting the soul in what then becomes compulsive behavior—drug, alcohol and sugar addictions, et cetera, or even demon possession, crime, child molesting and every form of vice. Once in control of the conscious mind, the dweller takes over the whole house, attracting discarnates and demons that bring death and destruction to many innocent bystanders before the victim, himself but a tool of the sinister force, succumbs.

Supposedly, in our society, the difference between someone who is sane and someone who is insane would be the control or non-control of that Loch Ness monster, that dweller-on-the-threshold that dwells in the sublevels of the emotional body. The person who makes the conscious decision not to allow the carnal mind to vent itself in the ups and downs of life is sane because he, and not the beast, is in command.

Many people are entirely dominated by the carnal mind and extremely sane at the same time, or at least sane-appearing. When you get to know them, you don't think they're quite sane, but they do manage to run banks and big businesses and all kinds of corporate enterprises on this planet; and the planet manages to survive, and we survive. And sometimes we wonder why and how it all works.

The Face-to-Face Confrontation

There comes a time in the life of the individual who contacts the Path, the Masters or their representatives when he comes face-to-face with Christ and anti-Christ—Christ in the person of the man of God and anti-Christ in the personal dweller-on-the-threshold within himself. And he may see both face-to-face.

This usually does not happen the very day of the encounter with the Great White Brotherhood, but by and by, it does occur. And sometimes people manage to follow the Masters and the Path and the Teachings for many years without experiencing the confrontation. Either they avoid it or they try to avoid the appearance of having had the confrontation, but ultimately, when the Masters determine to do so, they will force the confrontation and force their chelas to make a choice between the Christ Self and the dweller.

This may occur at any time on the Path. People sense this, and therefore they may avoid all contact with the Great White Brotherhood or its agents. They even take up arms against it, thinking to thwart the Law and the inevitable day of reckoning.

This was so in the case of Saul on the road to Damascus. In this case, it was the Master Jesus who forced the encounter in which Saul was blinded in the alchemical process of the Light confounding the Darkness. Jesus made Saul choose between his dweller, the anti-Christ or anti-Self who was persecuting the Christians, and his Real Self personified and represented in the Ascended Master Jesus Christ.

When he chose his Lord, he chose the path of discipleship leading to individual Christhood. And the Master bound his dweller until he himself should slay it "in the last day" of his karma. Endued with the power of Christ in his Guru Jesus,

Saul, now called Paul, having put off the old man and put on the new, went forth to witness to the Truth that had set him free from his own momentum of human creation and the human mind that created it—the dweller-on-the-threshold.[12]

From his personal confrontation and conversion by the Lord, Paul was later able to tell the Romans with the conviction that comes only from experience: "To be carnally minded is death; but to be spiritually minded is life and peace. Because the carnal mind is enmity against God: for it is not subject to the law of God, neither indeed can be."[13]

Daily Choices on the Path

In the matter of Christ and the dweller, then, we all have an opportunity that we are given, in the meditation of our own heart, in the private, patient communion of God with us, little by little to make choices without being under the pressure of Joshua's immediate command: "Choose you this day whom ye will serve!"[14]

We may spend years or even embodiments exercising our free will, because the Law is very gracious to us in allowing us to figure out this problem of our own being, enabling us to see clearly that we have some element of human creation, some character trait that we definitely do not like. We know we don't want it, we smash it every time we see it. It reappears now and then, we smash it again. God knows we're trying and we're not fooling, and he leaves us alone. He lets us conquer, he lets us overcome.

Then there's the other situation where people will hide from God, will tarry, will procrastinate too long, and the Great Law says, "Thus far and no farther. You have indulged your human creation for thousands of years. You have acted out your rebellion against God for too many lifetimes, *and this time this is it!* Your decision and your decree in this situation will be the telling one." And the Master will challenge his chela: "Either you renounce your recalcitrance and make an about-face now, or you may no longer be considered a chela of the Great White Brotherhood."

This action is taken by the Great Law because the Master has borne his chela's karma for the duration of certain centuries, and the cycles of his sponsorship of the chela are spent. He has no choice but to compel the chela to come up higher. If he does not respond, the Master must leave him to his own devices until the day the chela chooses to stand, face and conquer on his own, and thereby earn the right to the Master's grace once again.

The Initiation of the Slaying of the Personal and Planetary Dweller

Then there is, of course, on down the road of self-mastery, the initiation that comes nigh the point of the crucifixion, when the individual has considerable Christ attainment as well as balanced karma and is required to slay that dweller totally and utterly.

Jesus could not have been on the cross had he not slain the dweller. As a matter of fact, his illustration of slaying the dweller was his wilderness confrontation with Satan three years before the crucifixion.[15] And that was the planetary dweller-on-the-threshold: Satan himself—the personification and sign of everyone's personal dweller.

Later the Son of God dealt with the planetary dweller again in his confrontation with the Watchers and the Nephilim —the chief priests and Pharisees, the elders of the people and the powers of Rome. This was possible only because he had already slain the personal dweller. This is why he said, "The prince of this world cometh and hath [findeth] nothing in me."[16]

The planetary momentum of the dweller-on-the-threshold, i.e., the collective undefined unconscious of all evolutions of the planet, can and does move against the individual who has not yet slain his personal carnal mind. What this means is the obvious: that most people come under the influence of the mass consciousness daily. And the more they have conquered the wiles of their own not-self, the less influenced they will be by the ups and downs of world turmoil.

Nevertheless, the planetary momentum will tie into and activate the personal anti-Christ to catch off-guard even the souls nearest their victory over the beast. At that moment, the individual must slay not only the personal carnal mind, but in so slaying it, drive back the planetary momentum and overcome the original Liar as well as the lie that the originator of Evil has propagated in his seed.

Now, you may day by day resist the temptations of your carnal mind and of the planetary dweller, but you may not have completely slain the personal representative of the Evil One. Thus, there is a point of winning on each occasion of the overcoming, and then there is the point of winning ultimately because the entire beast has been slain.

The Y on the Path

There comes a time when individuals on the Path have had the fullness of the Teaching, the Light, the Masters and the love of the community. That fullness is not gauged by years but by the evolution of the lifestream. It may be one year, it may be three years, it may be twenty years, it may be many embodiments. But there comes a point when the individual has full awareness of the Christ in the Masters, in the Messenger, full awareness of what the darkness is and what the carnal mind is. And he must come to the place of deciding for or against his mighty I AM Presence, the Brotherhood, for or against the false hierarchy. This is known as the Y. The Y in the Path is the point of the initiation where one actually becomes Christ or Antichrist.

One may refuse to surrender that dweller—to bind it, slay it, and send it to judgment aforehand—i.e., before the soul must give her accounting to the Karmic Board at the conclusion of this life. Jesus taught this law of karma to Paul, who wrote of it to Timothy: "Some men's sins are open beforehand, going before to judgment; and some men they follow after."[17]

Instead of surrendering it at the Y, the initiate may, instead, embrace the dweller. Instead of eating the flesh and drinking the blood of the Son of God[18] (assimilating the Light of Alpha and Omega in the Body of Christ), he literally drinks the cup of the blasphemy of the fallen angels and eats at their board the infamy of their anti-Word.

By taking the wrong way, the initiate actually puts on, personifies, identifies with and is now become the dweller-on-the-threshold incarnate. The soul and the cancer of the carnal mind have grown together and are no longer separable. Such an individual would then be on the *left-handed path*. His will, not God's, is supreme. An adept on the left-handed path is called a black magician.

Now, these events may happen very quickly, even overnight. The opportunity for service to the Master during which an individual walks the Path of discipleship in grace as a follower of Christ, still enjoying the protection and the sponsorship of the Brotherhood, continues right up until the hour of decision.

One day one sees the chela as a part of the community and

in the grace of the Masters, enjoying Maitreya's Mystery School and the opportunity to balance through service, right deeds and decisions, the karma borne during his apprenticeship by the Guru. But the next, the day of decision is upon him. The individual may be confronted at any level of his being, not necessarily *by* the Messenger, although it may be *through* the Messenger. And he may at that moment decide that he will not give in to his Lord and Master. He will not bend the knee; he will not confess the supremacy in his life of his Holy Christ Self. Instead, he considers himself—his untransmuted willful self—to be that Christ.

Confusing the lower self for the Greater Self through his own self-created spiritual blindness, he enthrones the dweller-on-the-threshold in the place of his Holy Christ Self. His personality, his psyche, his stream of consciousness all flow into the not-self. Instead of saying, "I and my Father are One,"[19] he declares, "I and my ego are one," and it is so. Behold mechanization man! Behold Rudyard Kipling's "man who would be king" who meets his fate in the abyss of the astral plane.[20] Though he thinks he is in control, the nonentity eventuates in nonexistence.

The Fate of Those Who Choose the Dweller

This is happening on planet Earth every day to people who have chosen to embody the anti-Buddha force. These are advanced initiations, but then, planet Earth is host to very old souls whose hour has come. As Jesus said to the chief priests, the elders and captains of the temple who could have chosen Christ but, in murdering him, solidified their position with Satan and made their whole house his: "This is your hour"—to choose to be or not to be in the Christ consciousness—"and the power of darkness,"[21] i.e., the power of the darkness of your own dweller-on-the-threshold and your karma. "Now I, the One Sent, charge you to bind and cast out that carnal mind that is enmity with God, if you would dwell forevermore with the Father and the Son."[22]

Jesus' incarnation of the Word forced the confrontation, the choice and the judgment of these ancient ones who knew full well at all levels of their consciousness who he was and who they were. And in their hour, they made their choice. It was a fair test—fair and square—and they failed it.

Likewise, your holy Christ Self will force the confrontation, the choice and the judgment not only of the dark ones, but of your own soul as well. Let us therefore judge righteous judgment.[23] For we know, beloved, that with what measure we mete justice unto one another, it shall be meted upon our own heads from on high.[24] The Law does not fail to reward each one, mercy for mercy.

It is very burdensome to our hearts to see anyone reject Reality for unreality. But this is not new to us. We have observed over the years betrayers of the Light in all walks of life turn into the darkest of Darkness overnight and become archdeceivers of innocent hearts.

These people, therefore, have become their dweller-on-the-threshold. They no longer even *pretend* to follow the true Teachings of Christ taught by the Brotherhood. They deny that the Teachings are true, they deny that the Masters are Real, and they deny the path of initiation under Maitreya through the embodied Guru.

And what's more, they embrace a false doctrine of Christ's accountability for their sin—for all past sins of all previous lives, mind you—saying, "Jesus died for my sins; I am free from all my karma. I am exonerated; there is nothing I can or should do to balance my debts to Life. My belief is my passport to the kingdom."

It is of no concern to them that they are in the very act of karma-making. In fact, they have so personified the dweller, and they are so pleased to be free to indulge that dweller with all its appetites and vehemence against the Law of Life, that they are either unconcerned or else unaware that they are on a collision course with destiny.

This cycling out of the planes of actuality into "outer darkness" or the self-extinguishment of the "second death" — two very specific doctrines of Jesus that cannot be rationalized away by the fallen ones[25]—may take many, many cycles according to cosmic law. The point here, which is made eloquently by Paul in his epistle to the Romans, is that the Adamic man cannot survive—neither here nor in the hereafter—unless he becomes the spiritual man, renewed, Spirit-filled and walking in full communion with God.

In the meantime, the "ex-disciple" of Christ who is now the servant of the natural man[26]—its wants and pleasures and superior knowledge—fashions a strong outer personality made in the likeness of the carnal mind—a "good human being," achieving and acceptable in the circles of all who likewise have abandoned the Road of Eternal Accountability that leads inevitably to the confrontation with Christ and the surrender of all sin against the Holy Ghost.

This is an altogether simplistic and temporary resolution of the schism between Christ and the dweller that yet exists within the psyche. This avoidance of accountability for one's actions and for the decision not to slay the dweller at the Cross and the crossroads of life is indulged by the false pastors and their false doctrine of salvation. While perfunctorily and intellectually observing the rites of worship, they tolerate everyone's carnal mind, including their own, and fail to present the real challenge of the path of personal Christhood that Jesus taught.[27]

The decree "I Cast Out the Dweller-on-the-Threshold!" has to do, then, with the confrontation—by those students of Light who have chosen the path of discipleship under Jesus Christ or one of the Ascended Masters—with embodied individuals who have elected by free will to merge with their own carnal mind in rejection of Christ and his Messenger—whoever that one who comes in the name of the Lord may be—and to become, in fact, the dweller.

These sincere students may not have come to the Y themselves. They may be God's precious children who have not the attainment to fully incarnate the Christ. They may not be at that point of Christic initiation. They may not be a Christed one who has the ability either to fight the personal or planetary dweller or to defend himself against the Antichrist.

Nevertheless, these dedicated souls are, in fact, being confronted and moved against by those self-serving ones who have embodied the dweller-on-the-threshold, yet cleverly disguise themselves as benign, concerned citizens working for the freedom of all. Jesus tagged them so we would not be fooled by their too kind words: "wolves in sheep's clothing," devils posing as deliverers. And there is more truth to those words than many are prepared to deal with.

You see, the one who embodies that dweller—being self-willed and inordinately imposing his will on others—the base definition of black magic—having passed the point of the Y—is actually incarnating that momentum of Evil that is the equivalent of the Light he had when he departed from the temple and fell from grace. In other words, he has inverted his original dispensation of Light to generate Evil. Moreover, he has deified that Evil and himself as its progenitor.

A Devil Is One Who Has Deified Evil

Now Evil, in itself, is misqualified energy, the malintent behind it, and the entity encompassing both. By the very nature of the Liar and his lie—the consciousness behind it— Evil at its inception is deceptive and deceitful. In fact, it is a veil of illusion—an energy veil, or *e-veil,* enshrouding the Deity and all his marvelous works. Illusion, or *maya,* as the Hindus call it, then appears more real than Reality itself. In fact, men's illusions become their gods, and Evil is deified.

Now, what is plain to see is that a devil *(d-evil)* is one who has deified Evil and the entire energy veil. A devil is one who has deified the dweller-on-the-threshold to the position of Christ and has declared himself master and saviour of the world, whether in politics or art or in the philosopher's chair or at the head of the PLO, the Baader-Meinhof gang, or in the Pentagon.

A devil is the Adamic man self-proclaimed as a messiah by his own ego-energy in the place of salvation by The Lord Our Righteousness. Thus, we have those who deify the energy veil of the dweller posing as the deliverers of the race—and if we follow them instead of "Christ in you, the hope of glory,"[28] we shall all fall into the ditch that empties into the River Styx.

Now, since the one who embodies the dweller, thereby deifying Evil, may have been a Watcher[29] or a fallen angel, the attainment at the point of the Fall may have been very great— for these fallen ones once had a great Light, dwelling as they did in the courts of heaven with our Father and Mother. So the greater the Light at the point of the Fall, the greater the Fall, and the longer the extension of time and space in which to repent. For God in his truly great mercy gives to that one an opportunity commensurate with his office in Hierarchy at the time of the Fall to repent and to return to Him.

Those who once had great Light may be given even a

longer opportunity to balance their karma and return to the throne of grace than those who had less. This is a corollary to the law of karma, as it is written: "For he that hath, to him shall be given: and he that hath not, from him shall be taken even that which he hath."[30]

And so, we know that the opportunity given to some of the fallen ones has been very, very, *very* long, until even the Psalmist thousands of years ago cried out, "How long, O LORD, how long shall the wicked triumph?"[31] For the power of their dweller-on-the-threshold seems endless as they move against the children of God who seem so much less powerful and often helpless.

Indeed, the fallen angels who swore their eternal enmity against God in heaven—in the full presence of his Glory!—move freely on Earth, embodying the dweller with bravado, sophistication, wealth and worldly wisdom until they should be confronted by someone in embodiment—someone who has the courage to be the spokesman for the Elect One.[32] For by definition, by the very science of Being, that Elect One who cometh in the name of the LORD I AM THAT I AM has the attainment of Light physically manifest equal to the dark ones. The One Sent did not fall from grace but took incarnation for the express purpose of challenging the seed of the wicked on behalf of the shorn lambs of God.

This is why John the Baptist and Jesus Christ as well as the prophets and the Avatars of all ages have come to the Earth: "For judgment I am come into this world."[33] They come because they want to give a reprieve to the blessed children of God who are tormented by these fallen ones and yet have not the ability—the externalized Christ consciousness—to move against them.

The Science of the Spoken Word for Judgment

Now in this hour of the Aquarian age and the dispensation of Saint Germain, we find that by the Science of the Spoken Word, when we give our dynamic decrees in the name of the Christ, in the name of the entire Spirit of the Great White Brotherhood or any of the Ascended Masters, we are decreeing in the full magnitude of their attainment sealed in their Causal Body of Light.

When you decree in the name of Saint Germain, instantaneously you have behind your call the full power of the Light qualified by the Ascended Master Saint Germain for thousands of years. His purple fiery heart multiplies the power of your heart, and it is as though Saint Germain and you were one. In fact, you *are* one.

Therefore, when you confront the Adversary within or without, you know that Saint Germain has the equivalent or greater of the power, let's say, of the Archangel (or any other fallen one) when he fell. And therefore, Saint Germain is able to fulfill the decree of the Word through you, even if your own externalized Light is not adequate to the encounter with Antichrist.

This is why little children of the Light, those who've not balanced the threefold flame, those who have recently come into the Teachings of the Ascended Masters, may in Jesus' name give his decree for the binding and casting out of the dweller-on-the-threshold and, as representatives of the Elect One, become a part of our concerted efforts to move against world situations of organized crime, war, massive forcefields of negative energy, problems in the economy—which to a great extent are controlled by Watchers and fallen ones who long ago chose to embody the dweller-on-the-threshold and have actually gone unchallenged in this physical octave (i.e., on this Earth) since the last Christed one appeared.

As a result of the dispensation of Jesus' judgments, his call to our Father, and his Presence with us whereby we may now indeed challenge by Christ's power the evildoers, we are seeing unprecedented planetary changes. The fallen ones are shocked and affrighted. They cannot believe that they could be challenged and that the Light—or the "Light-bearer"—could win, so accustomed are they to look down upon and to control by intimidation the children of God who do not have nearly the momentum on creating Good that they have on creating Evil. (That is, the children of God do not have on the right-handed path of Light—of Absolute Good—the momentum that the fallen ones have on the left-handed path of Darkness—of Absolute Evil.) But then, they never really counted on The Faithful and True[34] saving the day for the LORD and his anointed!

At whatever point the reprobate decided to embody the dweller, at that point on the Path he inverted the Light he had acquired up to that moment. If he succeeded in stealing the fruit of the tree of the knowledge of good and evil, and was not then and is not now challenged by a son of God, he will go on misappropriating the Light, turning it to greater Darkness —"If the light that is in thee be darkness, how great is that darkness!"[35] Thus he practices karma-dodging by devices of deceit, fooling the children of the Light, inciting them to accuse one another, to argue with each other, to be discordant, to engage in wars and genocide in defense of Nephilim divide-and-conquer political schemes, and generally to get into a heap of troubles.

This inequity between the children of Light and the children of this world (the seed of Christ and the seed of the Watchers and Nephilim) led Jesus to admonish: "The children of this world are in their generation wiser than the children of light.... Be ye therefore wise as serpents, and harmless as doves."[36]

Making karma by their foolishness, putting their attention upon the fallen ones through idolatry, the children of Light unwittingly give them their energy. It is the law of karma: what we place our attention on, or give our devotion to, we become; i.e., energy flows to the object of our attention and devotion.

The Incarnate Dweller-on-the-Threshold

The fallen ones make a spectacle of themselves, preferring politics, the media and entertainment as center stage. Focusing our attention on their outrageous, hilarious or spectacular antics, they rake in our money and our Light. And therefore, a fallen one walking the Earth today as the incarnate dweller-on-the-threshold, though spiritually bankrupt, may actually be gathering more power and more Light unto himself, which he turns into Darkness to control and destroy the very ones from whom he has taken it by the schemes he has perpetrated.

Many of these schemes center on money, because money is power. Money, even if it is paper, represents gold; it represents energy, it represents supply, the abundance of God, and it has a worth that is determined solely by the sacred labor of the people and by their trust. "In God we trust."

When money is amassed by those who have chosen to embody the dweller instead of Christ, that means power. Money and power are necessary coordinates of control. It is plain to see that the "serpents" (a scriptural term for embodied fallen angels who have misqualified the Kundalini,[37] the "serpent force," to control others through the misuse of the chakras) have used their power, gained as money, to turn world conditions and world events toward themselves and to propagate after their kind. And so, as like attracts like, their offspring are also those who have chosen to embody the dweller-on-the-threshold.

Thus the dynasties of the powered and moneyed interests carry on "the tradition," reincarnating until the law of cycles decrees their judgment by the Sons of God, Ascended and unascended. And so the cycles of manipulation continue until the one aligned with the Great White Brotherhood raises his right hand, lifts up his voice unto the LORD God, the Almighty One, and says: "In the name of Jesus Christ, Thus far and no farther! Enough!" and then gives the decree for the binding and the casting out of the dweller-on-the-threshold of the manipulators of the people.

This is a very important call, because when we say, "I cast out the dweller-on-the-threshold," we're talking about the personal and planetary dweller, we're talking about everyone on Earth in or out of embodiment who has raised a clenched fist to dare the Almighty to strike him dead, everyone who has hated the Light, declared war against The Faithful and True and spilled the blood of his sons and daughters in the rites and revenge of Hell.

Whoever the perpetrators of Evil are (and we ourselves need not know), the angels of the Lord Christ—the legions of the Archangels and Elohim—bind and render inactive the core of Absolute Evil within them and all that which is aligned with it. This is the true and righteous judgment that cleaves asunder the Real from the unreal, thereby opening the door to salvation to millions of oppressed peoples worldwide, and saving the world from the ultimate revenge of the false gods: planetary holocaust.

It is our earnest prayer that those whose ungodly deeds

are challenged by our call—even those allied with nefarious practices—might be liberated from the strong delusions of the dweller and make an about-face to serve the living God. In giving this call, we are champions of the soul and the defenders of the right of the individual to be free from the sinister strategies of the carnal mind—free to be his Real Self. This is a rescue mission on behalf of all caught in the grips of the illusions of the astral plane and its denizens.

This call is Jesus' sword. With it he goes forth to save the "lost sheep of the house of Israel" who have fallen into the cult of success, status, hedonism and excessive materialism. With all of his heart's love, our Master asks us to pray without ceasing for those who cannot see that they are enslaved by their own indulgence in the not-self. And see they must, before they can believe.

This is the increase of the Christ consciousness on Earth. The judgment call and the dweller decree are given by the Son of God as the signal to his angels that the consummation of the age of Pisces is at hand and the harvest of the tares sown among the wheat is nigh.

It is time for the bands of angels known as the Reapers to gather the seed of the children of the Wicked One sown among the good seed of the Son of man.[38] When both calls dictated by Jesus are combined with calls to the Elohim Astrea, Archangel Michael, the call to reverse the tide, and the violet flame (see pages 127–29, 253, 67), you will find that the Archangels can move in to do a wondrous work for God and his children of Light on Earth!

Jesus' prayers are Life-giving, not death-inducing. They are the fulfillment through his disciples in the ending of Pisces and the beginning of Aquarius of his eternal reason for Being: "I AM come that they might have life, and that they might have it more abundantly."[39] To have Life and that in full abundance, we need the sacred fire, the all-consuming fire of our God[40] to consume the shroud of death. And that's all the dweller is—the mask of death you tear off on Halloween and cast into the freedom flame.

We are charged to make the call, and the armies of heaven under the Archangels are charged to implement the answer, subject to the will of God and the adjudication of the Son, in Jesus and in us. Praise God that only the will of Christ can manifest, and that neither our human opinion nor anyone else's can alter the divine edict that was spoken by the Father in the Beginning and is ratified by the Son in the ending.

We are sons of God; we work on the yellow ray of Christ-illumination. The Elohim work on the blue ray, the power ray of the Father, and the angels work on the pink ray of the Holy Spirit. The three are one through their universal devotion to the Cosmic Virgin. If we fulfill our office through the Mind of God, the angels will perform their work through his love, and the Elohim and the elementals will perform theirs through his supreme edicts. We need only be certain that we invoke the necessary protection from the Hosts of the LORD in our daily service and decrees.

The Judgment

WHEN WE WENT FORTH AS living souls from the flame of Alpha and Omega, we were given an allotment of energy equivalent to a certain number of cycles of evolution in time and space. This could amount to several hundred thousand years, several million years—the figure doesn't matter. The principle is that we have free will and the right to experiment with free will for only a certain span of time and space. At the conclusion of the soul's passing through these cycles, then, is the judgment. And that judgment is known as the final judgment—the final tallying of what has been done cycle by cycle.[1]

If 51 percent of the energy allotted to the soul has been qualified with Light, the soul has earned the right to retain an identity. She is accorded the ascension in the Light. She becomes a part of the I AM Presence and then a permanent atom in the Body of God forevermore. One with God, sealed and fired in God, she can nevermore go out. She remains in the consciousness of God, expanding throughout eternity.

If there is not the sign of a sufficient amount of effort placed on the side of Light, if the soul cannot show just cause as to why her existence ought to be perpetuated, if she has been continually using Light to reinforce the ego and the worship of the ego, at the end of that cycle the soul stands before the high tribunal of the Four and Twenty Elders, which is located, in this sector of the galaxy, on the God Star Sirius. It is the Court of the Sacred Fire. The Four and Twenty Elders are Cosmic Beings, twelve sets of twin flames who represent the Twelve Hierarchies.

The soul stands on the dais of the Court. If the Court decides, in consonance with the Christ Self of the soul, that the soul has not shown just cause why her identity should be continued, then the flame of Alpha and Omega is passed through the dais and the identity of the soul is canceled out. The Christ Self of that lifestream merges with the Universal Christ; the I AM Presence of that lifestream merges with the Universal I AM Presence. All the energy that was used to create the soul and the energy that was used by the soul in her miscreations is withdrawn back to the God Star for requalification. The requalification occurs in a giant forcefield of the sacred fire that is named in the Book of Revelation as the "lake of fire."[2]

The vision of this lake of fire and the knowledge of the lake of fire by the fallen ones has resulted in their development of the doctrine of hellfire and damnation—eternal punishment in the fires of hell. It is the fallen ones who have created this false theology. They have purveyed it to the holy innocents.

In fact, the moment that any misqualified energy comes in contact with the lake of fire, the sacred fire consumes the cause and core of the misqualified substance. The energy is restored to the perfection of God, returned to the Fiery Core of the Great Central Sun Magnet as part of the Source of Life, and used again, even as the potter remolds the clay that he has fashioned into a form that he desires to now cancel out. So as far as eternal damnation goes, this is the desire of the Wicked to threaten the children of the Light with eternal suffering. The children of the Light need to be concerned with the fate of the soul, not with the doctrine of the Luciferians.

Time in Space to Repent

In his dictation announcing the judgment of Lucifer, Alpha explained that Lucifer, the Fallen One, at the time of his rebellion, had a certain quantity of Light that had been qualified as Good, as Light, while he had been in the service of God. That momentum of energy plus his attainment before the Fall qualified him to have a certain period of time in space to repent, to return to the worship of Almighty God. That period of time has been very long for the innocents, for the children of God. It has been going on for thousands of years upon the planetary body.

During that period of time, because of the tremendous prior attainment of Lucifer, his ability to manipulate energy, and because young souls do not have that attainment, it was Lucifer and the fallen ones who actually controlled life in the planes of Matter—not to the extent, however, that souls could not rise. During that period of tribulation, many souls overcame the carnal mind within and the Fallen One without; and through suffering and trial and temptation—overcoming all—they passed through the ritual of the ascension and returned to God as Ascended Beings.

The Judgment of Lucifer

Now it is the end of the Piscean dispensation, the end of the period when Jesus came to prove the Christ, to manifest the Light that Lucifer could not challenge, could not defeat. So at the end of this dispensation, it has come to pass that Lucifer's time was up—no more cycles allotted to him, no more opportunity.

Furthermore, he misused his position in Hierarchy, which he was not permitted to do, by coming forth and challenging the Messengers of the Great White Brotherhood. The manifestation of the Law is such that those who represent the Great White Brotherhood have protection from the Fallen One. Likewise, the Fallen One cannot be touched by the Messengers, because it is up to mankind to choose whom they prefer—the Messengers of the Christed ones or the carnal mind. At any moment, then, when the Fallen One, Lucifer, would go forth in a direct attack on the Messengers, a certain allotment of his opportunity and energy would be taken. This occurred increment by increment over a period of fifteen years, until finally that full portion of 51 percent of the Darkness of Lucifer was seized from him by the Lords of Karma.

It happened, then, that Lucifer was called to judgment, bound by Archangel Michael in answer to the calls of the Christed ones and taken to the Court of the Sacred Fire to stand trial before the Four and Twenty Elders. His trial lasted for ten days, and during that period, an examination of the total record of the actions of Lucifer and the fallen ones was taken by the Twenty-Four Elders. The testimony of many souls of Light in embodiment on Terra and other planets and systems in the galaxy were heard, together with that of the Ascended Masters, Archangels and Elohim.

A review was made. At the conclusion of the review, the

opportunity for repentance was given to Lucifer to bend the knee before the Christ, before Almighty God, and to worship the I AM Presence. He blasphemed before the Twenty-Four Elders and declared he would never worship the image of the Christ. His time was up. As he stood on the dais, the energy of Alpha and Omega passed through his form and canceled out the one who was once known as Son of the Morning.[3]

The Seed of Antichrist

Alpha was very concerned in making this announcement that the children of the Light, the students of the Ascended Masters, not become complacent, not consider that the victory is won. This is only the beginning; the warfare is now in the soul of everyone. In the four quadrants of being, we are required to exorcise the Antichrist, the seeds of Antichrist, of rebellion, that have been planted there by our association with the fallen ones, with the laggard generation.

When the fallen ones were cast down into the Earth, many were forced to take embodiment by edict of the Lords of Karma; and therefore they walk among us. There are fallen angels in embodiment who are the ones who instigate the philosophies and the movements that are Antichrist, leading the children of God into all manner of perversions, instigating corruption in government, in the economy, in every nation on Earth. They are a very dangerous group of individuals because they have that power of the angelic hosts and they convey tremendous feeling through the emotional body because that was their momentum before incarnation.

After they incarnated, many of the angelic hosts of Light who did not fall volunteered to take incarnation to offset the work of the fallen angels. And therefore, we have also abiding on Earth many angels of Light who serve the Light, who help mankind, who carry the flame of love, who are teachers. And many of these angels of Light are among the student body of the Ascended Masters' chelas, because they are the ones who desire to have the Teaching to teach mankind the way.

Now therefore, since our incarnation upon the planet, no matter what category we fit into—whether of the sons and daughters of God, the children of the fourth, the fifth and the sixth root races, whether we are of the angelic hosts who came to rescue mankind, whether we came with Sanat Kumara or whether we came from other planets on the rescue mission— most of us, until this time of the revelation of the Ascended Masters' Teachings, have forgotten all of this history of the Fall, all of this history of why we are here, what is happening, why we love the Light and yet find ourselves entangled with skeins of Darkness and in a situation of having karma with souls of Light and souls of Darkness.

The Lie of the Fallen Ones

We come to the place, then, of seeing that after we came on this rescue mission one way or the other, after taking incarnation, we forgot why we were here and who we were. No one told us we had an I AM Presence, and the veil of maya became very thick. Without a Teacher, we could not know the way. We believed the lie of the fallen ones that there was only one Son of God. We accepted the mass condemnation of the Luciferians, of whom it is spoken in the Book of Revelation, "This is the accuser of the brethren which accused them before our God day and night."[4] The "accuser of the brethren" is another name for Lucifer, who accuses, or condemns, souls of Light, continually amplifying and magnetizing condemnation until the children of Light feel totally worthless, allow themselves to be absorbed in the mass consciousness, and no longer take a stand for Truth because they do not understand that the Truth is within them.

We find that through intermingling, we have made karma. We have reacted to the fallen ones. We have been seized by their anger; we have responded in revenge. And therefore the skeins of karma have woven us, tied us, to the fallen ones, sometimes in a very personal way in a family situation. This is why you see in many families people of Light and people who don't love the Light; you see schism and division.

We find, therefore, that almost without exception—and it is important not to have that spiritual pride that makes us think we are the exception—the children of the Light on Terra have absorbed the influences of the fallen ones. Without even realizing it, we have taken in at subconscious levels their philosophies, their way of life, their morality, their accent on "the good life."

"Eat, drink and be merry, for tomorrow you die" is the byword of the Luciferians, because they know ultimately they will pass through the second death. So they teach that doctrine to the children of Light, and they draw the children of Light into a pleasure cult, a cult of sensual thralldom, and thereby cause the children of Light to lose their souls.* The fallen ones, knowing that they will be canceled out, have only one goal. They say, "If we're going anyway, we're going to take the children of Light with us." And so this is why they continue in their ways.

They have set up false forms of government. They have drawn individuals into their camp. Nazism is a clear example of a government of the fallen ones, of a black magician incarnate being used to take millions of children of Light into

---

* The philosophies and strategies of the pleasure cult are discussed in "The Cult of Hedon" in book 6 of the Climb the Highest Mountain Series, *Paths of Light and Darkness*.

the camp by the sounding of the fierceness of the voice, the beating of the drum, the military rhythm and the exultation of the concept of a superrace.

Appealing to the pride that the Luciferians had already implanted in the children of Light, they make them come into this mass hypnosis; they draw them in by the magnetism of pride. This has happened over and over and over again. Civilizations have risen and fallen as the result of the Luciferians entering into the top echelons of government and only slightly perverting the true philosophy of the Christ and of Almighty God.

The Dragon, the Beast, the Great Whore and the False Prophet

Unless people understand clearly and accurately that the battle is in the four lower bodies and the soul, the second death of Lucifer, the entire victory of Armageddon, even the victory of a Golden Age, will not mean the winning of immortality by the individual soul.[5] Each individual soul, because she elected to go forth from the Fiery Core of Oneness, must make the decision herself. She must sit in the center of the Christ flame even as the Four and Twenty Elders sit in the Court of the Sacred Fire on Sirius. The soul must invoke the Christ Self to manifest the judgment of the dragon, the beast, the great whore and the false prophet. Each of these perversions of the Godhead controls one of the four lower bodies.

If you study the Book of Revelation, beginning with chapter eleven, you can read of the mission of the Two Witnesses who are the Messengers for the Great White Brotherhood—the two prophets who bring the Teaching of the Ascended Masters to the age.[6] They come and they deliver the Teaching, and they also face the challenge of the dragon.

Then there is the coming of the Woman in chapter twelve —a "woman clothed with the sun, and the moon under her feet, and upon her head a crown of twelve stars," [7] the twelve stars denoting her mastery under the Twelve Hierarchies of the Sun. Chapter twelve is the sign of the Aquarian age, the coming of the Feminine Ray, the elevation of the Feminine Ray. And when the Feminine Ray is elevated, it brings forth the Christ, the Manchild, who is the fulfillment of the mission of the Divine Mother in all of us. [8]

Chapters thirteen, fourteen, fifteen and sixteen speak of the dragon, the beast, the great whore and the false prophet. And of course, the Book of Revelation is written in code. It is cryptic. It was delivered by Jesus' angel to John. The final verses say that if any man should tamper with the Book of Revelation in any way, his name should be removed from the Book of Life. [9]

That's a pretty strong warning to all of those who were in their cells in the last several thousand years rewriting the sacred scriptures and to the fallen ones who infiltrated the churches and removed from the Teachings of Christ and the Teachings of the Old Testament those scriptures that clearly revealed the nature of the Fall of the Luciferians, the nature of their creation, which clearly revealed the Teaching on reincarnation, the laws of karma. All this was at one time in our sacred scripture. All this has been tampered with.

There are some who say that sacred scripture is the absolute Word of God. Well, where it is the Word of God, it is the Word of God. Where it isn't there, it isn't there. And that is the problem we face—that people try to piece together a theology and a doctrine that they say we cannot stray from, when they do not have the whole writing of the Law and the Word.

Jesus, of course, knew that they would do this. Jesus didn't even bother to write the books—did you notice? He gave the Teaching; he let his disciples write it down. He knew that the Teaching would carry only in the flame within the heart, from fire to fire to fire. That is what apostolic succession is intended to be: the carrying-down of the tradition of the true Teaching of Christ—not of the dead ritual, not of the untempered zeal, not of the fanaticism, but of the Flame. That is what the true priests and priestesses at the altar of God are intended to convey to the people.

Instead, the Flame was lost. The Teaching was tampered with. So when Jesus dictated that Book of Revelation to John on the Isle of Patmos just shortly before John's ascension, he included this warning. And so they didn't tamper with it. It's there intact. But it is cryptic. And the reason it is cryptic, in code, is that you can't tamper with code, because those that would tamper with it are actually too ignorant to know what to change.

And that's what happened in the visions of Ezekiel and of Daniel in the Old Testament.[10] Those writings couldn't be tampered with, because they seem inane on the face of it to the fallen ones and the rebellious ones, since you have to be in the Holy Spirit to understand them. Let's talk now about the battle of Armageddon in your forcefield.

The Dragon: Perversion of the Father

We place the dragon on the twelve o'clock line (see figure 2, page 224). The dragon is the ultimate perversion of God as Father, God as lawgiver, God as power. The dragon, in its immensity, symbolizes that forcefield, that vortex of energy that has taken the power of God and created the image of the beast; it has created this monstrous form. And that dragon consciousness, the direct opposite of God the Father, initiates dark cycles and gives the perverted power to the beast. On the twelve o'clock line is the accuser of the brethren referred to in the Book of Revelation.

The perversion of God-power is condemnation. That condemnation is the pounding, the aggression on the mind that is continually downing you, telling you that you can't succeed, permeating the mass consciousness with the will to fail. It is the pressing-down of the crown chakra, the pressing-down of the energies of the crown into the lower chakras and then, by the action of the dragon, causing those energies to be misused in lust and sensuality.

This is the quadrant of the etheric body, the fire body. We learn that the dragon is the perversion of fire, of the fohat of creation. The creation of the beast itself and the dragon is the misuse of the sacred fire of man and woman, of the Elohim, of the seed and the egg of the Father-Mother God, creating this monstrous form that is seething with all of the accumulation of the rebellion of the fallen ones. This vibration will act in the subconscious, in your own etheric body, as self-condemnation, as condemnation of others, as the denial of God.

See how many among mankind under the influence of this dragon within their own subconscious deny God. Maybe it's not an outright denial—"God doesn't exist"—not as blatant as atheism. But maybe it comes under a perversion of Pisces—as doubt in the existence of God, fear that God will punish us, fear that he will not be just, a trembling, or a consideration that God is remote, that God is a hateful god (the perversion of Aquarius), that he is not a God of love.

Relegating God to a distant cosmos where he has no part of our personal lives—this is the denial of God. This is anti-God substance, very subtle. After all, if the dragon popped out of your subconscious, appeared on the screen before you,

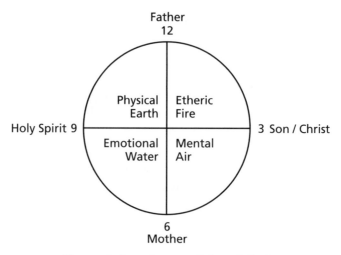

Figure 1 Four Personalities of God

The One God manifests in four personalities: Father, Mother, Son and Holy Spirit. These personalities correspond to the four planes of Matter and the four lower bodies of man. As the four quadrants, frequencies of God's energy, are further divided, the trinities of each quadrant become the twelve God-qualities shown in figure 3.

Figure 2 Four Personalities of Antichrist

Opposing the four personalities of God, both within the Macrocosm of the universe and the microcosm of the being of man, are the four personalities of Antichrist, described in Revelation 13–16 as the dragon, the great whore, the beast and the false prophet.

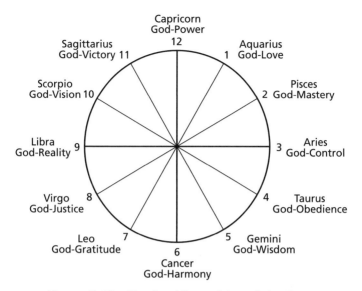

Figure 3 The Twelve Hierarchies of the Sun
The Twelve Hierarchies of the Sun are twelve mandalas
of Cosmic Beings ensouling twelve facets of God's consciousness, holding the
pattern of that frequency for the entire cosmos. They are identified by the
names of the signs of the zodiac.

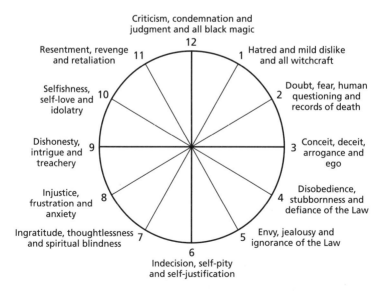

Figure 4 Misuses of the Twelve God-Qualities

talked to you and said, "Now I'm the dragon, I'm the perversion of God, and I'm going to see to it that you fail," you would take up your sword and slay the dragon! But the dragon is subtle: it is our own carnal consciousness.

It is simply the doubt that the I AM Presence is Real. It's the doubt that the I AM Presence can fulfill the Law of Being within us. It is the doubt that the I AM Presence will come through every time we make a call. It's the doubt that the I AM Presence will be able to completely defeat the world dragon, the world momentum and the mass collective subconscious.

Let us understand, then, when we feel that momentum of condemnation of ourself or other parts of life, of hatred of ourself or mild dislike of ourself or other parts of life, of doubt and death and belief in death—all of this is the dragon consciousness stealing the fire of our etheric body, depriving us of the glorious victory of the Light of the solar hierarchies in that body.

This is a consciousness, a very subtle consciousness, of *malice.* It is malice beneath the surface. It is not often active except in the insane or those who are suddenly seized to commit mass murders and crimes. But it is there. It's like a silvery black forcefield at subconscious levels that comes up and pricks and incites these sometimes aggressive emotions and energies that we suddenly feel coming through us. We actually don't come face-to-face with this type of force until we challenge it, until we totally and wholeheartedly accept God and the Teachings and the Path and the goal of the ascension. Because as long as we are not on the Path, we are part of the mass consciousness.

There are only two places you can be—either on the Path or in the mass consciousness. There is no middle ground. The middle ground is a very deceptive place. People think they are in the middle, but they aren't. They're really in the mass consciousness. So only when you decide to go against the mainstream of the mass consciousness do you confront all these forces, who then become very, very uncomfortable and begin to bellow their death cries and their death throes within your consciousness. And that's when you experience the battle of Armageddon and the confrontation with Antichrist.

People come into the Masters' Teachings and they think: "When I was in this or that church, I didn't have any problems at all. Now I'm in the Masters' Teachings, and all kinds of things are happening to me, and it's really a struggle to maintain my Light. What's happening to me?" And so because people don't like the struggle, they often go back to the calm and the ease and the downstream of orthodoxy, that aspect of orthodoxy that is the perverted Teachings of the Brotherhood.

The Exorcism of the Dragon

To set the record straight in the etheric body, the dragon must be exorcised. How do we exorcise it? You have the decree, "Round the Clock Protection" (page 255). You have the violet flame. You have Mighty Astrea (page 127). You have your own Christ Self and your own I AM Presence. And you can release the fiat:

In the name of the Christ, in the name of the I AM THAT I AM, I demand the binding of the dragon within my etheric body. I demand the transmutation of the cause and core of the consciousness of the dragon, the seed of the dragon and the egg of the dragon, and all that remains of the influence of the dragon in my subconscious. Let it be done this hour in the name of Jesus the Christ! And let Archangel Michael and Mighty

Astrea come into my etheric body this day and purge me
of the cause and core of all that is less than my I AM
Presence and my Christ Self! I accept it done this hour in
the full power of the threefold flame within my heart.

Now make your own prayer, make your own call, and
make it fervently. Apply the Teachings of the Brotherhood.
Get down on your knees, if necessary, when you feel the
temptation and the force of the dragon, and refuse to let it
overtake you. Call to Archangel Michael to take his sword
and slay that dragon. The entire Spirit of the Great White
Brotherhood will reinforce the call of the son of God who
desires to make secure the forcefield of his own microcosm.

The Antichrist and the Beast:
Perversion of the Christ

Standing on the three o'clock line challenging the Christ is
Antichrist himself. This Antichrist, from that point of the three
o'clock line of the Christ, is that which gives birth to all of
the other perversions of the Godhead—the dragon, the false
prophet and the great whore. Antichrist is the fulcrum of all
that is "anti-." That which is on the twelve o'clock line is anti-
Father. That which is on the six o'clock line, as the great
whore, is anti-Mother. And that which is on the nine o'clock
line opposing the Holy Spirit is anti-Spirit, or anti–Holy Spirit.
It is simply a frequency that is the exact opposite of the
frequency of Light, which opposes the forcefield.

Also on the three o'clock line, serving under the Antichrist,
is the beast. And in the Book of Revelation there are two
beasts listed—the beast that riseth up out of the sea and the
beast that cometh up out of the earth.[11] These are the two
beasts who, under the Antichrist, pervert the emotional body

and the mental body. The beast is the carnal mind—the serpent that crawled on its belly before Eve, now full-grown. The beast of Revelation is the mature adult of that serpent of Genesis, and it grew by the acceptance of souls. As we accepted the lie of the compromise of relative Good and Evil, we fed the serpent, and the serpent grew into the beast.

The beast controls almost the entire astral belt and mental plane of the planet. Not quite all, because those who are the Christed ones and who have the true Light and have the true Teachings (and this is not only those who are students of the Masters, because in every walk of life, in every church and in every religion, there are real souls who have the real Light, who are real devotees) are there and they hold the flame and they do not allow the emotional body or the mental body to become polluted.

But for the most part, the mental plane is polluted with the beast of intellectual pride and ambition and competition, and the beast polluting the astral plane is the pollution of all misuses of the flame of the purity of the Divine Mother. Saint Germain has said that the astral plane is the sewer of mankind's consciousness. And by the temptations of the beast leading to all forms of perversion and misuse of God's energy, the astral plane is what it is today.

Many people who study the Book of Revelation go into naming names of people in embodiment who personify the dragon, the beast, the false prophet and the great whore. It is not necessary to do that. There may be one or several individuals on the planet who can claim a greater concentration of the beast, the dragon, the great whore, and so forth, than the rest of us and might stand out among us as having that greater mastery and forcefield of the energy veil. But pointing the finger at anyone, even pointing the finger at Lucifer, diverts us from the victory and from the battleground of our own soul.

It's very dangerous to say, "The Devil made me do this and the 'force' made me do this and So-and-so made me do this, and so I sinned and so I fell." That's exactly what Adam said, "Eve gave me the apple and I ate it." And Eve said, "Well, the Serpent tempted me and I ate it." And everybody blames everybody else for the departure from consciousness.

So we look within. We examine our own mental body. We look at the lines of our own clock. We say: "Am I outpicturing God-control in the Divine Ego or am I prancing around like a peacock with my human ego, trying to impress everybody with my spiritual knowledge, getting myself all kinds of titles and things so that I can become a teacher and let everybody see how great I am?" Have you asked yourself, "Is it the human ego or the Divine Ego that has set itself up?" We have to think about these things. We have to know that when we are on the Path, nothing is going to be obvious—everything is going to be subtle.

That is why we have to study to show ourselves approved unto God[12]—because these are subtleties of vibration. And the ego goes around looking benign, smiling and saying that it is so wonderful and so lovely and such a perfect example of this or that teacher or teaching, making a great impression on all kinds of people. But it doesn't have the Flame. That's why Jesus warned of the false teachers that come as the Antichrist —come in the name of the Christ and yet have not the Flame.[13]

The question is, Can the teacher deliver the Flame? Does the Light flow? The teacher should only be a clear pane of glass. If the teacher takes any credit unto himself, the glass has a smudge on it. If you and your soul take credit for anything and give not the glory to God, you are reserving an identity separate from God. "The Father worketh hitherto, and I work. I of my own self can do nothing. It is the Father in me which doeth the work."[14]

Let us beware of the Antichrist within. Let us see that it does not manifest as that puffed-up pride carefully hidden on the three o'clock line or as rebellion against the Law of God on the four o'clock line or as jealousy and envy of the sons and daughters of God who have attained, on the five o'clock line. Let us see, then, that we clear the mental belt and clear the way for the coming of the Teaching, clear the way for the sacred fire of Alpha to be lowered into the mental plane.

The Great Whore: Perversion of the Mother

Now let us see on the six o'clock line how the great whore swallows up the image of the Cosmic Virgin. The signet of the Cosmic Virgin is the Teaching of the Divine Mother, the wisdom of the Mother. We are counseled in the book of Proverbs to seek out Wisdom, to follow her.[15] This is the counsel of the Father to the son—counseling him to seek out the learning of the Divine Mother. It is the Divine Mother who holds in her hand the teachings of the Father whereby the children of God can return to the flame of Alpha.

Coming in the name of the Mother is the great whore. It comes as organizations. It comes as large mass movements that, almost like a giant blowfish, suck the children of God into a teaching, into a doctrine, into a political theory that, instead of taking them to the sacred fire, takes them outside the circumference of God's Being. The great whore is all that goes against the purity of the Mother within us. It is the perversion of the Mother flame. It is the perversion of the Life-force.

It takes courage to kick out the great whore. Every perversion of the Feminine Ray in man and woman must go. On a mass scale we see it as pornography. We see it as the abuse of the body of the Mother in advertising, the promotion of sex everywhere, the misuse of sex. We see it in the destruction of the children of the Mother of all ages in this period when the Mother flame is rising.

It is rising like a continent, like Lemuria. It is pressing up in all mankind relentlessly. It cannot be turned back. But as it rises, it comes in contact with all that has opposed it in all centuries. And so there is cataclysm in consciousness, there is upheaval, there is insanity; and that flame keeps rising and it keeps rising. We either blend with it, move with it, determine to govern our energies, or we will find ourselves aligned with the great whore and not even realize that the precious energies of the Mother have been seized from us.

So let us beware the subtleties: all inharmony in the feeling body, ingratitude, anxiety, nervous tension, the sense of injustice. When we shake our fist at God and say: "It isn't fair! It isn't fair what you've done to me! You've killed my mother, you've killed my father, you've taken my child, you've given me this terrible disease, this terrible misfortune!"—that sense of injustice, of rebellion against our karma, is rebellion against the Mother, rebellion against God, against the Law of Life that coalesces in us through the Mother. Let us beware then. The entire astral plane of the planet is the great whore, the perversion of the Mother.

The Elohim Astrea gives us a teaching on the binding of the great whore: "You have heard of the fallen ones and that many have been brought to judgment in recent months. Now comes the judgment of the great whore and the impostors of the Divine Mother and the impostors of Kali and Durga and Mother Mary and all who implement the will of the Cosmic Virgin! Now judgment is spoken this day and the action of Astrea goes forth to *bind* the great whore!... It is done in the name of the living Christ by the action of Purity and Astrea according to judgment and justice this day implemented by the Four and Twenty Elders. Those impostors of the Feminine Beings of Hierarchy, those whose time has come, must go to the Court of the Sacred Fire for judgment in this hour."[16]

This judgment parallels the judgment of Lucifer. It means that key impostors of the Divine Mother on the astral plane— as Lucifer was on the astral plane, not in physical embodiment —have been taken to judgment. The judgment of those who live in physical bodies awaits the time of the fulfillment of their cycle, of their allotment of energy.

Judgment has come in the Macrocosm. The fiat has gone forth. The judgment will not come within our four lower bodies until we ratify it, until we kick out the great whore and enshrine the Divine Mother. God acts, and we must act to ratify his actions, or we will find ourselves separated and apart from the flow of the great cosmic sea.

The False Prophet: Perversion of the Holy Spirit

On the nine o'clock line is the false prophet and all of the line of false teachers. When each Avatar, each Christed one, takes his leave of the planet in the ritual of the ascension, the threefold flame within the heart merges with the threefold flame of the Christ and with the threefold flame of the I AM Presence. This trinity of action assumes the totality of the soul back into the I AM Presence. When this goes up, there is a release from the Presence that comes down to fill the vacuum and fill the void, to comfort those who are left, to comfort the disciples. Hence, the Holy Spirit is known as the Comforter.

In the last days of Jesus' mission in the Holy Land, he told his disciples what would come—that he would leave, that he must go, that he must be crucified that the Law and the

Prophets should be fulfilled—but they should not be heavy and sorrowful, because when he would go he would send them another Comforter, and "he shall teach you all things."[17] So it was on that day of Pentecost that the disciples were gathered, and there was the rushing of the mighty wind and the coming of the Holy Spirit.[18] It was the same vibration of the ascension spiral. And that Comforter gave them gifts of the Spirit to be teachers, gave them the gift of tongues, gave them the gift to go forth and fulfill their mission. It was the anchoring in their hearts of the mantle of the Christ.

The true Teacher of all mankind is the Holy Spirit. When we pray to the entire Spirit of the Great White Brotherhood, we are praying to the focalization of the Holy Spirit that each and every Ascended Master has left behind for the comfort of the disciples on the way. That Spirit appears on the nine o'clock line under the hierarchy of Libra for the precipitation of God as Father, God as Christ, God as Mother in the physical plane.

We cannot understand and receive the Teachings of the Ascended Masters unless we have the Holy Spirit. Unless we have the flame, the essence of the radiance, we cannot sit in a room and even comprehend or retain the words of the dictations. We cannot even read the words of the Masters and click into them unless the flame within our heart and soul responds.

Jesus also knew that inasmuch as the Comforter would come, all manner of false teachers and false prophets would also come. So throughout the New Testament, we are warned of the false prophets, the false teachers. "Wherefore by their fruits ye shall know them."[19] They say all the right things, they quote all the right words; yet they set themselves up independent of Hierarchy, independent of the Great White Brotherhood. They draw disciples to themselves, and they allow their disciples to give them the glory for the Light. They control the lives of their pupils; they interfere with the free and natural flow of the Light of the Presence and the Christ Self.

Some of them even know of what I speak, and that this is the mark of the false prophet. And therefore, they carefully camouflage the fact that this is taking place. With their mouth and with their words, they say they give glory; but in their feelings and in their subconscious and in their hearts, they are puffed up with the vanity of the fallen ones.

The only way to isolate the false teacher is by the flame of the Holy Spirit within you. Only by the testing and the continual testing of the vibration, only by keeping yourself unspotted from the world, by going through the battle of the four quadrants, by exorcising these four aspects of Antichrist from within yourself, will you be able to identify those who have not exorcised these forces. As long as they remain within, you may very well be the victim of these forces in the subconscious of others. But the innocence of your soul will always be protected by fervent prayer, by the intercession of Archangel Michael, by the Great White Brotherhood, until you come of age in the wisdom of the Mother whereby you have that perfect discernment and Christ-discrimination.

The Judgment in the Macrocosm Must Be Ratified in the Microcosm

When Alpha announced the judgment of Lucifer, he also explained the work that we must do: "The challenge of the hour is the consuming by the sacred fire of the cause, effect, record and memory of all that has been impressed upon the body of the Mother—that body the entire cosmos—by the fallen ones. Now let us behold how the Fallen One has left seeds of rebellion even in the four lower bodies of the children of God. And so the Evil One came and sowed the tares among the wheat.[20]

"Now let the sons of Light go forth! Let them go into the fields white with the harvest. Let them, as the reapers with the angelic hosts, separate the tares from the wheat. And let it be done by the fiat of Alpha and Omega! Let it be done by the action of the flow of sacred fire from the I AM Presence of each one!

"More dangerous even than the Fallen One are the seeds of rebellion that remain to be consumed, for the seed contains within itself the pattern of the whole. And therefore I release the Light of the fiery core of the flow of our Oneness for the canceling-out of the seed of the Fallen One. I release this energy to the level of the etheric plane, the plane of fire. Farther it cannot go without the assent of your free will and your invocation, for the sacred fire will burn and consume the wheat with the tares unless it first be assimilated in the consciousness of the Lightbearers.

"Let the sacred fire, then, in the increment that can be borne by each one, be sealed in the third eye and the crown and in the heart as a trinity of action that can be called forth and released in the plane of the mind and the mental belt of a cosmos. It is the Mind of Christ that the fallen ones have determined to seize, to misuse. They have no power from Alpha and Omega; yet the fiery core of Life within the children of the sun has been used to affirm that power, to acquiesce to it and to reinforce it.

"I say then, withdraw by the authority of your free will all affirmation, all consent that you have given unto the fallen ones, unto their rebellion, unto the seed and unto the carnal mind of your own creation. Only thus will the mental belt be cleansed of the remnant of the Fallen One.

"Now let the beast that occupies the bottomless pit of the

subconscious and the desire body be exposed also! And let it be seen that this creation instigated by the fallen ones has also received the seal of your approval. For that which remains untransmuted, which you have failed to challenge, that which exists in consciousness, is therefore the creation of free will. And until you will to call it back, to undo it, to restore it to the fiery core for transmutation, it remains a blight on the whole of cosmos.

"Only when you challenge the dweller-on-the-threshold of your own cosmos and your own consciousness—the rebellious one—can you breathe the breath of Life and know 'I AM free!' Therefore, that judgment that has come to the Fallen One, meted out by Alpha and Omega, must also resound within the consciousness of every living soul. And the Alpha-to-Omega, the atom of identity in the fiery core of your own being, must release the spiral that renders the judgment whereby the dweller-on-the-threshold passes through the second death and is no more and has no longer any habitation in the whole consciousness of that life that you call your own, but which I am here to tell you is my very own—mine to give, mine to take. And I can claim that fiery core, that replica of the Great Central Sun, when the cycles roll and the Law of Being returns the drop unto the Ocean.

"You have a cosmos! You have an energy field assigned to you! Let the four quadrants of your creation be purged of every residue of the Fallen One! Let them be purged by your free will aligned with my own, aligned with the Four and Twenty Elders who render judgment in the God Star. And let the earth body as well be free of the impressions of rebellion and the ego that is set apart from the Divine One!

"Let all be alert! Let all know that the passing from the Macrocosm of the one who instigated the rebellion of the angels is a point for the release of great Light in the Macrocosm.

You are globules of identity suspended in the Macrocosm of my own self-awareness. And that Light, which inundates the cosmic sea, cannot penetrate the sphere of identity that you are unless you will it so. Therefore I come to say: Ratify and confirm the judgment within your own being; and only then be satisfied in the Law and in the victory.

"Judgment is nigh. Understand that unless you release the judgment in your own microcosm and withdraw all support of the energy veil, when the judgment comes and the skeins of consciousness are found to be woven inextricably with skeins of evil, then the entire globule must pass through the spirals of Alpha and Omega. And this is the ritual, then, of the canceling-out of that which cannot be absorbed into the sea; for by free will it has not willed it so.

"You are set apart as a diamond suspended in crystal, suspended in ruby, suspended in agate. See how the crystallization of the God flame that I AM must be made your own. You determine the fate of your own cosmos. So let it be. So receive the warning that perhaps there is even greater danger now than when the Adversary was personified before you; for now it remains only the subjective awareness, and that subjectivity is the burden of the soul that longs to be extricated from that substance that has no part with Light.

"I AM Alpha! I AM Omega! When you know that you are Alpha, that you are Omega, then—and only then—will you find yourself in the white-fire core of the Great Central Sun. Children of the One: Forge your God-identity!"[21]

The Invocation of the Judgment

This is the hour of the fulfillment of the prophecy of Daniel: "And at that time shall Michael stand up, the great prince which standeth for the children of thy people; and there shall be a time of trouble, such as never was since there was a nation even to that same time: and at that time thy people shall be delivered, every one that shall be found written in the book.

"And many of them that sleep in the dust of the earth shall awake, some to everlasting life, and some to shame and everlasting contempt. And they that be wise shall shine as the brightness of the firmament; and they that turn many to righteousness as the stars for ever and ever."[22]

This is the hour of the awakening of the sleeping serpent of the dweller-on-the-threshold; this is the hour of judgment for those who choose not to be God but to be the embodiment of Evil; this is the hour of the judgment of many who have chosen the left-handed path, many who have become one with Antichrist, many who have inverted the Light to create the monster.

This is the hour when Jesus Christ has sent forth his call to the Father to bind them and cast them into the outer darkness, the astral plane, which they themselves have created; for these fallen ones are the creators of that Death and Hell, which itself shall be cast into the Lake of Sacred Fire.

We know not how God will accomplish his purpose or how the holy angels will implement the judgments of the Son. We have no desire to see anyone go through a physical death or even the second death: This is not the purpose of the Judgment Call or the Dweller Decree! It is for the life of the soul in the grips of the toiler that we cry out to God for salvation through his great and marvelous works—beginning with his perfect judgment. We are charged to make the call, and the armies of heaven under the Archangels are charged to implement the answer, subject to the will of God and the adjudication of the Son, in Jesus and in us.

Fully clothed upon with the armour of God, give your Tube of Light Decree (see page 42) and calls to Archangel Michael (page 129) before giving Jesus' Judgment Call or the decree for the casting out of the dweller-on-the-threshold.

The Judgment Call
"They Shall Not Pass!"
by Jesus Christ

In the Name of the I AM THAT I AM,
I invoke the Electronic Presence of Jesus Christ:
They shall not pass!
They shall not pass!
They shall not pass!
By the authority of the cosmic cross of white fire it shall be:
That all that is directed against the Christ
within me, within the holy innocents,
within our beloved Messengers,
within every son and daughter of God,
[by the Nephilim gods, their genetic engineering,
population control, and contrived wars,
slaughtering the sons of God and children of the Light
on the battlefields of life]*
Is now turned back
by the authority of Alpha and Omega,

---

* At the places indicated, you may give the suggested calls shown in brackets, or include your own calls for the Hosts of the LORD to take command of conditions of personal and planetary injustice that you name.

by the authority of my Lord and Saviour Jesus Christ,
by the authority of Saint Germain!

I AM THAT I AM within the center of this temple
and I declare in the fullness of
the entire Spirit of the Great White Brotherhood:
That those who, then, practice the black arts
against the children of the Light
[namely, the entire interplanetary conspiracy of
the fallen angels and their mechanization man]*
Are now bound by the Hosts of the LORD,
Do now receive the judgment of the Lord Christ
within me, within Jesus,
and within every Ascended Master,
Do now receive, then, the full return—
multiplied by the energy of the Cosmic Christ—
of their nefarious deeds which they have practiced
since the very incarnation of the Word!

Lo, I AM a Son of God!
Lo, I AM a Flame of God!
Lo, I stand upon the Rock of the living Word
And I declare with Jesus, the living Son of God:
They shall not pass!
They shall not pass!
They shall not pass!
ELOHIM. ELOHIM. ELOHIM. (chant this line)

Taken from a dictation by Jesus Christ, August 6, 1978, Camelot, California, "They Shall Not Pass!" Posture for giving this decree: Stand. Raise your right hand, using the *abhaya mudra* (gesture of fearlessness, palm forward), and place your left hand to your heart—thumb and first two fingers touching chakra pointing inward. Give this call at least once in every twenty-four-hour cycle.

"I Cast Out the Dweller-on-the-Threshold!"
by Jesus Christ

In the name I AM THAT I AM ELOHIM
>Saint Germain, Portia, Guru Ma, Lanello,
In the name I AM THAT I AM SANAT KUMARA
>Gautama Buddha, Lord Maitreya, Jesus Christ
I CAST OUT THE DWELLER-ON-THE THRESHOLD of _____.*

In the name of my beloved mighty I AM Presence and Holy Christ Self, Archangel Michael and the Hosts of the LORD, in the name Jesus Christ, I challenge the personal and planetary dweller-on-the-threshold, and I say:

You have no power over me! *You* may not threaten or mar the face of my God within my soul. *You* may not taunt or tempt me with past or present or future, for I AM hid with Christ in God. I AM his bride. I AM accepted by the LORD.

You have no power to destroy me!

Therefore, be *bound!* by the LORD himself.

Your day is *done!* You may no longer inhabit this temple.

In the name I AM THAT I AM, be *bound!* you tempter of my soul. Be *bound!* you point of pride of the original fall of the fallen ones! You have no power, no reality, no worth. You occupy no time or space of my being.

You have no power in my temple. You may no longer steal the Light of my chakras. You may not steal the Light of my heart flame or my I AM Presence.

Be *bound!* then, O Serpent and his seed and all implants of the sinister force, for I AM THAT I AM!

I AM the Son of God this day, and I occupy this temple fully and wholly until the coming of the LORD, until the New Day, until all be fulfilled, and until this generation of the seed

---

* Here insert your specific calls for the Hosts of the LORD to take command of conditions of personal and planetary injustice that you name.

of Serpent pass away.

Burn through, O living Word of God!

By the power of Brahma, Vishnu, and Shiva, in the name Brahman: I AM THAT I AM and I stand and I cast out the dweller.

Let him be bound by the power of the LORD's host! Let him be consigned to the flame of the sacred fire of Alpha and Omega, that that one may not go out to tempt the innocent and the babes in Christ.

Blaze the power of Elohim!

Elohim of God—Elohim of God—Elohim of God

Descend now in answer to my call. As the mandate of the LORD—as Above, so below—occupy now.

Bind the fallen self! *Bind* the synthetic self! Be *out* then!

Bind the fallen one! For there is no more remnant or residue in my life of any, or any part of that one.

Lo, I AM, in Jesus' name, the victor over Death and Hell! (2x)

Lo, I AM THAT I AM in me—in the name of Jesus Christ —is *here and now* the victor over Death and Hell! Lo! it is done.

The Victory of Christ

T
RULY, "FLESH AND BLOOD cannot inherit the kingdom of God,"[1] and it follows as the night the day (or the day the night) that regeneration is the requirement of every hour. In the Christ is the power of regeneration. Change, then, must come about, and that change must be in the person of each individual. If the change is of God and is activated by the Christ, it will be permanent, blessing all mankind and blessing Universal Life. If it is of the character and quality of defamation, it will be against all that for which the Christ stands—thus, Antichrist.

There are many individuals of an intellectual nature who find it difficult to understand the things of the invisible world. What they cannot touch, taste, see, feel or handle to them is nonexistent. They patiently wait for the development of those faculties of being that are encoded or locked within the sympathetic nervous system and the endocrine glands. Then a stepping-up of their energies can occur that will cause them to develop not psychic faculties but highly spiritualized qualities, permitting them to sense the activities of what we will call the "inner world" of divine Reality. But they do not reckon with the long journey that they have had into the night of human despair; they do not have enough patience to wait for the uncoiling of the spring and the transmutation of undesirable energies.

The Plot of Antichrist

It is difficult, then, at times for intellectual individuals to realize the tremendous plot in which the Antichrist is engaged. They do not realize that energies from all over the Earth of a negative or positive kind come together and form a conglomerate mass. They can understand that an ocean can pile up upon the landed surface of the Earth and large bodies of water can exist. They can understand how the tides and winds are born, but they do not understand how the tides of human negation and banal influences actually exist, how they are empowered by grossness and widespread activity of a negative sort, how they can actually attack the very roots of spirituality, how various branches of the humanities are used against nature, against society, against man and against God.

Commercial success can hardly be equated to success in the spiritual domain. For Life is total in its aspects, and men must seek the totality of living that is found in the divine experience. This does not mean economic failure; it means total success. And it includes the spirituality of Life and the understanding and manifestation of the Christ.

All branches of the sciences and the humanities—including social sciences and cultural activities in the fields of art, drama, literature and music—are intended to be adjuncts and assistants to the expansion of the fine faculties of the soul. Yet much of the music of the world that has come forth of late has keyed man into Antichrist responses. These responses have made man dependent upon drugs that have unleashed from his subconscious mind the primitive states of struggle that go back in history into past eras of human decadence.

There is a culture of darkness in the world today that is the spawn of satanic energies and lifestreams whose rebellion has fomented in their souls for a prolonged period of time, bringing hidden discomfort first of all to themselves. This consciousness seeks to make itself then a catalyst in the world at large. The motive is the destruction of the beauty of the Christ and the dream of the living God to restore man to Eden.

"It Is the Father's Good Pleasure to Give You the Kingdom"

Therefore, men must be "wise as serpents and harmless as doves."[2] Truly, the Divine Image must be adored. Men must understand that God who lives in them lives in all, even in these—yet all do not live in Him. Let us develop, in the name of God and for humanity, that discrimination that is the gift of God to everyone who loves enough that we may continue to know the Truth that will set us free, even as we were born free.

Yes, Antichrist has come into the world—but we must never forget that the Christ was here first, that the Christ is the Light that lighteth every man, that the Christ is the greater Light even as Antichrist is but the reflected light. We must discern the Lord's Body, understand what hidden motive is, examine our own motives and desires, our sincerity and the mirror in which we gaze that it may become refined as true perception. Thus shall the radiance of the living Christ so dazzle us with God-reality that Antichrist shall pale into the shadows of insignificance for the whole world. This is God's desire.

The Bible says, "The soul that sinneth, it shall die."[3] The soul is the potential of free will to elect to become one with God, to elect to become God. When the soul elects to unite with the living Spirit of the I AM THAT I AM, then and only then is she hid with Christ in God,[4] is she permanent, does she become a part of Immortal Life.

We are on Earth with a gift of free will to choose to be or not to be. There are powerful influences that are determined that you and I will choose not to be, to cease to be by partaking of their death culture. And we see this death culture upon our youth. In the face of all of this, what have the people to do and where have they to go?

The key that God has given us today is the liberating power of the Word. Children of the Light, awake to your divine destiny! Today the power of God is available to you as never before. The sword of Armageddon is the *Sacred Word*. Its science is taught to us by the true Sons of God who have not fallen from the skies in their UFOs. They are the Ascended Masters moving in our midst as our elder brothers and sisters.

Like the prophet Samuel of old, they are God's own representatives to his people. They are our Teachers, the way-showers and the true Hierarchy of heaven—not the false hierarchy who fell from grace and are still disguising themselves as prophets, patriarchs and benefactors of our society.

The LORD is calling you and me today to be the remnant who will use his name, the sacred name of AUM, the sacred name of the I AM THAT I AM, the sacred name of Jesus Christ, of Gautama Buddha, and every saint. He is calling us to use the sacred name, to intone the Word, and thereby release the Light for the healing of the nations. God has given us the answer. It is this liberating power of the Word—the greatest and yet most simple mystery of Life itself. It is the gift of God to his children now.

When Jesus our Lord revealed to his disciples the nature of this interplanetary conspiracy of the fallen ones, he concluded with the comforting words: "Fear not, little flock; for it is your Father's good pleasure to give you the kingdom."[5] If we fail to remember our ancient heritage as sons and daughters of the Most High and the all-power of heaven and earth that he gave to us in the Beginning, if we fail to remember the wickedness of the wicked clearly recorded on Sumerian tablets and in the records of akasha, if we fail to remember the countless Avatars who have come to expose the fallen ones and been murdered over and over again by them, if we fail to perceive their present massacre of our holy bands, then we will be condemned as the generation of Lightbearers who lost an age, an entire evolution and perhaps our very own souls.

Those who have the will to choose to do something about the persecution of the people of this planet by the Nephilim councils of war and their building of armaments of war, nation by nation, and their intended destruction of a people and an entire planet must turn swiftly to call upon the name of the LORD, to invoke a higher science and a higher law. This is the only means whereby this Earth and her evolutions and their very souls can be saved.

The Confrontation of Light and Darkness

In his manifesto on mechanization man, the Great Divine Director is very careful to immediately point to the propensity of human nature to rise up in indignation, in hate and hate creation, or in revenge or vengeance against the oppressors.

This has often happened in revolutions and wars that have been fought where the children of the Light get all mixed-up and move against the supposed enemies of their Light, often confusing the fallen ones and the sons of God.

Heads from all sides have rolled in revolutions and on the battlefields of life. Children of Light, side by side with the mechanical creation, have fought for the causes of the fallen ones in spite of themselves because they have been so brainwashed to align themselves in defense of absolute Evil instead of absolute Good.

Therefore, the Great Divine Director says that the only way to rid the Earth of mechanization man is transmutation—the violet flame, calls to Astrea, calls for the judgment. Those entrusted with this understanding, then, must have no sense of vendetta or a personal need to exact retribution from the forces of Evil. Such an attitude of mind and heart will only bind you to these fallen ones for centuries and millennia to come. Therefore, the purified heart is necessary. And if, at any time or in any space, you are so tempted to react humanly against the forces of Evil, remember that this is the most dangerous state of consciousness that you can entertain, because you are instantly bound to those against whom you would direct your warfare.

Truly, the attainment of the flame of peace from the heart of Jesus Christ and Gautama Buddha has been the legacy for us to embody for more than two thousand years and more. We have been nobly prepared for the confrontation. And the only state of mind that is acceptable is nonattachment, desirelessness, absolute love, and the absolute awareness that God himself, as the Universal Light, will—in his own time and space—burn the tares and separate the wheat and draw that wheat into his garner.[6]

The Means of Transmutation

I would remind you that Jesus came and he stated his purpose. He said, "For judgment I AM come."[7]

Why did he allow himself to be crucified by the fallen ones? Because in crucifying the Son of God, they are brought to their ultimate judgment. This is why God has continually sent his saints into the world and allowed them to be martyred; because by the spilling of the blood of the Son of God Incarnate, these fallen ones may then go before the Court of the Sacred Fire for the final judgment and, ultimately, the second death.

We have the advocate with the Father, the living Christ within our hearts. We have the Hierarch of the age, Saint Germain, who has given to us, through the violet flame and the sacred fire, the means of transmutation so that we can pass through the initiation of the crucifixion and yet remain in life in physical embodiment. The violet flame enables us to pass through this manifestation of the judgment and yet retain hours and decades of life with which to execute the divine plan.

In the Last Supper, Jesus assigned to his disciples the office of carrying out the judgment of the twelve tribes of Israel—and, I might add, of Earth's evolutions. It was not alone to the apostles. Apostleship, being an initiation above that of disciple, implies that the child of God, the disciple of the Master, has now accepted his joint heirship with Christ and with God and has graduated to the position of Son of God. It is therefore the Sons of God in the Earth (of which there were originally 144,000) that are entrusted with the invocation of the Word of judgment. With the Lord Jesus Christ, these Sons of God declare, "For judgment I AM come." They are male and female in embodiment, but they are called the Son of God because they manifest the fullness of their Christ Self.

The Sons of God, those who manifest the Christ consciousness, are the only ones who have the authority, in the name of Jesus Christ, to invoke the judgment. The children of God may do so, but they always preface their dynamic decree with the phrase "In the name of my beloved mighty I AM Presence and Holy Christ Self," so that the Christ Self and the mighty I AM Presence will speak the Word through them even though they have not the authority or the initiation. Therefore, we see the essential purpose of our life: to walk the path of initiation, to increase Light, to be endowed with Sonship, and finally, then, to be able to fulfill the requirements of the Law.

It is written in the New Testament that the Father has given unto the Son the office of judge.[8] Paintings of the Apocalypse include the figure of the Lord Jesus Christ enacting the judgment. Planetary Evil, the Evil of solar systems and galaxies, can only be checked by those in embodiment, and specifically those in embodiment who have passed the initiations of the Sons of God. This enables you to understand that all of the Ascended Masters and Cosmic Beings and Elohim cannot interfere with the increase of Light or the increase of Darkness except through those who cooperate in embodiment.

Does that mean that if there are not any in embodiment that God has no recourse? No.

God's recourse, if there are not those in embodiment to call forth the Flame, is to simply breathe the great inbreath with his cyclic regularity, drawing back to himself the entire Matter universe, passing this through his great heart as the Great Central Sun. Then all creation within the Matter universe that has not become God-identified is simply cancelled out.

We are not at that moment. We are in the moment when

we can manifest in the Matter sphere, in the entire Matter cosmos, the Light of God that swallows up the Darkness. And it is our goal that rather than being dissolved in the heart of God, the Matter universe in its entirety shall ascend.

Not only the ascension of the individual or a planet or a solar system or a galaxy, then, is our goal, but the ascension of the Matter sphere! If this occurs, there is a stupendous expansion of God consciousness, as God draws into himself the net gain of universal Life ascended; and in the outgoing of cycles once again, there is a grander and more vast manifestation of the next level of Matter qualification (or of Mother manifestation) for increased lifewaves to evolve.

We are in the moment of Armageddon that determines whether the Sons and Daughters of God shall take dominion in the Matter sphere and therefore preserve opportunity for the children of Light to continue their initiations. It is, to our understanding, a foregone conclusion that the Hierarchies of Light and the Sons of God will vanquish error. But it is not predestined—it is forged and won day by day through free will and its correct exercise.

Even though we see the divine plan of the victory that is held invincibly in the immaculate heart of Alpha and Omega, it is our outpicturing of that divine plan that will be the final sealing of the flame of victory.

Reverse the Tide

In the name of the beloved mighty victorious Presence of God, I AM in me from the Great Central Sun, my own beloved Holy Christ Self and Holy Christ Selves of all mankind, beloved Goddess of Light, beloved Queen of Light, beloved Goddess of Liberty, beloved Goddess of Wisdom, beloved Cyclopea, thou Silent Watcher for the Earth, beloved seven mighty Elohim, beloved seven Chohans and Archangels, the Great Divine Director, Ascended Master Cuzco, beloved Mighty Astrea, beloved Lanello and K-17, the entire Spirit of the Great White Brotherhood and the World Mother, elemental life—fire, air, water and earth! I decree:

TAKE DOMINION NOW OVER:

[Give one or more of the following inserts, or compose your own prayer for the specific situation you are working on.]

INSERT A: all lying entities, psychic riptides, black magic and witchcraft directed against elemental life or the Light and the freedom and illumination of all mankind—with their causes and cores.

INSERT B: all racial violence, civil disorders, rioting, insurrection, international terror, treason, anarchy, fanaticism, insanity, plots of assassination, plots to overthrow our federal government, plots to vampirize and destroy the Light of America, and plots to unleash nuclear warfare between the nations—with their causes and cores.

INSERT C: the cause and core of the conglomerate of the dweller-on-the-threshold, personally and in a planetary sense, of the false hierarchy of this system of worlds and all other galaxies, specifically in their plots against the sons of God on the path of the ascension.

* Reverse the tide! (3x)
  Roll them back! (3x)
  Reverse the tide! (3x)
   Take thy command!
  Roll them back! (3x)
  Set all free! (3x)
  Reverse the tide! (3x)

(*Repeat this section 3, 12 or 36 times.)

Replace it all by the glorious principles of God-freedom, of cosmic liberty for the expansion of the Christ flame in every heart and for the mighty plan of freedom for this age from the heart of beloved Saint Germain!

Unite the people in liberty! (3x)
By God's own love now set them free! (3x)
Unite the Earth and keep it free (3x)
By each one's I AM victory! (3x)
   Expose the Truth! (12x)
   Expose the lie! (12x)

And in full faith I consciously accept this manifest, manifest, manifest! (3x) right here and now with full power, eternally sustained, all-powerfully active, ever expanding and world enfolding until all are wholly ascended in the Light and free!

Beloved I AM! Beloved I AM! Beloved I AM!

———————

The following decree invokes the Ascended Masters who represent the Twelve Solar Hierarchies to this planet (listed in section A) to assist us in embodying the twelve God-qualities (section B) and overcoming the negative perversions of each of these qualities (section C). Diagrams of the twelve God-qualities and the Twelve Solar Hierarchies may be found on page 225 of this book. Further information about them may be found in the book *Predict Your Future*, by Elizabeth Clare Prophet.

Round the Clock Protection

In the name of the beloved mighty victorious Presence of God, I AM in me, Holy Christ Selves of all mankind, all great powers and legions of Light,

A (12) Beloved Great Divine Director and the seven Archangels
  (1) Beloved Saint Germain and the angelic hosts of Light
  (2) Beloved Jesus and the great hosts of Ascended Masters
  (3) Beloved Helios and the Great Central Sun Magnet
  (4) Beloved God Obedience and the seven mighty Elohim
  (5) Beloved El Morya and the legions of Mercury
  (6) Beloved Serapis Bey and the great Seraphim and Cherubim
  (7) Beloved Goddess of Liberty and the Lords of Karma
  (8) Beloved Lord Lanto and the Lords of Wisdom
  (9) Beloved Mighty Victory and the Lords of Individuality
  (10) Beloved Mighty Cyclopea and the Lords of Form
  (11) Beloved Lord Maitreya and the Lords of Mind

Beloved Lanello, the entire Spirit of the Great White Brotherhood and the World Mother, elemental life—fire, air, water and earth! I decree: Seize, bind and lock! Seize, bind and lock! Seize, bind and lock!

B (12) all criticism, condemnation and judgment and all black magic
  (1) all hatred and mild dislike and all witchcraft
  (2) all doubt, fear, human questioning and records of death
  (3) all conceit, deceit, arrogance and ego
  (4) all disobedience, stubbornness and defiance of the Law
  (5) all envy, jealousy and ignorance of the Law
  (6) all indecision, self-pity and self-justification
  (7) all ingratitude, thoughtlessness and spiritual blindness
  (8) all injustice, frustration and anxiety

(9) all dishonesty, intrigue and treachery

(10) all selfishness, self-love and idolatry

(11) all resentment, revenge and retaliation

and all that is not of the Light into mighty Astrea's cosmic circle and sword of blue flame of a thousand suns, and lock your cosmic circles and swords of blue flame of thousands of suns from the Great Central Sun and blaze megatons of cosmic Light, blue-lightning rays, and violet fire in, through and around all that opposes or attempts to interfere with the fulfillment of

C (12) my God-power and my divine plan fulfilled in all cycles

(1) my God-love and my divine plan fulfilled in all cycles

(2) my God-mastery and my divine plan fulfilled in all cycles

(3) my God-control and my divine plan fulfilled in all cycles

(4) my God-obedience and my divine plan fulfilled in all cycles

(5) my God-wisdom and my divine plan fulfilled in all cycles

(6) my God-harmony and my divine plan fulfilled in all cycles

(7) my God-gratitude and my divine plan fulfilled in all cycles

(8) my God-justice and my divine plan fulfilled in all cycles

(9) my God-reality and my divine plan fulfilled in all cycles

(10) my God-vision and my divine plan fulfilled in all cycles

(11) my God-victory and my divine plan fulfilled in all cycles

and my victory in the Light this day and forever.

And in full faith ...

Note: The decree may be given one of four ways: (1) Following the preamble, give sections A, B and C straight through, ending with the closing; (2) give the decree twelve times, using one insert each time from sections A, B and C, beginning with number 12; (3) give the trines on lines 12, 4, 8; 1, 5, 9; 2, 6, 10; 3, 7, 11, in sections A, B, and C; or (4) give the crosses on lines 12, 3, 6, 9; 1, 4, 7, 10; 2, 5, 8, 11, in sections A, B and C.

Chapter 4

The Summit

And he carried me away in the spirit to a great and high mountain, and shewed me that great city, the holy Jerusalem, descending out of heaven from God.

REVELATION

And it shall come to pass in the last days, that the mountain of the LORD's house shall be established in the top of the mountains, and shall be exalted above the hills; and all nations shall flow unto it.

And many people shall go and say, Come ye, and let us go up to the mountain of the LORD, to the house of the God of Jacob; and he will teach us of his ways, and we will walk in his paths: for out of Zion shall go forth the Law, and the Word of the LORD from Jerusalem.

ISAIAH

# The Summit

F OR THOUSANDS OF YEARS, humanity has been blessed with countless visitations of highly evolved souls—Avatars, Christs and Cosmic Beings. Angels have indeed walked with men. Truly God has sent his Son, his Light, his radiance to the Earth in every generation. Yet, for the most part, as the apostle John so aptly phrased it, the Light shone in the darkness, and the darkness comprehended it not.[1]

A Ray of Hope

In this age of self-sufficient technology, orthodox theology and all-embracing materialism, when the forces of Darkness threaten to utterly destroy civilization, God has seen fit once again to send a ray of hope to a darkened world. In August of 1958, the Darjeeling Council of the Great White Brotherhood endorsed the plan of the Ascended Master El Morya to found The Summit Lighthouse, and the Karmic Board granted the necessary dispensation for its formation. That month, the first *Pearl of Wisdom* was published in Washington, D.C.

Pearls of Wisdom are weekly releases of Ascended Master instruction. They are released under the direction of the Ascended Masters through the Darjeeling Council of the Great White Brotherhood. Concerning these releases, El Morya has said: "Our ideas are born within the flaming heart of Truth itself; and fortunate is every one of you who can share in the glorious karma of producing the perfection that we shall externalize through you—if you care willingly and lovingly to serve this cause in the name and by the authority of divine love itself."[2]

Master Morya, founder of The Summit Lighthouse, is Lord of the First Ray and Chief of the Darjeeling Council. Through many embodiments he was a dedicated servant of the Light. He was the son of Enoch who "was translated that he should not see death."[3] Morya was a seer who penetrated into the higher octaves of Light in the ancient land of Ur of the Chaldees; he was a Persian who worshipped the One God, *Ahura Mazda.* In these and other embodiments, he became increasingly aware of the spiritual power flowing through man, and he learned to experiment with these divine electricities. Later he mastered the constructive use of fohat, the electric power of cosmic consciousness, which, when called into action by divine fiat, will accelerate the evolution of a universe, of a galactic or solar system, or even of a human being, bringing to it its divine completion. The science of fohat is only given to the highest initiates, because it can be used to destroy as well as to create life.

It is well for us to acquaint ourselves with the founder of The Summit Lighthouse, for through many embodiments, El Morya has prepared to sponsor this world movement. And in his dedication and his life pattern, we come to understand the meaning and purpose that are embraced in the concept of The Summit Lighthouse.

Embodiments of Service

El Morya was embodied as Abraham, the ancient patriarch who emerged from Ur of the Chaldees to become the prototype and progenitor of the twelve tribes of Israel. Jews, Christians and Moslems accord him the place in history as the first to worship the one true God.

Returning as Melchior, one of the three wise men of the East, he followed the star that portended the birth of the best of his seed, who would fulfill all the promises of God unto his spiritual descendants. The Master has said, "Long ago, when my name was known as Melchior and I came with Kuthumi and Djwal Kul as one of the wise men of the East, as I came riding upon a camel to lay my offering at the feet of the Christ, I knew then that one day I should be devoted to the service of God's will. And so, beholding his Son as the epitome of good will, I journeyed to him with heart full of love to plight to him my hand and heart and head in the divine dimension. I pledged it all to the young babe, and I remembered and recalled the will of God as it manifested in the angelic ministrants' song coming through the heavens with paeans of praise to God: 'Glory to God in the highest.' "[4]

Morya was later King Arthur, who drew together his Knights of the Round Table as a nucleus of brotherhood under the Fatherhood of God, dedicated to the Christ and the search for the Holy Grail. While he wore the crown, unity, order and peace prevailed in England.

As Sir Thomas More (1478–1535), the Master served as Lord Chancellor of England under King Henry VIII. He discharged his duties wisely and well, but was beheaded because he failed to support the king in his departure from the laws of the Church regarding his marriage to Ann Boleyn. He was beatified by the Roman Catholic Church in 1886 and canonized in 1935. More's most famous work, *Utopia,* is an attempt to depict an ideal society, one in which men live in harmony under the holy will of the Most High God.

El Morya reembodied as Akbar (1542–1605), the greatest of the Mogul emperors of India. Akbar demonstrated a genius for administration and an appreciation of the good in all religions.

The Master was also the Irish poet Thomas Moore (1779–1852), many of whose songs are still favorites. In writing so movingly about the ancient glories and wrongs of his native Ireland, Moore did his country a great service.[5]

El Morya's Dream

El Morya is first and foremost a statesman of the highest order. As the representative of God's will, he has served since his ascension in 1898 to guide the governments of the nations from his retreat in Darjeeling. He wore the crown of authority in numerous lifetimes, exacting obedience not to his human will, but to the will of God. He considers government to be *God over men* and true statesmen to be *God's overmen.*

For this reason, through the Theosophical movement in the latter part of the nineteenth century, he sought to acquaint mankind with a broader understanding of the Reality of God, of the Ascended Masters and of the assurance of "Life everlasting" for all who would respond to God's will. He sought to encourage universal brotherhood, an interest in and cooperation among different religions and wide study of the latent divine powers in man.

Now, as an Ascended Being, he honors the Christ in all men and invites the Ascended Hosts and the spiritually elect among unascended mankind to attend in their finer bodies his council meetings at his retreat, the Temple of God's Holy Will in Darjeeling. There, seated about the fireside of their gracious host, these seek to foster God-government, good will and universal brotherhood among mankind.

After centuries of service to the will of God, El Morya saw what great spiritual power could be utilized for the salvation of the planet if all of mankind's energies were focused in the worship of the One God. And he nurtured a dream in his heart. That dream was to gather lifestreams from many spiritual endeavors and to offer them the opportunity of channeling their own Christ Light into one great fountain of spiritual effusion—a lighthouse whose powerful beams would sweep over the dark sea of humanity as a beacon light of eternal hope—until unity replaced diversity and the transcendent understanding of the One LORD who is all love would be known throughout the earth, until the Golden Age would blossom with God-happiness and the Ascended Ones would walk and talk with men as in ages gone by. That dream of the ages has been realized in the formation and continuing expansion of The Summit Lighthouse activity.

The Master Contacts His Messengers

When the Master contacted us, we offered ourselves to the service of God, conscious that it is "not by might. nor by power, but by my spirit, saith the LORD of Hosts"[6] and hoping that he would use us to lift the burden of the world, to foster understanding between peoples, to spread the illumination of Truth and to educate mankind in the mysteries of the Great Law.

Both of us had been under the tutelage of Master Morya since childhood, but it was Mark who established The Summit in 1958. Elizabeth was called in 1961 to assist the expansion of the activity as co-Messenger. El Morya said that our service would involve a lifetime of associated endeavor, and therefore we were married with his blessing in 1963. When The Summit Lighthouse was incorporated later that year, the Master named Mark as Chairman of the Board and Elizabeth as President. He vested us with his authority as twin rays, in order that the fullness of his plan might manifest in the balanced action of the Masculine and Feminine Rays.

Although we recognized the achievements of the established religions and their contributions to civilization, we also realized the limitations inherent in the existing structures. We appreciated all of God's revelation to man, but we realized that his revelation must of necessity be progressive. We saw the workings of divine Law in the churches, yet we also perceived therein the blocks to free thought. To be sure, the Masters' Teachings could not be disseminated through existing channels; for to some the Masters' work poses a threat to established dogma, and instead of longing for some new insight from the throne of God, they proceed with fear to defend the bastions of their faith, which have now become prison walls.

As we discussed this "closed door" policy with the Masters, we were reminded of the words spoken by the Pilgrim minister John Robinson before the Pilgrims embarked on that memorable journey to the New World: "The Lord has more truth yet to break forth out of His holy Word.... If God shall reveal anything to you by any other Instrument of his, be as ready to receive it as ever you were to receive any truth by my Ministry.... I beseech you remember it is an article of faith of your church covenant, that you be ready to receive whatever truth shall be made known to you."[7]

Fostering Spiritual Understanding

On October 14, 1967, Archangel Jophiel gave the reason for the founding of The Summit Lighthouse from the standpoint of the evolution of spiritual understanding on the planet:

"The great cosmic Reality of the Wisdom Teachers is not yet in full bloom before the eyes of mankind because there are many people on this planetary body who have never even heard of the Ascended Master Jesus the Christ.... How, then, can men who are concerned with the link to Cosmic Hierarchy expect for one moment that mankind, who know not the Reality of Jesus the Christ, will know about the Archangels or about the angelic hosts or about the Ascended Masters? Today, only a few in America, by a relative sense, are able to have a composite picture of the Great White Brotherhood.

"When Madame Helena Petrovna Blavatsky in 1875 revealed the Ascended Masters of Wisdom through the Theosophical Order, it was a nova bursting upon the metaphysical sky.... The founders continued to work for world enlightenment and to pour out an increasing measure of Teachings and techniques blessed by the Hierarchy of Light. As a countermeasure, the brothers of the shadow released other information as a sham manifestation, a pseudoactivity designed to pull men away from the great Mother lodestone manifest in the Divine Theosophia....

"The Ascended Masters have found it expedient through the years to create new activities of Light and to endow them with specific functions in the name of holy progress. I shall explain:

"On the planetary body individuals of a very devout nature, when they become attached to a specific segment of holy instruction from 'on high,' are often concerned with the enormous responsibility involved in keeping pure the Teachings that are vouchsafed to them. Therefore, in their desire to do just that, they close themselves off and they deny to their followers the right to alter or to change the power structure, the revelatory structure and the messianic message in any way from its original dispensation.

"The Brothers of Wisdom are of the opinion that there is much wisdom in this action. However, because of the rigid (i.e., orthodox) stand that is taken by the followers of a specific movement, from time to time it becomes expedient, in order to break the old matrices of thought and feeling, that a new activity of Light should be launched so that the Ascended Masters may take by the hand and head those avant-garde individuals who are willing to be God-taught in every age, who are willing to behold the great onrush of Cosmic Reality as it parades across the sky of their minds, infusing them with ever-new flashes of intuitive intelligence and teaching them spiritual techniques destined in the future to give to the children of the coming race a new glimpse of Divine Reality.

"This, then, is the reason why in 1958 The Summit Lighthouse activity was endowed by the Cosmic Hierarchy with the right to function, ordained by God, so that Messengers, two in number, should go forth and proclaim to the world (because of their previous training in connection with the great temple at Tell el-Amarna[8]) the manifestation of the monotheistic technique of the Ascended Masters under the rule of the cosmic panoply, or Hierarchy of Masters, teaching both the Law of the One and its corollary in the law of the many manifestations emanating from the One.

"For it must always be remembered that as God is One, this God that is One has seen fit in his greater holy wisdom to extend himself forth in a manifestation of the many, and therefore to mankind is given the opportunity to be brought into captivity to Divine Love whereby the love they bear within themselves for the Divine does capture their whole hearts and cause them to welcome with open arms the ministering love and service, the holy wisdom that descends from on high.

"Thus are men drawn out of the mass sea of miasma and human emotion and raised up to a place where they can clasp to their hearts and minds holy Truth and understand its role in freeing them from the shadow of the present age."[9]

We Stand for Truth

We wish to make clear that The Summit Lighthouse is by no means a by-product of or a protest movement to any previous religious organization. If its teachings are similar to those of other groups, it is only because these also reflect Truth. The Summit Lighthouse stands upon the Truth that has been revealed through prophets and Teachers of all ages. We follow the saints and sages of all religions insofar as they themselves embrace Truth. There is, then, no outer connection between The Summit Lighthouse and any other movement or organization; but there is a definite inner connection between The Summit Lighthouse and the age-old activities of the Great White Brotherhood.

Many have asked whether The Summit Lighthouse is Christian. It is Christian in the truest sense of the word, for our Christianity is founded on the Rock of Ages, the Christ who overcame the world and who "shall so come in a like manner as ye have seen him go."[10] It is founded on the original Teachings of Jesus, not on the narrow dogma that men have made of them.

Just as The Summit Lighthouse is broad in its acceptance of Truth as it has been revealed through prophets in all religions, and just as it is tolerant in its outreach to all of God's children upon Earth, so it is narrow in its adherence to the spectrum of pure Truth that unfolds the Laws of God. Jesus said, "strait is the gate, and narrow is the way, which leadeth unto life."[11] We are willing to follow the lonely road that departs the highway of well-traveled religious thought and leads to the spiritual heights of Christ-regeneration.

Our activity is called The Summit Lighthouse because it is destined to be a beacon light in the history of the evolution of man's religious thinking. The Summit is dedicated to expanding the Light of God among mankind, and the truth it expands must be Truth without compromise. Jesus said, "Ye are the light of the world. A city that is set on a hill cannot be hid."[12]

Firmly established upon the rock of the Christ, the Lighthouse beams to the stormy sea of human struggle the message, "Peace, be still."[13] The Light from the tower is a beacon of hope to a troubled world that yet looks without for a luminary in the social or intellectual sky. It is the Light of the Christ that says, "The Light that ye seek is ever the Light that is in thee."

The standard of Truth must be upheld and the true Teachings of the Christ must be proclaimed. Only the whole Truth will set men free. Therefore, we strive to uphold the standard of excellence, to be The Summit Lighthouse, to lead every man into communion with his own Christ Self.

Only then can he become a Lighthouse himself—a veritable house of Light; only then can he find the Summit of his own Being—the Presence of God within him. The God Presence in man is a tower of strength, a pillar in the temple of Being. His Causal Body is a guiding Light for everyone who would follow the star to the place where the Christ is cradled in his own conscious individuality.

> Let us then be up and doing,
> Holding consort with the few.
> By election, now we're viewing
> All that God was wont to do.

By his Light our souls are nourished;
Our delight is in his Law.
Let his kingdom, then, now flourish—
Fill the hearts of men with awe.

Reverence, love and honor shew forth—
We will do it, in God's name.
By the fire of heaven's Spirit
Let us all now keep his flame.

Hold it high, aloft to vision;
Let all see and know precision.
Capture, then, his plan for fusion—
'Tis the end of all confusion.

By the Light of oneness showing,
Winds of delusion long now blowing
Will be stilled by Light now showing
All the way—O peace, be still.

Take Him by the hand and hold it;
Ne'er let go, our Father dear,
Thy great love within us glowing—
Perfect love casts out all fear.

Rectify and purify the world of men;
By the flame of Truth impart
Perseverance from beginning—
Start it now within each heart.

Move it forward by thy power,
Let its Light forever shine;
Beam it forth, reveal the flower*
Heaven-sent by hand divine.

---

* The threefold flame is the "divine spark," also called the Christ flame and
the liberty flame. It is literally a spark of sacred fire from God's own heart,
your soul's point of contact with the supreme Source of all Life. Its three
plumes embody the three primary attributes of God: blue, God's power,
Father; yellow, God's wisdom, the Son; and pink, God's love, the Holy Spirit.

Goals of The Summit Lighthouse

The goals the Masters have proposed for The Summit are many. These include the preparation of the Christ children, the Buddhas and the incoming Avatars for their mission and for the initiations leading to their ascension, as well as the preparation of all who are willing to undergo the rigors of initiation prescribed by the Hierarchy for acceptance into the Ascension Temple—either at the close of this embodiment or while the body is in sleep. Through the Teachings of the Masters published by The Summit Lighthouse, the requirements for the ascension will be made so plain that the Queen of Light's prophecy of mass ascensions from the hillsides will one day become a Reality.[14]

We must establish educational programs for all age levels from preschool to the university level—where parents will be taught to nurture the Christ in their children and in themselves, and where young people will be taught about the Christ and his Teachings on cosmic law.

We must sponsor the music of the spheres, which carries the matrix for the Golden Age. We must prepare the training of parents and teachers who will sponsor the seventh root race, and we must preserve the link with Hierarchy for coming generations. The Summit must leave a written record for those who have not been quickened by the Spirit, that they might find Truth in future embodiments.

Finally, the foundation must be laid for the Golden Age, setting forth the Teachings of the Brotherhood and writing the sacred scriptures for the next two-thousand-year cycle. We must write the Everlasting Gospel of God,[15] of which this series is the first chapter.

The Summit is an activity that promotes self-purification, self-mastery, preparation for the ascension and continual progression into greater Light and greater attunement with the

Presence. Through this activity, the Masters are constantly engaged in the recovery of the "Lost Word," in the regeneration of millions of lifestreams, and in the removal of subconscious barriers through the power of the sacred fire.

If some of our methods have been noted by other organizations, it is because at various times in history, the Hierarchy, through one or more prophets, has inspired mankind with certain knowledge. El Morya has told us that after a prophet passes from the screen of life, his followers often take license with his words and the Truth becomes distorted. Morya explained, "Consequently, from time to time we find it necessary, in adhering to the plumb line of principle, to reform the old in the miracle of newness and to empower individuals to go forth to form either a new religion or a new approach to thought." He said, "Truly, Truth is one, and all of God's Laws must of necessity adhere to the one."

It is possible to rephrase old Truths, cloaking them with the freshness of a new perspective. The Master reiterated, "Our goals are the salvation of the planet, the freedom of man and the perpetual joy of God that can be made known to all." He said, "There is a great treasury of wisdom concerning God's infinite Laws that has not yet been released unto mankind.

"However, for us to release the superstructure of the building without putting it upon a sound foundation would not be an orderly process. There must be relevance. Therefore, you must build upon the foundation of Truth that has already been revealed to the prophets of old and continue with the knowledge that we will unfold through you."

The Law of the I AM

The Master then proceeded to reveal to us the Law of the I AM. He said that the I AM Law is the highest and oldest

Law in creation. It was first affirmed in recorded history by Moses, who heard God say out of the burning bush, "I AM THAT I AM."[16]

El Morya told us that it is the Being of God that constitutes the Image of God, and inasmuch as man is made in the Divine Image, that Image is his sole Reality. God is the Word, and the Word is the Christ, and this Word, by whom all things were made,[17] went forth as the power of the I AM who said, "I AM the way, the truth and the life," and "I AM the resurrection and the life."[18]

The Master also reminded us that our Chart of Your Divine Self (facing page 12) could never convey to mankind any more than a symbol of the infinite Causal Body of man with its concentric spheres of color.

He said that the Chart should include a representation of the Christ Self (or Higher Mental Body) because man now lives in a time when the Second Coming of Christ may be seen as the Lord coming suddenly into his temple with the rush of a mighty wind.[19] God will claim the temple of man's being as the power of the Higher Mental Body and the Holy Paraclete (or Holy Spirit) enter the chalice, the body and being of man.

Because the dark and divisive forces work continually against the Law of the One—the law of man's being and his link with eternity—many attempts have been made to discredit those who in every age have stood for the principle of the I AM. However, inasmuch as I AM is the name of God, every man, woman and child upon Earth has the right to rejoice in it, to live in it and to change the world by it until the world reflects the splendor that is already within the Mind of God— as Above, so below.

The Summit as an Avenue
of the Great White Brotherhood

El Morya said, "Those who know the meaning of real love understand that the Great White Brotherhood has many avenues through which to express its many beautiful activities and refuses in the holy name of freedom and liberty to be limited in its approach to planetary assistance by mere human ideas of the self-styled elect!"

He continued, "As I have intimated before, the Brotherhood has only within the past few months and years begun to externalize through The Summit Lighthouse some of our most helpful ideas and plans for humanity. Our great hope is to create a haven of such Light that no human quality can ever enter in or abide.

"Wise men will understand its 'live and let live' policy as being of our making. They will not foolishly deem its attitude Pollyanna or weak, seeing rather that in unity with God, Truth and the Ascended Masters' way, there is strength victorious! As a potent, expanding facet of the Brotherhood, The Summit Lighthouse is one of our greatest avenues."[20]

Later Morya also said, "Understandable is it that each organization demands some form of loyalty of its adherents, but unfortunately 'all or nothing at all' seems to be the requirement of many religious orders. Only your mighty I AM Presence has the right to ask all of any part of Life.

"Loyalty to Truth, to your friends and to high standards or principles is good, but no one should ever permit himself to be dominated or controlled by any person, place, condition or thing except the Ascended Masters and their own God Presence I AM. Yet, of course, those of like mind should ever be willing to lovingly assist one another in effecting the many aspects of the eternal purposes.

"It does not appear to be clear to many people that the Ascended Masters and the Great White Brotherhood often have ordained or directed individuals in the past—even assisting them in forming an organization or group through which the Masters and the Brotherhood could disseminate information and render a profound service—and then find that at a later date the control of these same groups or organizations was wrested away from the Masters and the Brotherhood while the activity degenerated into a mere outer husk or shell of its former self. One thing that has made this particularly confusing is the fact that often these religious orders or philosophical groups continue to grow or prosper outwardly, still disseminating many of the Truths of the Great Ones.

"The key to all of this, dear hearts, lies in the free will that unascended beings have to choose what they will do. No Master or Brotherhood—even the greatest of all—has the cosmic right to hold control over individuals unless they are requested by them to do so!...

"I want to particularly point out that I do not want to seem an alarmist in issuing this information: on the other hand, I do feel it is good to discuss these aspects of Truth with the student body in order to keep them informed and under God-guard at all times. Whatever harmonizes and produces peace with dignity and Truth is of God; whatever divides for selfish intent is of deceit! I am confident the true-hearted chela will recognize the need to have an honest heart full of love for all—yet still be unafraid to make decisions for the Light's sake."[21]

Lord Lanto, Chohan of the Second Ray, explained: "Because this activity is builded so solidly upon the rock, I, Lanto, declare in wisdom's name, it shall stand to fulfill El Morya's dream, and those who have aided it shall be so grateful one day that they did, as they see just why Utopia did come into manifestation because of their cooperation, constancy and determination to *be* Christs in action."[22]

Weekly Outpouring of Wisdom

The Masters are making available the wisdom of the ages through the *Pearls of Wisdom*. Those who receive these releases from the Masters are bound by no rules of conduct or statement of faith. They are asked only to assist with the nominal publication and mailing costs. On November 10, 1959, El Morya said:

"Knowing that faith and harmony are ever a part of the Light and that The Summit Lighthouse asks no special fealty or allegiance other than your love for deeper contact with us, I trust that all of you who love the Truth of which I speak will continue to enjoy the *Pearls of Wisdom* for a long time to come until in God's memory-record of Light you become illustrious and in manifestation self-luminous. Then, as one of us, you will need no other 'thread of contact,' having attained the glory of full reunion for which you ever and always seek.

"The continuing support you give to the physical activity of The Summit Lighthouse in the future will, as it did in the past, make possible my continuing allotment of spiritual energy in the weekly releases of the *Pearls of Wisdom*. You see, we cannot give it all—the cosmic law decrees that part must come from your side of the veil. Whatever you do, do in goodwill; for in God one is indeed never alone, but all One!"[23]

Keepers of the Flame

On January 31, 1961, the Master authorized the formation of a specially dedicated group within The Summit Lighthouse called the Keepers of the Flame Fraternity. He said, "Class lessons are to be offered to the members of the Keepers of the Flame group.... Regardless of one's station, all those interested in both basic and advanced instruction ought to enroll in this dedicated group of servers for many reasons. A word to the wise is sufficient."[24] The members of this universal spiritual order have vowed to keep the Flame of Life blazing upon the hearts' altars of all mankind, to be their brothers' keepers[25] and to keep in mind and heart all that the Father has given into heart, head and hand for his glory and the swift externalization of his kingdom upon Earth.

It was the Ascended Master Saint Germain who, as Knight Commander, sponsored the organization of this group. In his *Pearl of Wisdom* dated September 17, 1967, he said:

"In this day and age we have entrusted the Teachings to no one man, but we have given finite portions of the Infinite, segments of Reality, to the planet as cosmic cipher, which the heart, when purified in any man, can readily decipher. In the *Pearls of Wisdom*, the Keepers of the Flame Lessons and other expressions that comprise the Teachings of The Summit Lighthouse, we have sought to integrate the wholeness of all genuine uplift movements that have ever existed upon the planet.

"Ours is the intent, as God wills it—if man wills it, too, and serves with God—to elucidate through the Keepers of the Flame Lessons such standards of elder beauty as have never before been known and experienced upon this planet. The day will come when those souls who are privileged to receive these communications will esteem them as the golden illumined Light of the hand of heaven reaching into the individual heart and saying, 'Know God, know thyself, know the law of thy being.'

"As never before we hope to open the ancient books—even the books of the Ancient of Days—to reveal that which has been kept secret since the foundation of the world....

"There is so much that is hidden, waiting to be revealed, that we can scarcely contain ourselves as we work under higher guidance to raise the consciousness of the aspirant toward the Light and away from the shadows that life has sought to impose upon him.... The sunlight of God's love is the sunlight of God's freedom. Into the dimensionless, limitless world of the Spirit, man must come, bearing in his hand the cup of his desire for God's wonderful revelation, for God's wonderful work to be made known unto him."[26]

Master Morya's statement of policy concerning the Fraternity could well serve as the cornerstone for The Summit Lighthouse organization:

"Knowing the pain of uncertainty, the travails possible to humanity and the hope of escape within the hearts of men, I pledge to leave no stone unturned to make the Teachings and services of the Keepers of the Flame Fraternity representative of the highest offering of the Great White Brotherhood and the sons of heaven.

"The Keepers of the Flame Fraternity and the Golden Age Teachings brought forth in these lessons are builded on the one foundation that many spiritual leaders have claimed as their own and to which, I am certain, by creative effort and divine attunement many have added beauty.

"Keepers of the Flame shall strive to use the eternal Light and Truth, expressed so ably in the past by great teachers and prophets, as stepping-stones today into greater spiritual progress, knowing with supreme certainty that much yet remains to be revealed to mankind.

"We, the Spiritual Board of Directors [of the Fraternity],[27] with the assistance of the entire Spirit of the Great White Brotherhood, do ordain and dedicate the Keepers of the Flame Lessons as an official channel that shall serve to further enlighten mankind and to vanquish ignorance by the Light and power of the God flame. The sacred knowledge of the flame that we are pledged to release in these lessons will provide a safe platform for ascending souls—one that is so well lighted that none who examine it with an objective heart need ever hesitate to cross the threshold into Life and Truth.

"The worth of this activity is in the completed structure, which is designed from its conception to hold the flames of Truth and freedom in constant view. For we who serve you from higher planes know that only the radiance of the eternal Logos can deliver the Earth into the breathing awareness of God that sustains peace, frees from every bondage and is the true knowing that at last brings eternal happiness to all."[28]

Members of the Keepers of the Flame Fraternity are free to retain membership in the church of their choice while belonging to the Fraternity. El Morya says:

"Men and women, then, of every faith or national origin: We appeal to you to see here an opportunity to express the highest tenets of your faith itself—which, if it exists at all, must be within your hearts—and therefore, the end result of peace and victory that we hope to obtain shall not come about alone because of either personality or organization, but because of the response of men's hearts! Do you see?

"The Summit Lighthouse itself *is* The Summit Lighthouse because it elects to stand for the highest and best in all men, in people of every faith and nation, for the purest victory for the Earth and her people. We intend not only the highest and best spiritually for all, but the release through this doorway of the finest and best educational material for all, which will help men to live in happiness and harmony forevermore."[29]

The Need for Expansion

Morya has also told us that "there is an ever-increasing need for expansion of the Ascended Masters' Teaching in opposition to all anti-Christ distortions and errors, and it was with this end in view that we secured the permission from Helios and Vesta and the Great Karmic Board to originally create The Summit Lighthouse[30]—not in order to necessarily absorb religions or ideologies, but rather to serve as a cosmic springboard where the forte of Truth would be expanded and expounded our way, free from commercialization or exploitation by the ego, and wherein the many thirsty travelers would find such refreshment of the Spirit in godly simplicity that a general expansion of divine world good would ensue quite naturally!"[31]

Lanto has expressed the concern of the Brotherhood over the fact that there is little they can do in times of world crisis because the Masters can answer only when called upon. He says:

"The key to it all lies in the expansion in the world of form of the knowledge about the Brothers of Light, about the Spiritual Hierarchy, about the Ascended Masters, about the natural unfoldment of the individual through his own I AM Presence.

"Unless this be done, the world will not suddenly turn to the Light. It has never been enough simply to produce great Lights in the world. Some of these go down in the halls of fame and are remembered in the annals of every age. But deeds are more important than names, and the face of pure Truth is more important than speaking about it.

"We urge upon those of you today with whom we have contact to understand that all of the glory that is held focused in all of our retreats in the world has little meaning for embodied mankind unless we can accomplish in your time one of two things: either (1) the broad expansion of the knowledge of our work, or (2) the laying of a foundation for that work to be expanded in succeeding generations."[32]

Outer Focuses of the Activity

In earlier years, The Summit Lighthouse activity maintained two focuses—one in Colorado Springs, Colorado, and one in Santa Barbara, California. The Masters selected the Santa Barbara location for several reasons. They intended not only to forestall the possibility of a West Coast cataclysm, but also to establish a point of Light between the vortices of negation in San Francisco and Los Angeles. Furthermore, there is an ancient focus of Lemuria in the hills above Santa Barbara, the radiance of which extends from the Aleutian chain to the southern tip of South America.[33]

In December 1975, Jesus directed that The Summit Lighthouse move to Los Angeles, the City of the Angels, and in 1976, the headquarters was moved to a leased campus in Pasadena, California. In 1977, the organization purchased from the Claretian Fathers the beautiful 218-acre Gillette estate in the Santa Monica Mountains near Malibu and named it Camelot. It served as international headquarters through 1986.

On January 14, 1979, Archangel Gabriel announced Mission Amethyst Jewel for the gathering of disciples to keep the Flame in their cities. Responding to Gabriel's call, Keepers of the Flame established new Study Groups and Teaching Centers around the world.

In September 1981, The Summit Lighthouse purchased the Royal Teton Ranch, bordering Yellowstone National Park in Montana. Camelot was sold in 1986 and the headquarters was moved to this property in Montana, which the Masters have called the Inner Retreat.

Djwal Kul gave a prophecy of the Inner Retreat in 1920. He spoke of a preparatory school close to but outside a large city and by the sea,* and then the Inner Retreat in the high mountains for initiates, far from the crowded places of the Earth. He said, "The sea or expanse of water close to a preparatory school will convey to [the student's] mind a constant reminder of the purification which is his paramount work, whilst the mountains will imbue the advanced student with cosmic strength and will hold steadily before him the thought of the mount of initiation, which he aims soon to tread."

A year before the property for the Inner Retreat was secured, the Goddess of Liberty spoke of some of the purposes it would fulfill: "We would see that Inner Retreat manifest and with all deliberate haste—paced, of course, to the rhythm always of the heartbeat of Saint Germain.

"We would see you come together in a greater under-standing of the true meaning of home and in all of those necessities of life that bring out the potential, the indepen-dence, the pioneer spirit.

"You are all pioneers from the Great God Star. And at this conclusion of an age, simultaneously with the dawn of another, it is the arcing of the Light of Sirius that is become your principal assignment, that the Great White Brotherhood and its God-government in the galaxies might have that physical focus that is necessary in order for those Beings of Light as well as the divine plan of God to manifest in the Earth.

"From century to century, emissaries of Sirius, sons of

---

* The prophecy of the center by the sea was fulfilled in Camelot, which was just outside Los Angeles and inland from the beaches of Malibu.

God, have sought to establish the nucleus of Light that would anchor that certain elevation of Light that is a certain key from the God Star in the very physical Earth itself. From time to time these have succeeded, but usually only temporarily.

"Thus with the going out of the Light of the nucleus of the God Star itself, there have come periods of darkness and misapplication of the Law, followed by chaos and old night and deterioration. Thus desolations, as the cold winds crossing the desert, have in their own time and space made the human consciousness itself a wasteland devoid of the cosmic connection with the God Star.

"Thus we plan ahead. Thus we come to inform you that the Great White Brotherhood, Surya, the Lords of Karma and the sponsoring Hierarchy of your own souls are ready to accelerate a physical location for the Inner Retreat as well as your own souls' development into the understanding of our molecule of Light."[34]

Maitreya's Mystery School

In 1984, Jesus spoke of the dedication of the Royal Teton Ranch as the Mystery School of Lord Maitreya: "I come to the reason for being of our oneness in this Heart [of the Inner Retreat]. For we are sheltered in the heart of Lord Maitreya. And he desires me, as his pupil, to announce to you that he is dedicating this Heart of the Inner Retreat and this entire property as the Mystery School of Maitreya in this age....

"I would tell you of our great joy and of the meaning of the securing of this place for the Mystery School. You realize that the Mystery School of Maitreya was called the Garden of Eden.[35] All of the Ascended Masters' endeavors and the schools of the Himalayas of the centuries have been to the end that this might occur from the etheric octave unto the physical

The Heart of the Inner Retreat

—that the Mystery School might once again receive the souls of Light who have gone forth therefrom, now who are ready to return, to submit, to bend the knee before the Cosmic Christ—my own blessed Father, Guru, Teacher and Friend.

"Beloved hearts, the realization of this God-goal and the willingness of Maitreya to accept this activity and Messenger and students in sacred trust to keep the flame of the Mystery School does therefore gain for planet Earth and her evolutions a dispensation from the Hierarchies of the Central Sun. For, you see, when there is about to become physical through dispensation of the Cosmic Christ the renewal of the open door whereby souls—as students of Light who apprentice themselves to the Cosmic Christ—may come and go from the planes of earth to the planes of heaven and back again, this is the open door of the coming of the Golden Age. This is the open door of the pathway of East and West, of the Bodhisattvas and the disciples.

"This being so, the planetary body, therefore, has gained a

new status midst all of the planetary bodies, midst all of the evolutionary homes. For once again it may be said that Maitreya is physically present, not as it was in the first Eden but by the extension of ourselves in form through the Messenger and the Keepers of the Flame. And as you have been told, this mighty phenomenon of the ages does precede the stepping through the veil of the Ascended Masters—seeing face-to-face their students and their students beholding them.

"All of the Ascended Masters' dictations over the years have been to that end. And with the inauguration of the mission of Maitreya in this century and then again in this hour, you see that the momentum of all Ascended Masters' dictations gone before does increase the momentum of Light and the ability of some, and *not* a few upon Earth, to actually maintain an etheric consciousness.

"Though they may not be aware of it, their hearts and minds tend to gravitate to the etheric octaves so apparent in the higher altitude and in the mountains and the snowy, fiery energies of the coolness of the mountains. For this fire of coolness is a stimulant of the chakras. It is a stimulant of the mind. It creates an acceleration of fire merely by the change of temperature of the four lower bodies....

"See, then, that Maitreya truly is more physical today than ever before since the Garden of Eden. For his withdrawal into higher octaves was due to the betrayal of the fallen angels and the acts of the fallen angels against Adam and Eve and others who were a part of that Mystery School.

"Thus, the long scenario of the fallen angels and their devilish practices against the pure and the innocent have ensued. And one by one, each must come to the divine conclusion of the Return. Each one is accountable for leaving the Mystery School, and each one is responsible for his own return and his making use of that which is available and accessible as the divine Word.

"Thus, Maitreya is truly with us.... [And this is the] Mystery School of the Garden of Eden come again, marked by the sign of the pillar of fire, Old Faithful, and the name recalled in the naming of the *Paradise* Valley."[36]

On December 31, 1985, Lord Maitreya announced that his twin flame had come forth from nirvana (where she had been since the birth of Christ) to join him in "a mighty work for this age."[37] Maitreya also explained his role in the reuniting of twin flames who were with him in the Lemurian Mystery School. And he magnanimously invited all students of the Ascended Masters to apply to become his chelas. He said:

"The world is waiting for Maitreya and Maitreya's co-workers and servants. And they are also waiting for my twin flame, whom they know not. Thus, out of the octaves of nirvana she has descended in a golden orb of Light. And you will see how this Presence of my beloved will multiply my action in your behalf.

"Now see the great Teams of Conquerors. You have called to them. They are here! And if you see them not, watch how you will develop your spiritual senses by divorcing yourself from the world of drugs and sugar and marijuana and alcohol and nicotine.

"Beloved, I long to see you free, and we are determined! And the Presence, then, in this golden sphere of the Causal Body of Light of my beloved does arc the Presence of the Lady Master Venus in that Retreat of the Divine Mother unveiled over the Inner Retreat so that Camelot, in this City of the Angels of the Christ and the Buddha, shall have that ray and that Light of my divine counterpart.

"And you will know the Truth of Maitreya. And you will receive the initiations individually from my heart daily if you but inscribe a separate letter to me this New Year's Eve addressed to your mighty I AM Presence and Holy Christ Self, to me and to my beloved twin flame.

"Then, beloved, you may apply to become my chela, my initiate. And watch well, for I AM determined to accept almost as many who call upon me, rather to give you the initiations and let you eliminate yourselves than to eliminate you without giving you a clean white page ... to begin anew where you left off on Lemuria.

"And I tell you, you did leave me in Lemuria, and I come to claim you again! And you may determine to move forward, for I will bring you to that point of the union, whether inner or outer, of twin flames as only my office can accomplish. For it is my office that was violated by twin flames in the Garden of Eden, and therefore you who left the Path under my tutelage must receive that reuniting through me."[38]

The Masters have plans for other focuses throughout the world as a preview to the time when their etheric retreats[39] will once again have physical outposts open to the masses. When the schools of the Brotherhood begin to flourish in the outer world, as they did in past Golden Ages, then we know that our victory is drawing nigh.

Summit University

The first session of Summit University (originally known as Ascended Master University) was held in Santa Barbara, California in July of 1970. At the Freedom Class of that year, El Morya said: "This activity is going forward to become a Light to the youth of this nation, to show them the way out of their current dilemma ... through beautiful music, beautiful thoughtforms and beautiful service to God to once again open up the glory and Light of the everlasting hills....

"We are determined that this shall be the most beautiful

body of the elect that has ever been upon this planetary body, and we are anxious to extend the borders of the kingdom of that election to the whole wide world."[40]

In September 1973, the first full-time, twelve-week session of Summit University was held at the Motherhouse in Santa Barbara. Summit University soon outgrew the Motherhouse; it was held in Colorado Springs from fall 1975 through spring 1976, and then settled at the Nazarene campus in Pasadena until the organization moved to Camelot in 1978. Starting in 1988, Summit University convened at the Inner Retreat and is now held each year there and in locations around the world.*

Beams from the Lighthouse

The purpose of this Ascended Master activity is to unite the hearts of all mankind by raising their consciousness to the common level of the Christ. Without this elevation, there can be no unity; and those who attempt to impose such a unity will find that without the leaves of the true knowledge of the Law, the brotherhood of man will never be accomplished.

Those who share in the consciousness of the Christ and the knowledge of their divine Sonship are One; they embrace one another in the bonds of their Father-Mother God; they break bread together as they serve in the brotherhood of angels, elementals and men. The kingdoms of God in mystical union shall become the kingdoms of this world because men hope, because they do not fail to pray, and because they keep the vigil through the long night of human error until the dawn of universal spiritual understanding appears. And that will appear when those who have pledged at inner levels the service

---

* For information on future Summit University retreats and seminars, see www.tsl.org/Summit_University, or call 1-800-245-5445 (U.S.A.), +1 406-848-9500 (international).

of heart, head and hand find their destiny in the Truth that is the Summit of every man's being.

The Summit Lighthouse activity derives its authority from and is sponsored by the Great White Brotherhood. As long as it upholds the tenets of that Brotherhood to the best of its ability, the Brotherhood will, in this age, and we hope in many to come, use the arm of the Summit to uphold the torch of enlightenment unto man.

We conclude with Henry Wadsworth Longfellow's poem "The Lighthouse," which is much too prophetic to be omitted from this chapter on The Summit.

The Lighthouse

The rocky ledge runs far into the sea,
  And on its outer point, some miles away,
The Lighthouse lifts its massive masonry,
  A pillar of fire by night, of cloud by day.

Even at this distance I can see the tides,
  Upheaving, break unheard along its base,
A speechless wrath, that rises and subsides
  In the white lip and tremor of the face.

And as the evening darkens, lo! how bright,
  Through the deep purple of the twilight air,
Beams forth the sudden radiance of its light
  With strange, unearthly splendor in the glare!

Not one alone; from each projecting cape
  And perilous reef along the ocean's verge,
Starts into life a dim, gigantic shape,
  Holding its lantern o'er the restless surge.

Like the great giant Christopher* it stands
  Upon the brink of the tempestuous wave,
Wading far out among the rocks and sands,
  The night o'ertaken mariner to save.

And the great ships sail outward and return,
  Bending and bowing o'er the billowy swells,
And ever joyful, as they see it burn,
  They wave their silent welcomes and farewells.

They come forth from the darkness, and their sails
  Gleam for a moment only in the blaze,
And eager faces, as the light unveils,
  Gaze at the tower, and vanish while they gaze.

---

* Saint Christopher is the patron saint of travelers. He is known in legend for having borne the Christ Child safely across the waters of a swift stream.

The mariner remembers when a child,
　On his first voyage, he saw it fade and sink,
And when, returning from adventures wild,
　He saw it rise again o'er ocean's brink.

Steadfast, serene, immovable, the same
　Year after year, through all the silent night
Burns on forevermore that quenchless flame,
　Shines on that inextinguishable light!

It sees the ocean to its bosom clasp
　The rocks and sea-sand with the kiss of peace;
It sees the wild winds lift it in their grasp,
　And hold it up, and shake it like a fleece.

The startled waves leap over it; the storm
　Smites it with all the scourges of the rain,
And steadily against its solid form
　Press the great shoulders of the hurricane.

The sea-bird wheeling round it, with the din
　Of wings and winds and solitary cries,
Blinded and maddened by the light within,
　Dashes himself against the glare, and dies.

A new Prometheus, chained upon the rock,
　Still grasping in his hand the fire of Jove,
It does not hear the cry, nor heed the shock,
　But hails the mariner with words of love.

"Sail on!" it says, "sail on, ye stately ships!
　And with your floating bridge the ocean span;
Be mine to guard this light from all eclipse,
　Be yours to bring man nearer unto man!"

Notes

Books referenced here are published by Summit University Press unless otherwise noted.

Preface

1. Eph. 6:12.
2. Rev. 14:6.

Introduction

1. Phylos the Thibetan, *A Dweller on Two Planets* (Los Angeles: Borden Publishing Co., 1952) pp. 46, 47.
2. Gen. 6:11–13.
3. 1 John 4:4.
4. Joel 2:28–32.

Chapter 1 · Prayer, Decrees and Meditation

Opening quotations: Isa. 55:11; 45:11.

1. John 1:1–3.
2. Gen. 1:3.
3. John 11:25.
4. Phil. 2:5.
5. Phil. 2:6.
6. "And God said, Let us make man in our image..." (Gen. 1:26).
7. Phil. 2:6.
8. Matt. 12:37.
9. "All things were made by him; and without him was not any thing made that was made" (John 1:3).
10. Ps. 91:1, 2.
11. Exod. 3:13–15.
12. Gen. 4:26; 12:8; 26:25; Ps. 99:6; Joel 2:32; Acts 2:21; Rom. 10:12, 13.
13. Exod. 13:21, 22; Num. 14:14; Neh. 9:12, 19; Ps. 78:14.
14. Matt. 6:19, 20; John 14:2.
15. Matt. 6:21; Luke 12:34.
16. Rev. 10:1.
17. James 4:8.
18. Eccles. 12:6.
19. Rev. 22:1.
20. John 4:14.

21. Matt. 28:18.
22. Job 22:28.
23. El Morya, "Heart, Head and Hand Decrees," in Mark L. Prophet and Elizabeth Clare Prophet, *The Science of the Spoken Word,* p. 32.
24. Jesus and Kuthumi, *Prayer and Meditation.*
25. Mark L. Prophet and Elizabeth Clare Prophet, *The Science of the Spoken Word.*
26. Phil. 4:8.
27. Kuthumi, "Meditation upon the Rainbow of Light's Perfection," in *Prayer and Meditation,* pp. 65–66.
28. Kuthumi, "Merging with the Impenetrable Light of the Atom," in *Prayer and Meditation,* p. 97.
29. Kuthumi, "A Journey into the Temple Most Holy," in *Prayer and Meditation,* pp. 80–81.
30. Phil. 2:5.
31. Ezek. 1:24; 43:2.
32. Ezek. 12:2.
33. Matt. 6:9.
34. Matt. 6:9–13; Luke 11:2–4.
35. Gen. 1:28; 9:1–3, 7.
36. Exod. 20:3; Deut. 5:7.
37. Deut. 6:4; Mark 12:29.
38. Heb. 9:23.
39. Rom. 3:4,
40. Matt. 21:21, 22.
41. Matt. 6:13.
42. Matt. 24:22.
43. Giving decrees 1.30C and 70.16 in "Prayers, Meditations, Dynamic Decrees for the Coming Revolution in Higher Consciousness" will greatly assist those who desire to implement the law of forgiveness.
44. Luke 22:42.
45. Kuthumi, "The White-Hot Heat of Meditation," in *Prayer and Meditation,* pp. 89–90.
46. Mark 14:36; Matt. 26:39; Luke 22:42.
47. Ps. 19:14.
48. John 5:17, 19, 21.
49. See *Saint Germain On Alchemy,* a complete course on the science of precipitation, published by Summit University Press.
50. Josh. 6:10–20; Heb. 11:30.
51. Mal. 3:10.
52. Job 37:2–5.
53. John 1:1–3; Heb. 11:3.
54. Saint Germain, "The Power of the Spoken Word," in *Science of the Spoken Word,* pp. 38–44.
55. Matt. 4:7.
56. Zech. 2:5.
57. 1 Cor. 15:31.
58. 1 Cor. 3:13.

59. Eph. 5:26.
60. Matt. 3:11; Luke 3:16.
61. Josh 6:20.
62. Kuthumi, July 3, 1962.
63. 1 Cor. 3:16.
64. John 11:41–43.
65. Mark 1:22.
66. Ps. 46:1.
67. John 14:6.
68. Available from Summit University Press.
69. Matt. 6:7.
70. Lord Maitreya, "The Overcoming of Fear through Decrees," in *Science of the Spoken Word,* pp. 23–24.
71. 1 Thess. 5:17.
72. Matt. 16:25; Mark 8:35; Luke 9:24.
73. Mark 1:35; 4:38; Luke 6:12; John 6:15.
74. John 12:31; 14:30; 16:11.
75. The attention of your mind controls and directs the flow of God's energy in your world.
76. Alfred, Lord Tennyson, *The Passing of Arthur,* line 414.
77. Jesus, "Unceasing Prayer," in Jesus and Kuthumi, *Prayer and Meditation,* pp. 8–10, 12.
78. Saint Germain, July 4, 1984, "May You Pass Every Test!" in Mark L. Prophet and Elizabeth Clare Prophet, *Lords of the Seven Rays,* book two, pp. 254–55, 257–59.
79. Job 3:25.
80. Lord Maitreya, "The Overcoming of Fear through Decrees," in *Science of the Spoken Word,* pp. 20–21, 22.
81. Ibid., p. 24.

Chapter 2 · Black Magic

Opening quotation: Matt. 11:22.
1. Acts 17:22–25, 27–28.
2. Rom. 7:23, 25; 8:2; 1 John 3:4.
3. Rom. 7:19.
4. Gen. 1:26, 28.
5. John 8:44.
6. El Morya, "New Lines of Battle in the Holy Cause of Freedom," *Pearls of Wisdom,* vol. 7, no. 16, April 17, 1964.
7. Luke 23:34.
8. Genesis 3:1.
9. Matt. 10:16.
10. Prov. 29:18.
11. Luke 16:8.
12. El Morya, "New Lines of Battle in the Holy Cause of Freedom."
13. Rom. 1:30.
14. The story of Peshu Alga concludes in 1984, with his final judgment

and second death. Archangel Michael speaks of the significance of this event: "Speaking now with the message of the Court of the Sacred Fire, the God Star Sirius, speaking in the name of the Four and Twenty Elders, I announce to you, O children of the Sun, the day of days. Thus, in this very hour, the Judgment—the final judgment and the second death—has come of that one you have known as Peshu Alga.

"Thus, the Keeper of the Scrolls has read these weeks record by record of the infamy of that fallen one in the trial at the Court of the Sacred Fire—that one who himself moved to tempt Lucifer away from the service of Light, that one who forever swore vengeance upon Almighty God because of the death of his only son, failing to apprehend eternal Life and the reappearance of the son. Thus, his sworn enmity was one of the turning points (if not *the* turning point) in the rebellion of those fallen angels who have also followed him to the Court of the Sacred Fire....

"Beloved ones, this judgment, long attended, has far-reaching ramifications across the galaxies. And in this very hour, beloved, there is a liberation and a freedom not known before to many of your own brothers and sisters who happen to be what seems to be so very far, far away....

"This is a day of cosmic celebration and burst of joy unto the Lord Christ in every heart! It is the hour of rejoicing for the binding of the old witch and witchcraft—of the old dragon and the tempter and the seed of Satan. This is the hour and the day when the Light going forth from the heart of Helios unto Vesta in this abode does truly win for God many souls lost—lost because they had lost their moorings in God, lost because they followed the maya and the magnetism and the bravado of these fallen ones.

"We have reached, therefore, the high point of darkness, and darkness now must recede. And now you will have the momentum of the victory of our God, the victory of our bands, and the removal of Darkness as impetus to thrust ho, to move forward, to act for the Light and for the Home, and to clear the way for many beings of Light to descend to Earth through the portals of birth.

"It is an hour for cosmic change if you will have it. But I must tell you truly in the honor of God, as in all time and space, the Law does require the spoken Word, the mantra, the call to me, and the call to God in order for Light to enter in. For you see, God has given to you absolute free will in the physical octave. If you desire change, you must call upon the LORD, your mighty I AM Presence, and call for the reinforcement of us as agents of Light and of the Father-Son-Holy Spirit-Mother complement of the Godhead" ("The Judgment of Peshu Alga," in *Pearls of Wisdom,* vol. 28, no. 2, January 13, 1985).

15. John 8:44.
16. John 3:19.
17. In his general audience on November 15, 1972, Pope Paul VI asked the question: "What are the greatest needs of the Church today?" He said: "Do not let our answer surprise you as being oversimple or even super-

stitious and unreal: one of the greatest needs is defence from that evil which is called the Devil. Evil is not merely a lack of something, but an effective agent, a living, spiritual being, perverted and perverting. A terrible reality. It is contrary to the teaching of the Bible and the Church to refuse to recognise the existence of such a reality or to explain it as a pseudo reality, a conceptual and fanciful personification of the unknown causes of our misfortunes. That it is not a question of one devil, but of many, is indicated by the various passages in the Gospel (Luke 11:21, Mark 5:9). But the principal one is Satan, which means the adversary, the enemy; and with him, many, creatures of God, but fallen, because of their rebellion and damnation—a whole mysterious world, upset by the unhappy drama, of which we know very little" (*L'Osservatore Romano,* November 23, 1972, quoted in Benedict Heron, *Praying for Healing: The Challenge,* ch. 7, at http://www.christendom-awake.org/pages/dombenedict/book-healing/healing-home.html).

18. Saint Germain, "The Doorway of Light," in *Keepers of the Flame Lesson 15,* pp. 28–29, 30.
19. Jesus' "Watch with Me" Vigil of the Hours, p. 21.
20. 2 Thess. 2:12.
21. Mark 5:9; Luke 8:30.
22. Lewis Spence, *An Encyclopaedia of Occultism* (New York?: University Books, 1960), p. 68.
23. Pallas Athena, "On Truth and Self-Deceit," in *Keepers of the Flame Lesson 15,* p. 10.
24. Matt. 6:24; Luke 16:13.
25. Suggested reading: C. S. Lewis, *The Screwtape Letters* (New York: Macmillan, 1968).
26. For teaching on cultivating discrimination, see Lord Maitreya. "Integration with God," *Pearls of Wisdom,* vol. 18, no. 50, December 14, 1975; and "At the Feet of Holy Reason for Self-Discernment," *Pearls of Wisdom,* vol. 8, no. 29, July 18, 1965.
27. On erroneous documents purportedly released through the Masters and the need for discernment on the part of the students, see Saint Germain, "The Truth Shall Make You Free!" *Pearls of Wisdom,* vol. 7, no. 33, August 14, 1964.
28. "For there shall arise false Christs, and false prophets, and shall shew great signs and wonders; insomuch that, if it were possible, they shall deceive the very elect" (Matt. 24:24).
29. Pallas Athena, "On Truth and Self-Deceit," in *Keepers of the Flame Lesson 15,* pp. 11–12.
30. Matt. 27:51; Mark 15:38.
31. John 19:30.
32. Mother Mary, *Pearls of Wisdom,* vol. 6, no. 38, September 20, 1963.
33. Matt. 6:23.
34. Eph. 6:12; 2 Cor. 11:14.
35. Matt. 6:24; Luke 16:13.
36. Matt. 7:16.

37. Mark 1:24; Luke 4:34.
38. El Morya, "New Lines of Battle in the Holy Cause of Freedom," *Pearls of Wisdom,* vol. 7, no. 16, April 17, 1964.
39. *The Martyrdom of an Empress,* pp. 188–90.
40. Matt. 6:23; Maha Chohan, October 4, 1975, "Gifts of the Spirit: Factors and Faculties to Be Considered in Aquarian Education."
41. Luke 8:43–46; Mark 5:25–31.
42. Some of Serapis Bey's teaching on this subject may be found in his book, *Dossier on the Ascension.*
43. The natural rhythm of the four-petaled base chakra is the 4/4. In rock music, the 4/4 beat is syncopated. With this shift in the rhythm, the energy of the spine does not rise in a natural flow, but it falls. The vibration of the energy descending becomes the synthetic experience, or the inverted experience, of the raising of the Kundalini fire. For additional explanation of the science of rhythm and the spiritual effects of rock music, see book 6 of the Climb the Highest Mountain series, *Paths of Light and Darkness,* pp. 72–76.
44. The embedding of subliminal messages in advertising has been analyzed in three books by Wilson Bryan Key: *Subliminal Seduction: Ad Media's Manipulation of a Not So Innocent America, Media Sexploitation* and *The Clam-Plate Orgy* (New York: New American Library, 1973, 1976, 1980). The Spring 1983 issue of *Heart* magazine includes a summary of Key's work and an account of the reaction it caused in the media. This magazine also includes an account of a meeting with a commercial artist skilled in inserting subliminal images and a demonstration of his techniques.
45. Matt. 16:26.
46. Matt. 10:16.
47. Matt. 7:22.
48. Gen. 6:5.
49. Ps. 91:1.
50. Gen. 3:22.
51. Matt. 24:15–16; Mark 13:14.
52. Rev. 3:11.
53. 1 Pet. 5:5; James 4:6.
54. Ps. 139:7–10.
55. Saint Germain, "The Doorway of Light," in *Keepers of the Flame Lesson 15,* pp. 32–35, 36–37, 40, 41–43, 30–32.

Chapter 3 · Antichrist

Opening quotation: 1 John 2:22

CHAPTER 3 · SECTION 1 · THE FALSE HIERARCHY

1. 1 John 2:18.
2. 2 Pet. 2:20.
3. John 8:58.
4. Rev. 13:8.

5. Exod. 7:8–12.
6. 2 Cor. 11:13–15.
7. The one great weakness in the consciousness of those who have taken the left-handed path is that through pride they think they are their forms (yin) and their experiences (yang). They do not identify with the Spirit of God but with the personal patterns of their mortal consciousness. This is their great undoing. Identification with form and experience is the foundation of human pride. Until man overcomes this propensity, he is chained to the world of maya.

When man identifies with his own form, he automatically identifies with the forms of all people (the mass consciousness is one). Therefore, he is susceptible to every limitation and disease to which the flesh is heir. He is not exempt unless he identifies with the Flame, for only then will the aggressive suggestions of the mass consciousness be consumed before penetrating his form consciousness—there to outpicture disease, decay and death.

Unless man consciously rejects mass thoughts and feelings, he will outpicture them in the plane of Matter. He must stand guard at the door of his consciousness as the watchman through the night, refusing entrance to the forms of Antichrist—all that betrays the patterns of the Christ in him.

Life is one. Therefore, when we identify others with their forms (characterizing this one as fat, another as ugly, that one as frail), we ourselves soon become that which we accept or acknowledge as their identity. We imprison ourselves in the matrices we hold for others. It is therefore enlightened self-interest to see others as the Flame, even as we see ourselves as the Flame. The practice of this aspect of the Golden Rule ensures that we as well as our posterity will inherit our immortal identity.

By surrendering his form and his experiences, man surrenders his ego and reaches a state of desirelessness. He is a flame merging with the Great Flame; therefore, he is not consumed. He is an observer of both the lower self and the Higher Self. He is suspended between the two as the Christ, and his immortal identity is preserved.
8. Mark 5:9; Luke 8:30.
9. If they cannot succeed in trapping the innocent through manipulation and imitation, they follow the course of pure Truth and logic for a time, until their followers are so sure they are on the right track that they are no longer careful to examine each release.

It is not difficult for individuals to procure the sacred scriptures of the world, to study them, to quote them, and to use those sacred writings according to their own purposes. Even later prophecy available today in our own material, released through The Summit Lighthouse and other constructive activities, is available to the public and can be studied by individuals who are connected with the false brotherhood and Antichrist activities. Upon studying any of these real and genuine releases, they find little difficulty either in fabricating other materials or in deluding themselves into using these releases as though they themselves originated them.

The flood prophesied in Revelation that is thrown out against the Christ, the Word of God, is the tremendous rehashing of spiritual material put out by the false brotherhoods in order to deceive humanity. They will often use pages of beneficial literature in order to entangle the reader in just one or two little points that may be dangerous, while apparently sugarcoating the whole bitter pill with a mountain of delightful material, similarly written according to Truth, Ascended Master Laws and God's Laws, which are one.

In the same manner, one unjust law may be carried through Congress or a lawmaking body in any nation, simply because it is tied to a most necessary bill for the good of the people. "If this bill would have been passed anyway by public demand," they reason, "why not railroad through some undesirable law that we want passed?" Thus they put man backward every step he moves forward.

10. Paramahansa Yogananda, *Autobiography of a Yogi* (1946; reprint, Los Angeles: Self-Realization Fellowship, 1977), p. 138.
11. Rom. 3:10.
12. Matt. 7:1.
13. 1 John 4:2–3.
14. John 6:56.
15. John 1:14.
16. Luke 15:11–32.
17. Luke 17:21.
18. Prov. 4:7.
19. Luke 23:34.
20. Matt. 25:40.
21. Exod. 13:21, 22; 14:24.
22. Col. 3:1.
23. John 10:30.
24. John 1:3.
25. John 3:14.
26. Gen. 3:15.
27. John Emerich Edward Dalberg, 1st Baron Acton, letter, April 3, 1887, to Bishop Mandell Creighton, in *The Life and Letters of Mandell Creighton,* ed. Louise Creighton (1904) vol. 1, ch. 13.

CHAPTER 3 · SECTION 2 · THE NEPHILIM AND THE POWER ELITE
1. Eccles. 1:11.
2. Zechariah Sitchin, *The Twelfth Planet* (New York: Avon Books, 1976), p. 49.
3. Ibid., p. 52.
4. Ibid., p. 89.
5. Ibid., p. 99.
6. "The Nephilim were on the earth at that time (and even afterward) when the sons of God resorted to the daughters of man, and had children by them" (Gen. 6:4, Jerusalem Bible).
7. "… the same became mighty men which were of old, men of renown"

8. (Gen. 6:4, KJV).
8. Sitchin, *The Twelfth Planet,* pp. 139–53.
9. The Greek Septuagint, a late translation of the Hebrew scriptures, rendered the Hebrew word *Nephilim* as "giants," and this term has been used in the King James version and other translations. In time, it appears that the original meaning of the term *Nephilim* became more generalized and applied to whoever was wicked. The term is used again in Numbers 13:33: "there we saw the Nephilim, sons of Anak, of the Nephilim; and we are in our own eyes as grasshoppers; and so we were in their eyes" (Young's Literal Translation).
10. Early in the twentieth century, when the Anglo-American Corporation was getting ready to commence mining operations in the African nation of Zambia, teams of archaeologists were first dispatched to the region to examine it for archaeological finds before the mining began. Their initial surveys showed evidence of prehistoric mining dating back to 7690 B.C. The archaeologists were amazed at the antiquity of these finds and extended their surveys to other sites. Carbon dating at Lion Peak pushed the date back to 41,250 B.C. South African scientists then investigated ancient mine sites in southern Swaziland, where they found artifacts dating back to about 50,000 B.C. The scientists estimated that mining had begun at these sites at least 70,000 years ago. Sitchin, based on his interpretation of the ancient texts, places the beginning of mining operations at more than 300,000 years ago. The challenge for archaeologists is to explain how and why men were mining for metals so early in what is conventionally thought of as the Stone Age. See Sitchin, *The Twelfth Planet,* pp. 324–25.
11. Ibid., pp. 333–35, 341.
12. Similar tales of man's creation by the gods are found in many ancient mythologies. The Mayan Popul Vuh also records the experiments of these "creators." In this Quiche narrative, the divine beings cast man in a "puppet mold." Here, as in other versions of the tale, it took the gods a few tries to get the right product. At first the workers were blind and could not turn their heads; they could speak (i.e., they had a well-developed vocal tract, which man's primate ancestors did not have) but they had no intelligence. Several experiments later, the demiurges of the Popul Vuh had finally created mankind. But there was a problem. The new creatures were too highly endowed; they knew too much. The gods were not pleased. "This is not well! Their nature will not be that of simple creatures; they will be as gods.... Would they perchance rival us who have made them, whose wisdom extendeth far and knoweth all things?" And so the gods "obscured the vision" of their new creation, significantly reducing their knowledge and wisdom. See Hartley Burr Alexander, *The Mythology of All Races in Thirteen Volumes: Latin American* (Boston: Marshall Jones Company, 1920), 11:162–63, 165–66.
13. Sitchin's account of the creation of a primitive worker has parallels in the revelations of Edgar Cayce, who spoke of a race of soulless beings that were created on Atlantis to perform manual labor. He called them

"automatons" or "things." See *Edgar Cayce on Atlantis* (New York: Paperback Library, 1968), pp. 101–6.

14. Werner Keller, *The Bible as History,* translated by William Neil 2d ed. (New York: William Morrow and Company, 1964) pp. 38–39. As well as the biblical account, stories of a great flood appear in sources as diverse as Norse, Greek, Chinese, Indian, Indonesian, Inca and Native American legends.
15. Gen. 6:5.
16. Gen. 6:1, 2.
17. Sitchin, *The Twelfth Planet,* p. 372.
18. Gen. 1:28.
19. Sitchin, *The Twelfth Planet,* p. 391.
20. Ibid., p. 401. The Ascended Masters have equated the biblical Flood with the sinking of Atlantis, the island continent that existed where the Atlantic Ocean now is. The continent has been vividly depicted by Plato, "seen" and described by Edgar Cayce in his readings, and recalled in scenes from Taylor Caldwell's *Romance of Atlantis.* James Churchward deduces from Plato's account that the continent sank about 11,600 years ago, which is quite close to the date that Sitchin determined from the geological record. (James Churchward, *The Lost Continent of Mu* [New York: Crown Publishers, 1931], p. 264.)
21. According to Sitchin, the Twelfth Planet has a very elongated elliptical orbit through the solar system. The orbit takes the planet far beyond Pluto at its furthest extent and within the orbit of the Earth at its closest approach to the sun. The period of the orbit is 3,600 years. Thus, once every 3,600 years, the orbit of the Twelfth Planet crosses that of Earth.
22. Sitchin, *The Twelfth Planet,* p. 397.
23. Ibid., p. 102.
24. Ibid., p. 398.
25. Ibid., p. 400.
26. Gen. 8:17; 9:1, 7.
27. Sitchin, *The Twelfth Planet,* pp. 420–421.
28. Matt. 23:27.
29. Gen. 3:4.
30. 1 Cor. 3:16.
31. Ps. 82:6, 7.
32. John 8:44.
33. Josh. 23:7, 12. See also Exod. 33:16; Lev. 20:24, 26; Ezra 10:11; Neh. 9:2; 2 Cor. 6:17.
34. For a detailed discussion of the account of the Garden of Eden, see book 2 of the Climb the Highest Mountain series, *The Path of Self-Transformation.*
35. Isa. 14:12.
36. Prov. 14:12.
37. Saint Germain, April 29, 1984, "The Ancient Story of the Drug Conspiracy," in Elizabeth Clare Prophet, *Saint Germain On Prophecy,* book 4, pp. 96–97.

38. One account of Lucifer's Fall is found in the early Christian text *Vitae Adae et Evae*. In chapters 11 to 16, we read: "And she [Eve] cried out and said: 'Woe unto thee, thou devil. Why dost thou attack us for no cause? What hast thou to do with us? What have we done to thee? for thou pursuest us with craft? Or why doth thy malice assail us? Have we taken away thy glory and caused thee to be without honour? Why dost thou harry us, thou enemy (and persecute us) to the death in wickedness and envy?'

"And with a heavy sigh, the devil spake: 'O Adam! all my hostility, envy, and sorrow is for thee, since it is for thee that I have been expelled from my glory, which I possessed in the heavens in the midst of the angels and for thee was I cast out in the earth.' Adam answered, 'What dost thou tell me? What have I done to thee or what is my fault against thee? Seeing that thou hast received no harm or injury from us, why dost thou pursue us?'

"The devil replied, 'Adam, what dost thou tell me? It is for thy sake that I have been hurled from that place. When thou wast formed, I was hurled out of the presence of God and banished from the company of the angels. When God blew into thee the breath of life and thy face and likeness was made in the image of God, Michael also brought thee and made (us) worship thee in the sight of God; and God the Lord spake: Here is Adam. I have made thee in our image and likeness.'

"And Michael went out and called all the angels saying: 'Worship the image of God as the Lord God hath commanded.' And Michael himself worshipped first; then he called me and said: 'Worship the image of God the Lord.' And I answered, 'I have no (need) to worship Adam.' And since Michael kept urging me to worship, I said to him, 'Why dost thou urge me? I will not worship an inferior and younger being (than I). I am his senior in the Creation, before he was made was I already made. It is his duty to worship me.'

"When the angels, who were under me, heard this, they refused to worship him. And Michael saith, 'Worship the image of God, but if thou wilt not worship him, the Lord God will be wrath with thee.' And I said, 'If He be wrath with me, I will set my seat above the stars of heaven and will be like the Highest.'

"And God the Lord was wrath with me and banished me and my angels from our glory; and on thy account were we expelled from our abodes into this world and hurled on the earth. And straightway we were overcome with grief, since we had been spoiled of so great glory. And we were grieved when we saw thee in such joy and luxury. And with guile I cheated thy wife and caused thee to be expelled through her (doing) from thy joy and luxury, as I have been driven out of my glory" (R. H. Charles, *The Apocrypha and Pseudepigrapha of the Old Testament* [Oxford: Clarendon Press, 1913]).

39. Isa. 14:12–15.
40. Rev. 12, 13, 20.
41. Rev. 12:7–9.

42. 1 Cor. 15:47.
43. Rev. 12:4.
44. Dan. 12:7; Rev. 12:14. A similar cycle is seen in Rev. 11:9, 11.
45. Isa. 9:6.
46. 1 Sam. 17.
47. Rev. 12:12.
48. Dan. 7.
49. Matt. 28:18.
50. John 5:30.
51. See "The Coming of the Laggards," in book 1 of the Climb the Highest Mountain series, *The Path of the Higher Self.*
52. Sanat Kumara (from the Sanskrit *sanat,* "from of old," "always," "ever" and *kumara,* "always a youth") is revered in Hinduism as one of the four or seven sons of Brahma; they are portrayed as youths who have remained ever pure. Sanat Kumara is said to be the oldest of the progenitors of mankind; in the Mahabharata he is called the "eldest born of Brahman." In some accounts he is considered to be the son of Shiva. In the Chandogya Upanishad Sanat Kumara is the teacher of the sage Narada, who learns from him that the highest truth can be attained only through true Self-knowledge. Sanat Kumara also takes on the role of the god of war and commander-in-chief of the divine army of the gods in his manifestation as Karttikeya or Skanda. He is often represented holding a spear and riding on a peacock and is sometimes shown with twelve arms holding weapons. He is said to have been reared by the six Pleiades, from which the name Karttikeya ("Son of the Pleiades") is derived. Some works also acclaim Karttikeya as the god of wisdom and learning.
53. John 3:17.
54. John 1:12.
55. Matt. 7:20.
56. The Great Divine Director, "Man," in Mark L. Prophet, *The Soulless One,* p. 108.
57. See Apollo, "An Increment of Light from the Holy Kumaras," in Elizabeth Clare Prophet, *The Great White Brotherhood in the Culture, History and Religion of America,* ch. 21.
58. Matt. 10:28.
59. Matt. 7:15–20.
60. Matt. 13:37–43.
61. Matt. 7:1; Luke 6:37.
62. "For we wrestle not against flesh and blood, but against principalities, against powers, against the rulers of the darkness of this world, against spiritual wickedness in high places" (Eph. 6:12).
63. Rom. 3:17.
64. Saint Germain speaks of the creations of genetic engineering on Atlantis, which included the crossbreeding of human and animal life: "The destructive use of the Life force on Lemuria and Atlantis is well known among students of cosmic history. The creation of animal forms by the black magicians who came with the laggards ... was fol-

lowed by the infusion of those created forms with Solar Energy in the process of crossbreeding human beings with animal life. This resulted in a frightful distortion of the divine plan, in violation of all of heaven's Laws, and brought on the Noachian deluge. The destruction of those forms through the Flood was nature's way of removing from the screen of life these gross and wicked 'imaginations of men's hearts,' which were so unlike the creation of God (Gen. 6:1–9, 17).

"In the mass memory of the race there remains some knowledge of the existence of these forms, some of which were, for example, part horse and part man. Ultimately, the mighty cosmic councils took steps to curb mankind's creative powers. It was therefore decreed that each seed should thenceforth bear 'after its kind'; and thus the prevention of the recurrence of this unholy activity was instituted by cosmic law" (Saint Germain, "The Science of the Ascension," in *Keepers of the Flame Lesson 13,* p. 30).

65. John 1:1–3.
66. Rev. 19:11.

CHAPTER 3 · SECTION 3 · THE ENEMY WITHIN

1. El Morya, July 2, 1984, "Message to America on the Mission of Jesus Christ," in *Pearls of Wisdom,* vol. 27, no. 47, September 23, 1984.
2. El Morya, April 4, 1997, "Stand, Face and Conquer the World of Self!" in *Pearls of Wisdom,* vol. 40, no. 40, October 5, 1997.
3. Some commentators have interpreted the quatrains of Nostradamus as predicting the coming of three Antichrists. Interpreters have speculated that the first two were Napoleon and Hitler, and that the third Antichrist will be a blue-turbaned Arab.
4. Jer. 23:6; 33:16.
5. 1 Cor. 3:13–15; 1 Pet. 1:7; 4:12.
6. See Lord Maitreya, January 1, 1986, "The Lord of the World's Path of the Six-Pointed Star," in *Pearls of Wisdom,* vol. 29, no. 22, June 1, 1986.
7. Isa. 34:8; 61:2; 63:4; Jer. 50:15, 28; 51:6, 11; Luke 21:22.
8. Matt. 14:28–31.
9. Gen. 4:3–8.
10. Jesus and Kuthumi, *Prayer and Meditation.*
11. Kuthumi, January 27, 1985, "Remember the Ancient Encounter," in *Pearls of Wisdom,* vol. 28, no. 9, March 3, 1985.
12. Acts 7:58–60; 8:1–3; 9:1–31; 13–28.
13. Rom. 8:6, 7.
14. Josh. 24:15.
15. Matt. 4:1–11.
16. John 14:30.
17. 1 Tim. 5:24.
18. John 6:53.
19. John 10:30.
20. Rudyard Kipling's short story "The Man Who Would Be King" tells the tale of two British adventurers who travel to a remote Asian

kingdom and succeed in convincing the natives that they are gods, one of them setting himself up as king. They are eventually exposed; the tribesmen turn against them, pursuing them through the surrounding mountains. The former king is forced onto a rope bridge spanning a deep gorge. He falls into the chasm when the ropes holding the bridge are cut. A film version produced in 1975 starred Sean Connery and Michael Caine.

21. Luke 22:53.

22. Rom. 8:7; Rev. 2:9; 3:9.

23. John 7:24.

24. Matt. 7:2; Mark 4:24.

25. Matt. 8:12; 22:13; 25:30; Rev. 2:11; 20:6, 14; 21:8. For further explanation of the second death, see book 7 of the Climb the Highest Mountain series, *The Path to Immortality,* ch. 3, "Immortality."

26. 1 Cor. 2:14–16.

27. Matt. 23:15; Luke 11:52.

28. Col. 1:27.

29. The Watchers are a particular band of fallen angels whose story is told in the Book of Enoch. See Elizabeth Clare Prophet, *Fallen Angels and the Origins of Evil.*

30. Mark 4:25.

31. Ps. 94:3.

32. "Elect One" is the term used in the Book of Enoch for the coming Avatar who would judge the fallen angels. See Enoch 45:3, 4; 50:3, 5; 51:5, 10; 54:5; 60:7, 10–13; 61:1, in Elizabeth Clare Prophet, *Fallen Angels and the Origins of Evil.* The original Greek manuscript of Luke 9:35 uses this term in reference to Jesus: "This is my Son, the Elect One. Hear him."

33. John 9:39.

34. Rev. 19:11.

35. Matt. 6:23.

36. Luke 16:8; Matt. 10:16.

37. *Kundalini:* lit., "coiled-up serpent"; coiled energy in latency at the base-of-the-spine chakra; the seal of the seed atom; negative polarity in Matter of the positive Spirit-fire that descends from the I AM Presence to the heart chakra. When the Kundalini is awakened (through specific yogic techniques, spiritual disciplines, or intense love of God) it begins to ascend the spinal column through the channels of the *Ida, Pingala* and *Sushumna,* penetrating and activating each of the chakras. The initiate who has taken the left-handed path at the Y uses the Kundalini to enhance his adeptship in the black arts. The false guru initiates the unwary in the rites of raising the Kundalini before the rituals of soul purification and transmutation of the chakras have taken place. This can result in insanity, demon possession, or uncontrolled and inordinate sexual desire or a perversion of the Life-force in all the chakras. The One Sent takes his disciples by the hand and leads them gently in the disciplines of self-mastery until they can deal with the great powers conferred by the Goddess Kundalini and use them to

bless and heal all life by the release of the sacred fire through all of the chakras—centering in the heart, which in the true initiate becomes the chalice for the Sacred Heart of Jesus Christ. The Kundalini is the Life-force, the Mother energy. When the base chakra and the Kundalini are mastered, they become the vessels for the ascension flame in the one preparing for this initiation.

38. Matt. 13:24–30, 36–43.
39. John 10:10.
40. Deut. 4:24.

CHAPTER 3 · SECTION 4 · THE JUDGMENT

1. Rev. 20:12, 13. Further teaching on the final judgment may be found in book 7 of the Climb the Highest Mountain series, *The Path to Immortality*, chapter 3, "Immortality."
2. Rev. 20:14, 15.
3. Lucifer was bound on April 16, 1975, and taken to the Court of the Sacred Fire, where he stood trial before the Four and Twenty Elders for a period of ten days. He was sentenced to the second death on April 26, 1975, by unanimous vote of the Four and Twenty Elders. His judgment was announced in a dictation delivered by Alpha on July 5, 1975. See Alpha, "The Judgment: The Sealing of the Lifewaves throughout the Galaxy"; and Elizabeth Clare Prophet, July 6, 1975, "Antichrist: the Dragon, the Beast, the False Prophet, and the Great Whore," in *The Great White Brotherhood in the Culture, History and Religion of America*, pp. 234–36, 239–49.
4. Rev. 12:10.
5. Rev. 16:14, 16.
6. Rev. 11:3–13.
7. Rev. 12:1.
8. Rev. 12:5.
9. Rev. 22:18, 19.
10. Ezek.; Dan. 7–12.
11. Rev. 13:1, 11.
12. 2 Tim. 2:15.
13. Matt. 24:11, 23–24; Mark 13:21–22. See also 1 John 2:18, 22; 1 Pet. 2:1.
14. John 5:17, 30; 14:10.
15. Prov. 4:5–9.
16. Purity and Astrea, May 25, 1975, "Releasing the Light of the Mother within You," in Elizabeth Clare Prophet, *The Great White Brother-hood in the Culture, History and Religion of America*, p. 264.
17. John 14:26.
18. Acts 2:2.
19. Matt. 7:20.
20. Matt. 13:24–30, 36–43.
21. Alpha, July 5, 1975, "The Judgment: The Sealing of the Lifewaves throughout the Galaxy," in Elizabeth Clare Prophet, *The Great White Brotherhood in the Culture, History and Religion of America*, pp. 234–37.

22. Dan. 12:1–3.

CHAPTER 3 · SECTION 5 · THE VICTORY OF CHRIST
  1. 1 Cor. 15:50.
  2. Matt. 10:16.
  3. Ezek. 18:20.
  4. Col. 3:3.
  5. Luke 12:32.
  6. Matt. 13:24–30, 36–43.
  7. John 9:39.
  8. John 5:22.

Chapter 4 · The Summit

Opening quotations: Rev. 21:10; Isa. 2:2–3.
  1. John 1:5.
  2. El Morya, letter to "Chelas Mine," August 8, 1958, in *Morya I*, p. xxv.
  3. Heb. 11:5.
  4. El Morya, July 3, 1965, "O Excalibur," in Mark L. Prophet and Elizabeth Clare Prophet, *Morya: The Darjeeling Master Speaks to his Chelas on the Quest for the Holy Grail*, pp. 298–99.
  5. Additional information about El Morya's embodiments may be found in Mark L. Prophet and Elizabeth Clare Prophet, *Lords of the Seven Rays*, book one, pp. 21–78.
  6. Zech. 4:6.
  7. John Robinson, farewell address to the Pilgrims at Leyden, July 1620, in *New Encyclopaedia Britannica*, 15th ed., micropaedia, s.v. "Robinson, John." Willison, George F., *Saints and Strangers* (New York: Time-Life Books, 1945), p. 127.
  8. The Messengers Mark L. Prophet and Elizabeth Clare Prophet were embodied as Ikhnaton and Nefertiti, who ruled Egypt in the fourteenth century B.C. Ikhnaton introduced a revolutionary religion into Egypt based on the worship of the one God. This God, known as "Aton," was represented in the symbol of a sun disc or orb with diverging rays, each of which ended in a hand bestowing blessings upon all life. Ikhnaton prohibited the worship of the old (Nephilim) gods of Egypt, particularly Amon, the chief god, and ordered their names and images erased from the monuments. Ikhnaton built a new city at Tel el-Amarna as the religious and administrative capital of his empire. The black priests of Amon viciously conspired against Ikhnaton and Nefertiti, eventually murdering them; they reestablished the former gods and obliterated from monuments and temples throughout Egypt the name and image of Aton and Ikhnaton.
  9. Archangel Jophiel, October 14, 1967, in Mark L. Prophet and Elizabeth Clare Prophet, *Lords of the Seven Rays*, pp. 66–68.
 10. Acts 1:11.
 11. Matt. 7:14.
 12. Matt. 5:14.

13. Mark 4:39.
14. El Morya, "Chelas Mine," p. xxvii; Queen of Light, July 3, 1969. For further teaching about the ascension, see book 3 of this series, *The Masters and the Spiritual Path,* chapter 2; book 7, *The Path to Immortality,* chapter 3; and Serapis Bey, *Dossier on the Ascension.*
15. Rev. 14:6.
16. Exod. 3:14.
17. John 1:1–3.
18. John 14:6; 11:25.
19. Acts 2:2.
20. El Morya, *Pearls of Wisdom,* vol. 3, no. 34, August 19, 1960.
21. El Morya, *Pearls of Wisdom,* vol. 3, no. 36, September 2, 1960.
22. Lanto, *Pearls of Wisdom,* vol. 4, no. 20, May 19, 1961.
23. El Morya, letter to "My Beloved Friends of Light and Love," November 10, 1959.
24. El Morya, letter to "Beloved Chelas of God's Own Will," January 31, 1961.
25. Gen. 4:9.
26. Saint Germain, "Know God, Know Thyself, Know the Law of Thy Being," *Pearls of Wisdom,* vol. 10, no. 38, September 17, 1967.
27. Morya explains that "Keepers of the Flame are responsible to the spiritual board of the fraternity, which is headed by the Maha Chohan, the Keeper of the Flame, and the Knight Commander, Saint Germain. The board of directors is composed of the seven Chohans, who direct various aspects of the unfoldment of the Law both through the printed instruction and through the individual training that Keepers of the Flame are given in the etheric retreats of the Great White Brotherhood. A special Committee for Child Guidance formed for the preparation of parents of incoming souls and for the proper education of children is headed by the World Teachers, Jesus and Kuthumi, together with Mother Mary" (El Morya, *The Chela and the Path,* p. 103).
28. El Morya, "Statement of Policy," in *Keepers of the Flame Lesson 1,* pp. 6–7.
29. El Morya, *Pearls of Wisdom,* vol. 4, no. 41, October 13, 1961.
30. On the thirty-third anniversary of The Summit Lighthouse, El Morya spoke of the original grant from Helios and Vesta for the founding of the activity and its renewal. See El Morya, August 11, 1991, "Let the Word Go Forth!" in *Pearls of Wisdom,* vol. 34, no. 51, October 23, 1991.
31. El Morya, *Pearls of Wisdom,* vol. 4, no. 32, August 11, 1961.
32. Lanto, "The Star of Universality," *Pearls of Wisdom,* vol. 10, no. 40, October 1, 1967.
33. In 1982, Saint Germain explained that the focus in Santa Barbara, known as the Motherhouse, had fulfilled its purpose: "You may remember when the Archangels sent forth the word that we would keep the flame of the Motherhouse in Santa Barbara until its purpose should be fulfilled. And one key purpose of that house was to keep a Light so that the darkness gathering in San Francisco and Los Angeles should not meet midpoint on that coast and cause cataclysm. There-

fore our witnesses, with determined Keepers of the Flame, set on the map a tiny pyramid of Light in the secret-ray chakra of that ancient city. And therefore, the darkness has not passed either from north to south or south to north.

"Subsequently, with the Messenger's ascension and the expansion by his heart of the gathering of forces, I sent forth the call for the Teaching Centers and the amethyst jewels. And therefore, strong focuses have been established in San Francisco and in Los Angeles, holding the balance against a mounting karma and a mounting disturbance in elemental life due to man's inhumanity to man....

"Weighing all things in the balance, we see that there has been a fulfillment of cosmic cycles within that property. And we are therefore ready for the very alchemy of which the Messenger has spoken—the drawing of the Light from that property and its consecration to the building of a new and a more useful place where all of you may come and realize that here at the Heart of the Inner Retreat and there in the outer ranch, you have a greater need for a Motherhouse than you now have individually for a Motherhouse in Santa Barbara" (*Pearls of Wisdom,* vol. 25, no. 63, 1982).

34. Goddess of Liberty, July 3, 1980, "The Greater Goal of Life: The Establishment of the Inner Retreat through the Cosmic Connection with the God Star," in *Pearls of Wisdom,* vol. 23, no. 34, August 24, 1980.

35. See book 2 of the Climb the Highest Mountain series, *The Path of Self-Transformation.*

36. Jesus, May 31, 1984, "The Mystery School of Lord Maitreya," in *Pearls of Wisdom,* vol. 27, no. 36, July 8, 1984. The Royal Teton Ranch is located in Montana's Paradise Valley, on the northern border of Yellowstone Park.

37. Lord Maitreya, January 1, 1986, "The Lord of the World's Path of the Six-Pointed Star," in *Pearls of Wisdom,* vol. 29, no. 22, June 1, 1986.

38. Lord Maitreya, December 31, 1985, "I Draw the Line!" in *Pearls of Wisdom,* vol. 29, no. 19, May 11, 1986.

39. For additional information about the retreats of the Masters, see Mark L. Prophet and Elizabeth Clare Prophet, *The Masters and Their Retreats.*

40. El Morya, July 3, 1970.

Publications of Summit University Press that display this crest are the authentic Teachings of the Ascended Masters as given to the world by Mark L. Prophet and Elizabeth Clare Prophet.

Glossary

Terms set in italics are defined elsewhere in the glossary.

Adept. An initiate of the *Great White Brotherhood* of a high degree of attainment, especially in the control of *Matter,* physical forces, nature spirits and bodily functions; fully the alchemist undergoing advanced initiations of the *sacred fire* on the path of the *ascension.*

Akashic records. The impressions of all that has ever transpired in the physical universe, recorded in the etheric substance and dimension known by the Sanskrit term *akasha.* These records can be read by those with developed soul faculties.

Alchemical marriage. The soul's permanent bonding to the *Holy Christ Self,* in preparation for the permanent fusing to the *I AM Presence* in the ritual of the *ascension.* See also *Secret chamber of the heart.*

All-Seeing Eye of God. See *Cyclopea.*

Alpha and Omega. The divine wholeness of the Father-Mother God affirmed as "the beginning and the ending" by the Lord *Christ* in Revelation (Rev. 1:8, 11; 21:6; 22:13). Ascended *twin flames* of the *Cosmic Christ* consciousness who hold the balance of the masculine-feminine polarity of the Godhead in the *Great Central Sun* of cosmos. Thus through the *Universal Christ* (the *Word* incarnate), the Father is the origin and the Mother is the fulfillment of the cycles of God's consciousness expressed throughout the *Spirit-Matter* creation. See also *Mother.*

Ancient of Days. See *Sanat Kumara.*

Angel. A divine spirit, a herald or messenger sent by God to deliver his *Word* to his children. A ministering spirit sent forth to tend the heirs of *Christ*—to comfort, protect, guide, strengthen, teach, counsel and warn. The fallen angels, also called the dark ones, are those angels who followed Lucifer in the Great Rebellion, whose consciousness therefore "fell" to lower levels of vibration. They were "cast out into the earth" by Archangel Michael (Rev. 12:7–12)—constrained by the karma of their disobedience to God and his Christ to take on and evolve through dense physical bodies. Here they walk about, sowing seeds of unrest and rebellion among men and nations.

Antahkarana. The web of life. The net of *Light* spanning *Spirit* and *Matter,* connecting and sensitizing the whole of creation within itself and to the heart of God.

Archangel. The highest rank in the orders of *angels.* Each of the *seven rays* has a presiding Archangel who, with his divine complement or *Archeia,* embodies the God consciousness of the ray and directs the bands of angels serving in their command on that ray. The Archangels and Archeiai of the rays and the locations of their *retreats* are as follows:

> First ray, blue, Archangel Michael and Faith, Banff, near Lake Louise, Alberta, Canada.
>
> Second ray, yellow, Archangel Jophiel and Christine, south of the Great Wall near Lanchow, north central China.
>
> Third ray, petal pink, deep rose and ruby, Archangel Chamuel and Charity, St. Louis, Missouri, U.S.A.
>
> Fourth ray, white and mother-of-pearl, Archangel Gabriel and Hope, between Sacramento and Mount Shasta, California, U.S.A.
>
> Fifth ray, green, Archangel Raphael and Mary, Fátima, Portugal.
>
> Sixth ray, purple and gold with ruby flecks, Archangel Uriel and Aurora, Tatra Mountains, south of Cracow, Poland.
>
> Seventh ray, violet and purple, Archangel Zadkiel and Holy Amethyst, Cuba.

Archeia (pl. **Archeiai**). Divine complement and *twin flame* of an *Archangel.*

Ascended Master. One who, through *Christ* and the putting on of that mind which was in Christ Jesus (Phil. 2:5), has mastered time and space and in the process gained the mastery of the self in the *four lower bodies* and the four quadrants of *Matter,* in the *chakras* and the balanced *threefold flame.* An Ascended Master has also transmuted at least 51 percent of his karma, fulfilled his divine plan, and taken the initiations of the ruby ray unto the ritual of the *ascension*—acceleration by the *sacred fire* into the Presence of the I AM THAT I AM (the *I AM Presence*). Ascended Masters inhabit the planes of *Spirit*—the kingdom of God (God's consciousness)—and they may teach unascended souls in an *etheric temple* or in the cities on the *etheric plane* (the kingdom of heaven).

Ascension. The ritual whereby the soul reunites with the *Spirit* of the living God, the *I AM Presence.* The ascension is the culmination of the soul's God-victorious sojourn in time and space. It is the process whereby the soul, having balanced her karma and fulfilled her divine plan, merges first with the Christ consciousness and then with the living Presence of the I AM THAT I AM. Once the ascension has taken place, the soul—the corruptible aspect of being—becomes the incorruptible one, a permanent atom in the Body of God. See also *Alchemical marriage.*

Aspirant. One who aspires; specifically, one who aspires to reunion with God through the ritual of the *ascension.* One who aspires to overcome the conditions and limitations of time and space to fulfill the cycles of karma and one's reason for being through the sacred labor.

Astral plane. A frequency of time and space beyond the physical, yet below the mental, corresponding to the *emotional body* of man and the collective unconscious of the race; the repository of mankind's thoughts and feelings, conscious and unconscious. Because the astral plane has been muddied by impure human thought and feeling, the term "astral" is often used in a negative context to refer to that which is impure or psychic.

Astrea. Feminine Elohim of the fourth ray, the ray of purity, who works to cut souls free from the *astral plane* and the projections of the dark forces. See also *Elohim; Seven rays.*

Atman. The spark of the divine within, identical with *Brahman;* the ultimate essence of the universe as well as the essence of the individual.

AUM. See *OM.*

Avatar. The incarnation of the *Word.* The avatar of an age is the *Christ,* the incarnation of the Son of God. The *Manus* may designate numerous Christed ones—those endued with an extraordinary *Light*—to go forth as world teachers and wayshowers. The Christed ones demonstrate in a given epoch the Law of the *Logos,* stepped down through the Manu(s) and the avatar(s) until it is made flesh through their own word and work—to be ultimately victorious in its fulfillment in all souls of Light sent forth to conquer time and space in that era.

Bodhisattva. (Sanskrit, "a being of *bodhi* or enlightenment.") A being destined for enlightenment, or one whose energy and power is directed toward enlightenment. A Bodhisattva is destined to become a *Buddha* but has forgone the bliss of *nirvana* with a vow to save all children of God on earth. An Ascended Master or an unascended master may be a Bodhisattva.

Brahman. Ultimate Reality; the Absolute.

Buddha. (From Sanskrit *budh* "awake, know, perceive.") "The enlightened one." Buddha denotes an office in the spiritual *Hierarchy* of worlds that is attained by passing certain initiations of the *sacred fire,* including those of the *seven rays* of the Holy Spirit and of the five secret *rays,* the raising of the Feminine Ray (sacred fire of the Kundalini) and the "mastery of the seven in the seven multiplied by the power of the ten."

Gautama attained the enlightenment of the Buddha twenty-five centuries ago, a path he had pursued through many previous embodiments culminating in his forty-nine-day meditation under the Bo tree. Hence he is called Gautama, the Buddha. He holds the office of *Lord of the World,* sustaining, by his *Causal Body* and *threefold flame,* the divine spark and consciousness in the evolutions of earth approaching the path of personal Christhood. His aura of love/wisdom ensouling the planet issues from his incomparable devotion to the Divine *Mother.* He is the Hierarch of Shamballa, the original *retreat* of *Sanat Kumara* now on the *etheric plane* over the Gobi Desert.

Lord Maitreya, the *Cosmic Christ,* has also passed the initiations of the Buddha. He is the long-awaited Coming Buddha who has come to the fore to teach all who have departed from the way of the Great *Guru,* Sanat Kumara, from whose lineage both he and Gautama descended. In the history of the planet, there have been numerous Buddhas who have served the evolutions of mankind through the steps and stages of the path of the *Bodhisattva.* In the East Jesus is referred to as the Buddha Issa. He is the World Saviour by the love/wisdom of the Godhead.

Caduceus. The Kundalini. See *Sacred fire.*

Causal Body. Seven concentric spheres of *Light* surrounding the *I AM Presence.* The spheres of the Causal Body contain the records of the virtuous acts we have performed to the glory of God and the blessing of man through our many incarnations on earth. See also *Chart of Your Divine Self;* color illustration facing page 12.

Central Sun. A vortex of energy, physical or spiritual, central to systems of worlds that it thrusts from, or gathers unto, itself by the Central Sun Magnet. Whether in the *microcosm* or the *Macrocosm,* the Central Sun is the principal energy source, vortex, or nexus of energy interchange in atoms, cells, man (the heart center), amidst plant life and the core of the earth. The Great Central Sun is the center of cosmos; the point of integration of the *Spirit-Matter* cosmos; the point of origin of all physical-spiritual creation; the nucleus, or white-fire core, of the *Cosmic Egg.* (The God Star, Sirius, is the focus of the Great Central Sun in our sector of the galaxy.) The Sun behind the sun is the spiritual Cause behind the physical effect we see as our own physical sun and all other stars and star systems, seen or unseen, including the Great Central Sun.

Chakra. (Sanskrit, "wheel, disc, circle.") Center of *Light* anchored in the *etheric body* and governing the flow of energy to the *four lower bodies* of man. There are seven major chakras corresponding to the *seven rays,* five minor chakras corresponding to the five secret rays, and a total of 144 Light centers in the body of man.

Chart of Your Divine Self. (See color illustration facing page 12.) There are three figures represented in the Chart. The upper figure is the *I AM Presence,* the I AM THAT I AM, the individualization of God's presence for every son and daughter of the Most High. The Divine Monad consists of the I AM Presence surrounded by the spheres (color rings) of *Light* that make up the body of First Cause, or *Causal Body.*

The middle figure in the Chart is the Mediator between God and man, called the *Holy Christ Self,* the *Real Self* or the *Christ* consciousness. It has also been referred to as the Higher Mental Body or one's Higher Consciousness. This Inner Teacher overshadows the lower self, which consists of the soul evolving through the four planes of *Matter* using the vehicles of the *four lower bodies*—the *etheric* (memory) *body,* the *mental body,* the *emotional* (desire) *body,* and the *physical body*—to balance karma and fulfill the divine plan.

The three figures of the Chart correspond to the Trinity of Father, who always includes the *Mother* (the upper figure), Son (the middle figure) and Holy Spirit (the lower figure). The latter is the intended temple of the Holy Spirit, whose *sacred fire* is indicated in the enfolding *violet flame.* The lower figure corresponds to you as a disciple on the *Path.*

The lower figure is surrounded by a *tube of light,* which is projected from the heart of the I AM Presence in answer to your call. It is a cylinder of white Light that sustains a forcefield of protection twenty-four hours a day, so long as you guard it in harmony. The *threefold flame* of life is the divine spark sent from the I AM Presence as the gift of life, consciousness and free will. It is sealed in the *secret chamber of the heart* that through the love, wisdom and power of the Godhead anchored therein the soul may fulfill her reason for being in the physical plane. Also called the Christ Flame and the Liberty Flame, or fleur-de-lis, it is the spark of a man's divinity, his potential for Christhood.

The silver cord (or *crystal cord*) is the stream of life, or *lifestream,* that descends from the heart of the I AM Presence to the Holy Christ Self to nourish and sustain (through the *chakras*) the soul and its vehicles of expression in time and space. It is over this 'umbilical cord' that the energy of the Presence flows, entering the being of man at the crown and giving impetus for the pulsation of the threefold flame as well as the physical heartbeat.

When a round of the soul's incarnation in Matter-form is finished, the I AM Presence withdraws the silver cord (Eccles. 12:6), whereupon the threefold flame returns to the level of the Christ, and the soul clothed in the etheric garment gravitates to the highest level of her attainment, where she is schooled between embodiments until her final incarnation when the Great Law decrees she shall go out no more.

The dove of the Holy Spirit descending from the heart of the Father is shown just above the head of the Christ. When the son of man puts on and becomes the Christ consciousness as Jesus did, he merges with the Holy Christ Self. The Holy Spirit is upon him, and the words of the Father, the beloved I AM Presence, are spoken: "This is my beloved Son, in whom I AM well pleased" (Matt. 3:17).

Chela. (Hindi *celā* from Sanskrit *ceta* "slave," i.e., "servant.") In India, a disciple of a religious teacher or *guru.* A term used generally to refer to a student of the *Ascended Masters* and their teachings. Specifically, a student of more than ordinary self-discipline and devotion initiated by an *Ascended Master* and serving the cause of the *Great White Brotherhood.*

Chohan. (Tibetan, "lord" or "master"; a chief.) Each of the seven *rays* has a Chohan who focuses the *Christ* consciousness of the ray. Having ensouled and demonstrated the law of the ray throughout numerous incarnations, and having taken initiations both before and after the *ascension,* the candidate is appointed to the office of Chohan by the Maha Chohan (the "Great Lord"), who is himself the representative of the Holy Spirit on all the rays. The names of the Chohans of the Rays (each one an *Ascended Master* representing one of the seven rays to earth's evolutions) and the locations of their physical/etheric focuses are as follows:

First ray, El Morya, Retreat of God's Will, Darjeeling, India
Second ray, Lanto, Royal Teton Retreat, Grand Teton,
    Jackson Hole, Wyoming, U.S.A.
Third ray, Paul the Venetian, Château de Liberté, southern
    France, with a focus of the *threefold flame* at the
    Washington Monument, Washington, D.C., U.S.A.
Fourth ray, Serapis Bey, the Ascension Temple and Retreat at
    Luxor, Egypt
Fifth ray, Hilarion (the apostle Paul), Temple of Truth, Crete
Sixth ray, Nada, Arabian Retreat, Saudi Arabia
Seventh ray, Saint Germain, Royal Teton Retreat, Grand
    Teton, Wyoming, U.S.A.; Cave of Symbols, Table
    Mountain, Wyoming, U.S.A.

Saint Germain also works out of the Great Divine Director's focuses—the Cave of Light in India and the Rakoczy Mansion in Transylvania, where Saint Germain presides as Hierarch.

Christ. (From the Greek *Christos* "anointed.") Messiah (Hebrew, Aramaic "anointed"); "Christed one," one fully endued and infilled—anointed—by the *Light* (the Son) of God. The *Word,* the *Logos,* the Second Person of the Trinity. In the Hindu Trinity of Brahma, Vishnu and Shiva, the term "Christ" corresponds to or is the incarnation of Vishnu, the Preserver; Avatāra, God-man, Dispeller of Darkness, *Guru.*

The term "Christ" or "Christed one" also denotes an office in *Hierarchy* held by those who have attained self-mastery on the *seven rays* and the seven *chakras* of the Holy Spirit. Christ-mastery includes the balancing of the *threefold flame*—the divine attributes of power, wisdom and love—for the harmonization of consciousness and the implementation of the mastery of the seven rays in the chakras and in the *four lower bodies* through the Mother flame (the raised Kundalini).

At the hour designated for the *ascension,* the soul thus anointed raises the spiral of the threefold flame from beneath the feet through the entire form for the transmutation of every atom and cell of her being, consciousness and world. The saturation and acceleration of the *four lower bodies* and the soul by this transfiguring Light of the Christ flame take place in part during the initiation of the transfiguration, increasing through the resurrection and gaining full intensity in the ritual of the ascension.

Christ Self. The individualized focus of "the only begotten of the Father, full of grace and Truth" (John 1:14). The *Universal Christ* individualized as the true identity of the soul; the *Real Self* of every man, woman and child, to which the soul must rise. The Christ Self is the Mediator between a man and his God. He is a man's own personal teacher, master and prophet.

Color rays. See *Seven rays.*

Cosmic Being. (1) An *Ascended Master* who has attained cosmic consciousness and ensouls the *Light*/energy/consciousness of many worlds and systems of worlds across the galaxies to the Sun behind the *Great Central Sun;* or, (2) A Being of God who has never descended below the level of the *Christ,* has never taken physical embodiment, and has never made human karma.

Cosmic Christ. An office in *Hierarchy* currently held by Lord Maitreya under Gautama *Buddha,* the *Lord of the World.* Also used as a synonym for *Universal Christ.*

Cosmic Clock. The science of charting the cycles of the soul's karma and initiations on the twelve lines of the Clock under the *Twelve Hierarchies of the Sun.* Taught by Mother Mary to Mark and Elizabeth Prophet for sons and daughters of God returning to the Law of the One and to their point of origin beyond the worlds of form and lesser causation.

Cosmic Egg. The spiritual-material universe, including a seemingly endless chain of galaxies, star systems, worlds known and un-known, whose center, or white-fire core, is called the *Great Central Sun.* The Cosmic Egg has both a spiritual and a material center. Although we may discover and observe the Cosmic Egg from the standpoint of our physical senses and perspective, all of the dimensions of *Spirit* can also be known and experienced within the Cosmic Egg. For the God who created the Cosmic Egg and holds it in the hollow of his hand is also the God flame expanding hour by hour within his very own sons and daughters. The Cosmic Egg represents the bounds of man's habitation in this cosmic cycle. Yet, as God is everywhere throughout and beyond the Cosmic Egg, so by his Spirit within us we daily awaken to new dimensions of being, soul-satisfied in conformity with his likeness.

Cosmic Law. The Law that governs mathematically, yet with the spontaneity of Mercy's flame, all manifestation throughout the cosmos in the planes of *Spirit* and *Matter*.

Crystal cord. The stream of God's *Light*, life and consciousness that nourishes and sustains the soul and her *four lower bodies*. Also called the silver cord (Eccles. 12:6). See also *Chart of Your Divine Self*.

Cyclopea. Masculine Elohim of the fifth ray, also known as the All-Seeing Eye of God or as the Great Silent Watcher. See also *Elohim; Seven rays*.

Deathless solar body. See *Seamless garment*.

Decree. A dynamic form of spoken prayer used by students of the *Ascended Masters* to direct God's *Light* into individual and world conditions. The decree may be short or long and is usually marked by a formal preamble and a closing or acceptance. It is the authoritative *Word* of God spoken in man in the name of the *I AM Presence* and the living *Christ* to bring about constructive change on earth through the will of God. The decree is the birthright of the sons and daughters of God, the "Command ye me" of Isaiah 45:11, the original fiat of the Creator: "Let there be light: and there was light" (Gen. 1:3). It is written in the Book of Job, "Thou shalt decree a thing, and it shall be established unto thee: and the light shall shine upon thy ways" (Job 22:28).

Dictation. A message from an *Ascended Master*, an *Archangel* or another advanced spiritual being delivered through the agency of the Holy Spirit by a *Messenger* of the *Great White Brotherhood*.

Divine Monad. See *Chart of Your Divine Self; I AM Presence*.

Electronic Presence. A duplicate of the *I AM Presence* of an

Ascended Master.

Elementals. Beings of earth, air, fire and water; nature spirits who are the servants of God and man. The elementals establish and maintain the physical platform for the soul's evolution. The elementals who serve the fire element are called salamanders; those who serve the air element, sylphs; those who serve the water element, undines; and those who serve the earth element, gnomes.

Elohim. (Hebrew; plural of *Eloah,* "God.") The name of God used in the first verse of the Bible: "In the beginning God created the heaven and the earth." The Seven Mighty Elohim and their feminine counterparts are the builders of form. They are the "seven spirits of God" named in Revelation 4:5 and the "morning stars" that sang together in the beginning, as the Lord revealed them to Job (Job 38:7). In the order of *Hierarchy,* the Elohim and *Cosmic Beings* carry the greatest concentration, the highest vibration of *Light* that we can comprehend in our present state of evolution. Serving directly under the Elohim are the four Hierarchs of the elements, who have dominion over the elementals—the gnomes, salamanders, sylphs and undines.

Following are the names of the Seven Elohim and their divine complements, the ray they serve on and the location of their etheric *retreat:*

First ray, Hercules and Amazonia, Half Dome, Sierra Nevada, Yosemite National Park, California, U.S.A.

Second ray, Apollo and Lumina, western Lower Saxony, Germany

Third ray, Heros and Amora, Lake Winnipeg, Manitoba, Canada

Fourth ray, Purity and *Astrea,* near Gulf of Archangel, southeast arm of White Sea, Russia

Fifth ray, *Cyclopea* and Virginia, Altai Range where China, Siberia and Mongolia meet, near Tabun Bogdo

Sixth ray, Peace and Aloha, Hawaiian Islands

Seventh ray, Arcturus and Victoria, near Luanda, Angola, Africa

Emotional body. One of the *four lower bodies* of man, corresponding to the water element and the third quadrant of *Matter;* the vehicle of the desires and feelings of God made manifest in the being of man. Also called the astral body, the desire body or the feeling body.

Etheric body. One of the *four lower bodies* of man, corresponding to the fire element and the first quadrant of *Matter;* called the envelope of the soul, holding the blueprint of the divine plan and the image of *Christ*-perfection to be outpictured in the world of form. Also called the memory body.

Etheric octave or etheric plane. The highest plane in the dimension of *Matter;* a plane that is as concrete and real as the physical plane (and even more so) but is experienced through the senses of the soul in a dimension and a consciousness beyond physical awareness. This is the plane on which the *akashic records* of mankind's entire evolution register individually and collectively. It is the world of *Ascended Masters* and their *retreats,* etheric cities of *Light* where souls of a higher order of evolution abide between embodiments. It is the plane of Reality.

The lower *etheric plane,* which overlaps the astral/mental/physical belts, is contaminated by these lower worlds occupied by the false hierarchy and the mass consciousness it controls.

Etheric temple. See *Retreat.*

Fallen angels. See *Angels.*

Father-Mother God. See *Alpha and Omega.*

Four Cosmic Forces. The four beasts seen by Saint John and other seers as the lion, the calf (or ox), the man and the flying eagle (Rev. 4:6–8). They serve directly under the *Elohim* and govern all of the *Matter* cosmos. They are transformers of the Infinite *Light* unto souls evolving in the finite. See also *Elohim.*

Four lower bodies. Four sheaths of four distinct frequencies that surround the soul (the physical, emotional, mental and etheric bodies), providing vehicles for the soul in her journey through time and space. The etheric sheath, highest in vibration, is the gateway to the three Higher Bodies: the *Christ Self,* the *I AM Presence* and the *Causal Body.* See also *Physical body; Emotional body; Mental body; Etheric body.*

Great Central Sun. See *Central Sun.*

Great Hub. See *Central Sun.*

Great White Brotherhood. A spiritual order of Western saints and Eastern adepts who have reunited with the *Spirit* of the living God; the Heavenly Hosts. They have transcended the cycles of karma and rebirth and ascended (accelerated) into that higher reality that is the eternal abode of the soul. The *Ascended*

Masters of the Great White Brotherhood, united for the highest purposes of the brotherhood of man under the Fatherhood of God, have risen in every age from every culture and religion to inspire creative achievement in education, the arts and sciences, God-government and the abundant life through the economies of the nations. The word "white" refers not to race but to the aura (halo) of white *Light* surrounding their forms. The Brotherhood also includes in its ranks certain unascended *chelas* of the Ascended Masters.

Guru. (Sanskrit.) A personal religious teacher and spiritual guide; one of high attainment. A guru may be unascended or ascended.

Hierarchy. The universal chain of individualized God-free beings fulfilling the attributes and aspects of God's infinite Selfhood. Included in the cosmic Hierarchical scheme are *Solar Logoi, Elohim,* Sons and Daughters of God, Ascended and unascended masters with their circles of *chelas, Cosmic Beings,* the *Twelve Hierarchies of the Sun, Archangels* and *angels* of the *sacred fire,* children of the *Light,* nature spirits (called elementals) and *twin flames* of the *Alpha/Omega* polarity sponsoring planetary and galactic systems.

This universal order of the Father's own Self-expression is the means whereby God in the *Great Central Sun* steps down the Presence and power of his universal being/consciousness in order that succeeding evolutions in time and space, from the least unto the greatest, might come to know the wonder of his love. The level of one's spiritual/physical attainment—measured by one's balanced self-awareness "hid with *Christ* in God" and demonstrating his Law, by his love, in the *Spirit/Matter* cosmos —is the criterion establishing one's placement on this ladder of life called Hierarchy.

Higher Mental Body. See *Chart of Your Divine Self.*

Higher Self. The *I AM Presence;* the *Christ Self;* the exalted aspect of selfhood. Used in contrast to the term "lower self," or "little self," which indicates the soul that went forth from and may elect by free will to return to the Divine Whole through the realization of the oneness of the self in God. Higher consciousness.

Holy Christ Self. See *Christ Self.*

Human monad. The entire forcefield of self; the interconnecting spheres of influences—hereditary, environmental, karmic—

which make up that self-awareness that identifies itself as human. The reference point of lesser- or non-awareness out of which all mankind must evolve to the realization of the *Real Self* as the *Christ Self.*

I AM Presence. The I AM THAT I AM (Exod. 3:13–15); the individualized Presence of God focused for each individual soul. The God-identity of the individual; the Divine Monad; the individual Source. The origin of the soul focused in the planes of *Spirit* just above the physical form; the personification of the God flame for the individual. See also *Chart of Your Divine Self;* color illustration facing page 12.

I AM THAT I AM. See *I AM Presence.*

Kali Yuga. (Sanskrit.) Term in Hindu mystic philosophy for the last and worst of the four yugas (world ages), characterized by strife, discord and moral deterioration.

Karmic Board. See *Lords of Karma.*

Keepers of the Flame Fraternity. Founded in 1961 by Saint Germain, an organization of *Ascended Masters* and their *chelas* who vow to keep the Flame of Life on earth and to support the activities of the *Great White Brotherhood* in the establishment of their community and Mystery School and in the dissemination of their teachings. Keepers of the Flame receive graded lessons in *cosmic law* dictated by the *Ascended Masters* to their Messengers Mark and Elizabeth Prophet.

Lifestream. The stream of life that comes forth from the one Source, from the *I AM Presence* in the planes of *Spirit,* and descends to the planes of *Matter* where it manifests as the *threefold flame* anchored in the heart chakra for the sustainment of the soul in Matter and the nourishment of the *four lower bodies.* Used to denote souls evolving as individual "lifestreams" and hence synonymous with the term "individual." Denotes the ongoing nature of the individual through cycles of individualization.

Light. The energy of God; the potential of the *Christ.* As the personification of *Spirit,* the term "Light" can be used synonymously with the terms "God" and "Christ." As the essence of Spirit, it is synonymous with *"sacred fire."* It is the emanation of the *Great Central Sun* and the individualized *I AM Presence*—and the Source of all Life.

Logos. (Greek, "word, speech, reason.") The divine wisdom manifest in the creation. According to ancient Greek philosophy, the Logos is the controlling principle in the universe. The Book of John identifies the *Word,* or Logos, with Jesus Christ: "And the Word was made flesh, and dwelt among us" (John 1:14). Hence, Jesus Christ is seen as the embodiment of divine reason, the Word Incarnate.

Lord of the World. *Sanat Kumara* held the office of Lord of the World (referred to as "God of the earth" in Rev. 11:4) for tens of thousands of years. Gautama *Buddha* recently succeeded Sanat Kumara and now holds this office. His is the highest governing office of the spiritual *Hierarchy* for the planet—and yet Lord Gautama is truly the most humble among the *Ascended Masters.* At inner levels, he sustains the *threefold flame,* the divine spark, for those *lifestreams* who have lost the direct contact with their *I AM Presence* and who have made so much negative karma as to be unable to magnetize sufficient *Light* from the Godhead to sustain their soul's physical incarnation on earth. Through a filigree thread of Light connecting his heart with the hearts of all God's children, Lord Gautama nourishes the flickering Flame of Life that ought to burn upon the altar of each heart with a greater magnitude of love, wisdom and power, fed by each one's own *Christ* consciousness.

Lords of Karma. The Ascended Beings who comprise the Karmic Board. Their names and the *rays* they represent on the board are as follows: first ray, the Great Divine Director; second ray, the Goddess of Liberty; third ray, the Ascended Lady Master Nada; fourth ray, the *Elohim Cyclopea;* fifth ray, Pallas Athena, Goddess of Truth; sixth ray, Portia, Goddess of Justice; seventh ray, Kuan Yin, Goddess of Mercy. The Buddha Vairochana also sits on the Karmic Board.

   The Lords of Karma dispense justice to this system of worlds, adjudicating karma, mercy and judgment on behalf of every *lifestream.* All souls must pass before the Karmic Board before and after each incarnation on earth, receiving their assignment and karmic allotment for each lifetime beforehand and the review of their performance at its conclusion. Through the Keeper of the Scrolls and the recording *angels,* the Lords of Karma have access to the complete records of every lifestream's incarnations on earth. They determine who shall embody, as well as when and where. They assign souls to families and communities, measuring out the weights of karma that must be balanced as the "jot and tittle" of the Law. The Karmic Board, acting in consonance with the individual *I AM Presence* and *Christ Self,* determines when the soul has earned the right to be free from the wheel of karma and the round of rebirth.

The Lords of Karma meet at the Royal Teton Retreat twice yearly, at winter and summer solstice, to review petitions from unascended mankind and to grant dispensations for their assistance.

Macrocosm. (Greek, "great world.") The larger cosmos; the entire warp and woof of creation, which we call the *Cosmic Egg.* Also used to contrast man as the microcosm ("little world") against the backdrop of the larger world in which he lives. See also *Microcosm.*

Mantra. A mystical formula or invocation; a word or formula, often in Sanskrit, to be recited or sung for the purpose of intensifying the action of the *Spirit* of God in man. A form of prayer consisting of a word or a group of words that is chanted over and over again to magnetize a particular aspect of the Deity or of a being who has actualized that aspect of the Deity. See also *Decree.*

Manu. (Sanskrit.) The progenitor and lawgiver of the evolutions of God on earth. The Manu and his divine complement are *twin flames* assigned by the *Father-Mother God* to sponsor and ensoul the Christic image for a certain evolution or lifewave known as a root race—souls who embody as a group and have a unique archetypal pattern, divine plan and mission to fulfill on earth.

According to esoteric tradition, there are seven primary aggregations of souls—that is, the first to the seventh root races. The first three root races lived in purity and innocence upon earth in three Golden Ages before the Fall of Adam and Eve. Through obedience to *cosmic law* and total identification with the *Real Self,* these three root races won their immortal freedom and ascended from earth.

It was during the time of the fourth root race, on the continent of Lemuria, that the allegorical Fall took place under the influence of the fallen angels known as Serpents (because they used the serpentine spinal energies to beguile the soul, or female principle in mankind, as a means to their end of lowering the masculine potential, thereby emasculating the Sons of God).

The fourth, fifth and sixth root races (the latter soul group not having entirely descended into physical incarnation) remain in embodiment on earth today. Lord Himalaya and his beloved are the Manus for the fourth root race, Vaivasvata Manu and his consort are the Manus for the fifth root race, and the God and Goddess Meru are the Manus for the sixth root race. The seventh root race is destined to incarnate on the continent of South America in the Aquarian age under their Manus, the Great Divine Director and his divine complement.

Manvantara. (Sanskrit, from *manv,* used in compounds for *manu,* + *antara,* "interval, period of time.") In Hinduism, the name used to refer to various cycles, especially the length of the cycle of four yugas (consisting of 4,320,000 solar years) and the length of the reign of one *Manu* (308,448,000 years). The reign of a Manu is one of the fourteen intervals that constitute a *kalpa* (Sanskrit), a period of time covering a cosmic cycle from the origination to the destruction of a world system. In Hindu cosmology, the universe is continually evolving through periodic cycles of creation and dissolution. Creation is said to occur during the outbreath of the God of Creation, Brahma; dissolution occurs during his inbreath.

Mater. (Latin, "mother.") See *Matter; Mother.*

Matter. The feminine (negative) polarity of the Godhead, of which the masculine (positive) polarity is Spirit. Matter acts as a chalice for the kingdom of God and is the abiding place of evolving souls who identify with their Lord, their *Holy Christ Self.* Matter is distinguished from matter (lowercase *m*)—the substance of the earth earthy, of the realms of maya, which blocks rather than radiates divine *Light* and the Spirit of the *I AM THAT I AM.* See also *Mother; Spirit.*

Mental body. One of the *four lower bodies* of man, corresponding to the air element and the second quadrant of *Matter;* the body that is intended to be the vehicle, or vessel, for the Mind of God or the *Christ* Mind. "Let this [Universal] Mind be in you, which was also in Christ Jesus" (Phil. 2:5). Until quickened, this body remains the vehicle for the carnal mind, often called the lower mental body in contrast to the Higher Mental Body, a synonym for the *Christ Self* or *Christ* consciousness.

Microcosm. (Greek, "small world.") (1) The world of the individual, his *four lower bodies*, his aura and the forcefield of his karma; or (2) The planet. See also *Macrocosm*.

Mother. "Divine Mother," "Universal Mother" and "Cosmic Virgin" are alternate terms for the feminine polarity of the Godhead, the manifestation of God as Mother. *Matter* is the feminine polarity of *Spirit*, and the term is used interchangeably with Mater (Latin, "mother"). In this context, the entire material cosmos becomes the womb of creation into which Spirit projects the energies of Life. Matter, then, is the womb of the Cosmic Virgin, who, as the other half of the Divine Whole, also exists in Spirit as the spiritual polarity of God.

Nirvana. The goal of life according to Hindu and Buddhist philosophy: the state of liberation from the wheel of rebirth through the extinction of desire.

OM (AUM). The Word; the sound symbol for ultimate Reality.

Omega. See *Alpha and Omega*.

Path. The strait gate and narrow way that leadeth unto life (Matt. 7:14). The path of initiation whereby the disciple who pursues the *Christ* consciousness overcomes step by step the limitations of selfhood in time and space and attains reunion with Reality through the ritual of the *ascension*.

Pearls of Wisdom. Weekly letters of instruction dictated by the *Ascended Masters* to their Messengers Mark L. Prophet and Elizabeth Clare Prophet for students of the sacred mysteries throughout the world. *Pearls of Wisdom* have been published by *The Summit Lighthouse* continuously since 1958. They contain both fundamental and advanced teachings on *cosmic law* with a practical application of spiritual Truths to personal and planetary problems.

Physical body. The most dense of the *four lower bodies* of man, corresponding to the earth element and the fourth quadrant of *Matter*. The physical body is the vehicle for the soul's sojourn on earth and the focus for the crystallization in form of the energies of the *etheric, mental* and *emotional bodies*.

Rays. Beams of *Light* or other radiant energy. The Light emanations of the Godhead that, when invoked in the name of God or in the name of the *Christ*, burst forth as a flame in the world of the individual. Rays may be projected by the God consciousness of Ascended or unascended beings through the *chakras* and the third eye as a concentration of energy taking on numerous God-qualities, such as love, truth, wisdom, healing, and so on. Through the misuse of God's energy, practitioners of black magic project rays having negative qualities, such as death rays, sleep rays, hypnotic rays, disease rays, psychotronic rays, the evil eye, and so on. See also *Seven rays.*

Real Self. The *Christ Self;* the *I AM Presence;* immortal *Spirit* that is the animating principle of all manifestation. See also *Chart of Your Divine Self.*

Reembodiment. The rebirth of a soul in a new human body. The soul continues to return to the physical plane in a new body temple until she balances her karma, attains self-mastery, overcomes the cycles of time and space, and finally reunites with the *I AM Presence* through the ritual of the *ascension.*

Retreat. A focus of the *Great White Brotherhood,* usually on the *etheric plane* where the *Ascended Masters* preside. Retreats anchor one or more flames of the Godhead as well as the momentum of the Masters' service and attainment for the balance of *Light* in the *four lower bodies* of a planet and its evolutions. Retreats serve many functions for the councils of the *Hierarchy* ministering to the lifewaves of earth. Some retreats are open to unascended mankind, whose souls may journey to these focuses in their *etheric body* between their incarnations on earth and in their finer bodies during sleep or *samadhi.*

Root race. See *Manu.*

Sacred fire. The Kundalini fire that lies as the coiled serpent in the base-of-the-spine chakra and rises through spiritual purity and self-mastery to the crown chakra, quickening the spiritual centers on the way. God, *Light,* life, energy, the *I AM THAT I AM.* "Our God is a consuming fire" (Heb. 12:29). The sacred fire is the precipitation of the Holy Ghost for the baptism of souls, for purification, for alchemy and transmutation, and for the realization of the *ascension,* the sacred ritual whereby the soul returns to the One.

Samadhi. (Sanskrit, literally "putting together": "uniting") In Hinduism, a state of profound concentration or absorption resulting in perfect union with God; the highest state of yoga. In Buddhism, samadhis are numerous modes of concentration believed to ultimately result in higher spiritual powers and the attainment of enlightenment, or nirvana.

Sanat Kumara. (From the Sanskrit, "always a youth.") Great *Guru* of the seed of *Christ* throughout cosmos; Hierarch of Venus; the Ancient of Days spoken of in Daniel 7. Long ago he came to earth in her darkest hour when all *Light* had gone out in her evolutions, for there was not a single individual on the planet who gave adoration to the God Presence. Sanat Kumara and the band of 144,000 souls of Light who accompanied him volunteered to keep the Flame of Life on behalf of earth's people. This they vowed to do until the children of God would respond to the love of God and turn once again to serve their Mighty *I AM Presence.* Sanat Kumara's retreat, Shamballa, was established on an island in the Gobi Sea, now the Gobi Desert. The first to respond to his flame was Gautama *Buddha,* followed by Lord Maitreya and Jesus. See also *Lord of the World.*

Seamless garment. Body of *Light* beginning in the heart of the *I AM Presence* and descending around the *crystal cord* to envelop the individual in the vital currents of the *ascension* as he invokes the holy energies of the Father for the return home to God. Also known as the deathless solar body.

Secret chamber of the heart. The sanctuary of meditation behind the heart chakra, the place to which the souls of Lightbearers withdraw. It is the nucleus of life where the individual stands face-to-face with the inner *Guru,* the beloved *Holy Christ Self,* and receives the soul testings that precede the alchemical union with that Holy Christ Self—the marriage of the soul to the Lamb.

Seed Atom. The focus of the Divine *Mother* (the Feminine Ray of the Godhead) that anchors the energies of *Spirit* in *Matter* at the base-of-the-spine chakra. See also *Sacred fire.*

Seven rays. The *Light* emanations of the Godhead; the seven *rays* of the white Light that emerge through the prism of the *Christ* consciousness.

Siddhis. Spiritual powers such as levitation, stopping the heartbeat, clairvoyance, clairaudience, materialization and bilocation. The cultivation of siddhis for their own sake is often cautioned against by spiritual teachers.

Solar Logoi. *Cosmic Beings* who transmit the *Light* emanations of the Godhead flowing from *Alpha and Omega* in the *Great Central Sun* to the planetary systems. Also called Solar Lords.

Spirit. The masculine polarity of the Godhead; the coordinate of *Matter;* God as Father, who of necessity includes within the polarity of himself God as *Mother,* and hence is known as the *Father-Mother God.* The plane of the *I AM Presence,* of perfection; the dwelling place of the *Ascended Masters* in the kingdom of God.

Spoken Word. The *Word* of the LORD God released in the original fiats of Creation. The release of the energies of the Word, or the *Logos,* through the throat chakra by the Sons of God in confirmation of that lost Word. It is written, "By thy words thou shalt be justified, and by thy words thou shalt be condemned" (Matt. 12:37). Today disciples use the power of the Word in *decrees,* affirmations, prayers and *mantras* to draw the essence of the *sacred fire* from the *I AM Presence,* the *Christ Self* and *Cosmic Beings* to channel God's *Light* into matrices of transmutation and transformation for constructive change in the planes of *Matter.*

The Summit Lighthouse. An outer organization of the *Great White Brotherhood* founded by Mark L. Prophet in 1958 in Washington, D.C., under the direction of the *Ascended Master* El Morya, Chief of the Darjeeling Council, for the purpose of publishing and disseminating the teachings of the Ascended Masters.

Threefold flame. The flame of the *Christ,* the spark of Life that burns within the *secret chamber of the heart* (a secondary chakra behind the heart). The sacred trinity of power, wisdom and love that is the manifestation of the *sacred fire.* See also *Chart of Your Divine Self;* color illustration facing page 12.

Tube of light. The white *Light* that descends from the heart of the *I AM Presence* in answer to the call of man as a shield of protection for his *four lower bodies* and his soul evolution. See also *Chart of Your Divine Self;* color illustration facing page 12.

Twelve Hierarchies of the Sun. Twelve mandalas of *Cosmic Beings* ensouling twelve facets of God's consciousness, who hold the pattern of that frequency for the entire cosmos. They are identified by the names of the signs of the zodiac, as they focus their energies through these constellations. Also called the Twelve Solar Hierarchies. See also *Cosmic Clock.*

Twin flame. The soul's masculine or feminine counterpart conceived out of the same white-fire body, the fiery ovoid of the *I AM*

Presence.

Unascended master. One who has overcome all limitations of *Matter* yet chooses to remain in time and space to focus the consciousness of God for lesser evolutions. See also *Bodhisattva.*

Universal Christ. The Mediator between the planes of *Spirit* and the planes of *Matter.* Personified as the *Christ Self,* he is the Mediator between the Spirit of God and the soul of man. The Universal Christ sustains the nexus of (the figure-eight flow of) consciousness through which the energies of the Father (Spirit) pass to his children for the crystallization (*Christ*-realization) of the God flame by their soul's strivings in the cosmic womb (matrix) of the *Mother* (Matter).

Violet flame. Seventh-ray aspect of the Holy Spirit. The *sacred fire* that transmutes the cause, effect, record and memory of sin, or negative karma. Also called the flame of transmutation, of freedom and of forgiveness. See also *Decree; Chart of Your Divine Self;* color illustration facing page 12.

Word. The Word is the *Logos:* it is the power of God and the realization of that power incarnate in and as the Christ. The energies of the Word are released by devotees of the Logos in the ritual of the science of the *spoken Word.* It is through the Word that the *Father-Mother God* communicates with mankind. The Christ is the personification of the Word. See also *Christ; Decree.*

World Teacher. Office in *Hierarchy* held by those Ascended Beings whose attainment qualifies them to represent the universal and personal *Christ* to unascended mankind. The office of World Teacher, formerly held by Maitreya, was passed to Jesus and his disciple Saint Francis (Kuthumi) on January 1, 1956, when the mantle of *Lord of the World* was transferred from *Sanat Kumara* to Gautama *Buddha* and the office of *Cosmic Christ* and Planetary Buddha (formerly held by Gautama) was simultaneously filled by Lord Maitreya. Serving under Lord Maitreya, Jesus and Kuthumi are responsible in this cycle for setting forth the teachings leading to individual self-mastery and the *Christ* consciousness. They sponsor all souls seeking union with God, tutoring them in the fundamental laws governing the cause-effect sequences of their own karma and teaching them how to come to grips with the day-to-day challenges of their individual dharma, the duty to fulfill the Christ potential through the sacred labor.

MORE VOLUMES IN THE
CLIMB THE HIGHEST MOUNTAIN SERIES

The Path of the Higher Self

This cornerstone of metaphysical literature explores many topics important to every spiritual seeker—the destiny of the soul, the difference between soul and Spirit, the role of the Christ, how to contact the Higher Self and the spark of God within the heart.
ISBN: 978-0-922729-84-5   528 pages

The Path of Self-Transformation

The Path of Self-Transformation reveals the true meaning of the biblical allegory of Adam and Eve. It answers profound spiritual questions such as: Who suppressed the concepts of karma and reincarnation and why are they key to our spiritual growth? Why wasn't sex the original sin?
ISBN: 978-0-922729-54-8   358 pages

The Masters and the Spiritual Path

In this intriguing work the reader will discover keys to his own spiritual path: the relationship between the ascension, nirvana and Samadhi, the parallel structure of the spiritual and material universes, the role of the spiritual Hierarchy and the Masters. Includes a meditation on the union with Spirit.
ISBN: 978-0-922729-64-7   360 pages

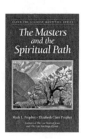

The Path of Brotherhood

Prior to the Fall, men and women lived in a golden age. Their souls evolved in love, peace and harmony, and everyone embodied the principle of being his brother's keeper. After the Fall, souls lost their sense of unity and oneness with God and with one another. Mark and Elizabeth Prophet demonstrate how brotherhood is possible, and crucial, today.

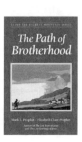

They speak of the golden-age family, and offer spiritual keys for achieving world brotherhood.
ISBN: 978-0-922729-82-1   264 pages

The Path of the Universal Christ

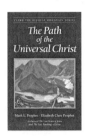

In this volume, the authors recapture the heart of the Master's message—that we, like Jesus, are meant to realize our innate divinity. Church fathers suppressed Jesus' original teaching on the Christ within. But today, Mark and Elizabeth Prophet reveal our true inner identity and the goal of our life on earth.
ISBN: 978-0-922729-81-4   288 pages

Paths of Light and Darkness

The battle of Light and Darkness is not new. It extends far beyond recorded history. It is fought on many fronts, but most importantly in the hearts, minds and souls of humanity. *Paths of Light and Darkness* reveals some of the key strategies in this battle—as well as spiritual solutions for our victory.
ISBN: 978-1-932890-00-6   480 pages

The Path to Immortality

This volume features profound and practical instruction on transcending the human condition. These ancient teachings, long hidden in the mystery schools, are essential for the serious seeker. They point the way to immortality—the ultimate freedom of the soul.
ISBN: 978-1-932890-09-9   352 pages

The Masters and Their Retreats

The great lights that have come out of the world's spiritual traditions and graduated from earth's schoolroom are known as Ascended Masters. What is not widely known is that they have retreats— temples and cities of light in the heaven world that we can visit during meditation or while we sleep. In this magnificent work, the authors describe the Masters, the stories of their lives and their incredible retreats.
ISBN: 978-0-9720402-4-2   560 pages

Mark L. Prophet and Elizabeth Clare Prophet are pioneers of modern spirituality and internationally renowned authors. Among their best-selling titles are *The Lost Years of Jesus, The Lost Teachings of Jesus, The Human Aura, Saint Germain On Alchemy, Fallen Angels and the Origins of Evil* and the Pocket Guides to Practical Spirituality series, which includes *How to Work with Angels, Your Seven Energy Centers* and *Soul Mates and Twin Flames*. Their books are now translated into more than twenty languages and are available in more than thirty countries.

FOR MORE INFORMATION

Summit University Press books are available at fine bookstores worldwide and at your favorite on-line bookseller. For a free catalog of our books and products or to learn more about the spiritual techniques featured in this book, please contact:

Summit University Press
63 Summit Way
Gardiner, MT 59030-9314 USA
Telephone: 1-800-245-5445 or 406-848-9500
Fax: 1-800-221-8307 or 406-848-9555
www.summituniversitypress.com
info@summituniversitypress.com